"*Too Big to Fall* is too important not to be read by elected and government officials and anyone who cares about the health of our cities, states, and country. LePatner, by concentrating on a major element of public works—our country's 600,000 bridges, brings into focus the causes and solutions that, if followed, in the long run would actually cost less and expose us to less risk. The release of this book could not be more timely. Thousands of local and state officials are facing record deficits. The easiest areas to cut are the nearly invisible activities of preventive maintenance. No large constituencies will be marching on city halls or statehouses to clamor to save the jobs of bridge painters or oilers. But at least government public works managers and citizens now have the source to educate elected officials and their bean counters in the penny-wise-pound-foolish choice of cutting maintenance now, only to face bigger costs and higher risks in just a few years. I was in charge of New York City's bridges after the fiscal crisis of the 1970s. On my watch in the 1980s, we had fatal collapses on the Brooklyn Bridge and the elevated FDR drive, as well as emergency closures of more than a score of other bridges. LePatner offers us a better choice."
—**Sam Schwartz**, Sam Schwartz Engineering

"Barry LePatner has emerged as one of the nation's leading advocates for infrastructure reform. *Too Big to Fall* provides a thought-provoking examination of America's infrastructure dilemma. It is eye-opening and sobering. Hopefully this work will resonate with those in authority to heighten their sense of urgency to aggressively address this threat to our nation's future."
—**Gary La Point**, Assistant Professor, Supply Chain Management, Syracuse University

"This book needs to be read by all those concerned about our transportation infrastructure, but especially those who are starting to realize that business as usual, with Uncle Sugar providing massive doses of feel-good funding, is over. The time for optimizing long-term transportation funding has begun, providing beleaguered taxpayers with much-deserved relief and achieving better results, supported by innovative technologies and enhanced business methods."
—**Peter J. Vanderzee**, President and CEO,
LifeSpan Technologies

"Barry LePatner makes an airtight case in *Too Big to Fall* that our nation's road infrastructure is becoming a liability, a drag on our productivity rather than an asset. His heavily researched book aptly warns us that if our nation's infrastructure continues to fail, so too does America. With China's rise, this book sends a timely warning of our need to compete with the East. LePatner's ultimate optimism and professional experiences lead us to a solution that we need to take to heart."
—**Dan McNichol**, bestselling author of *The Big Dig*,
*The Roads That Built America*, and *Asphalt in America*;
Columnist for *Rebuilding America's Infrastructure*

**Foster Publishing**

In association with

University Press of New England

www.upne.com

© 2010 Barry B. LePatner

All rights reserved

Manufactured in the United States of America

Typeset in Quadraat and Franklin Gothic by Copperline Book Services

University Press of New England is a member of the
Green Press Initiative. The paper used in this book meets
their minimum requirement for recycled paper.

For permission to reproduce any of the material in this book,
contact Permissions, University Press of New England, One Court Street,
Suite 250, Lebanon NH 03766; or visit www.upne.com

Library of Congress Cataloging-in-Publication Data
LePatner, Barry B.
Too big to fall : America's failing infrastructure and the way
forward / Barry B. LePatner.
    p. cm.
Includes bibliographical references and index.
ISBN 978-0-9844978-0-5 (cloth : alk. paper)
1. Transportation — United States — Finance.   2. Bridges—
Maintenance and repair —Economic aspects — United
States.   3. Roads — Maintenance and repair — Economic
aspects — United States.   4. Infrastructure (Economics) —
United States.   I. Title.
HE206.2.L47 2010
388.1'140973 — dc22      2010023137

5 4 3 2 1

# Barry B. LePatner

With Special Comments by
**Hon. James L. Oberstar,**
Chairman, U.S. House Committee on
Transportation and Infrastructure

Foreword by **Robert Puentes**,
Senior Fellow, Metropolitan Policy
Program, Brookings Institution

# Too Big to Fall

America's Failing
Infrastructure and
the Way Forward

**Foster Publishing** New York
In association with
University Press of New England
Hanover and London

# Too Big to Fall

# Contents

# Acknowledgments

During the two years of research and writing that made this book possible, I was aided by an astute group of individuals who helped me to sort through myriad issues that make our national infrastructure story so compelling. This book flowed out of *Structural and Foundation Failures*, which I wrote in the early 1980s on the many major building failures that captivated the nation and led the u.s. Congress to hold hearings into their cause. I was always fascinated by the failure of our nation's leaders to apply the lessons from that earlier story to our largest and most important transportation structures. By the time of the sudden, tragic collapse of the I-35W Bridge over the Mississippi River in Minneapolis on August 1, 2007—immediately following which I was interviewed on WCBS television in New York City—I had already begun researching just how perilous the situation had become.

In my search for clarification of the engineering technology that explained the physics of how and why bridges are designed and maintained, I was invaluably aided by a national coterie of experts. Each patiently expanded my understanding of the physical properties and the unique nature of each bridge in our nation. On more occasions than I can recount, Ramon Gilsanz sat down with me and took me through the fundamentals of structural design and the series of questions I would need to ask as my investigation continued. His assistance and friendship throughout the drafting and review of the manuscript was highly valuable. My interviews with the nationally known bridge designer, Ray McCabe, helped me to understand the role of the engineer who works as a consultant for state and federal agencies, a topic that became increasingly important as the manuscript proceeded.

Reaching an understanding of the intricacies of the collapse of a major structure such as the I-35W Bridge can be exhausting without the patient guidance of experts. As I studied the thousands of documents produced as a result of that failure, I turned to individuals such as Toader Balan, who had also begun to question the early findings of the National Transportation Safety Board (NTSB) as to the cause, and Peter Vanderzee, who, in a series of interviews, gave me insights and guidance that clarified many of the crosscurrents and eddies that seemed to send this story off in many directions. Peter was also instrumental in helping me to focus on the incredible way that our nation's transportation agencies have steered away from utilizing the latest technology in maintaining roads and bridges.

Steven B. Chase, research professor of civil and environmental engineering at the University of Virginia, provided an incredible wealth of insight and information with regard to decoding the often arcane data ensconced within the Federal Highway Administration National Bridge Inventory statistics. I am particularly thankful for the enormously important information he provided on the number of bridges that are both structurally deficient and fracture-critical, as that research—as much as anything else in this book—must be brought to the public's attention if we are to begin to grasp the enormity of the problem we are addressing with our nation's deteriorated bridge stock.

Critical in framing important issues that contributed to the book were my discussions with Ted Zoli, whose writings on bridge failures are essential reading in the field, and Herb Rothman, who took me through myriad structural concepts that proved to be highly insightful. Matthys Levy—who, along with my old and dear departed friend, Mario Salvadori, wrote a series of books for engineers and nonengineers alike on why structures fail—guided me along the path of understanding why structures deteriorate under the adverse impact of minimal maintenance.

My special thanks go to Sam Schwartz, who gave me invaluable time and resources from his personal library. He contributed in a major way to my understanding of the difficulties faced by transportation engineers who must deal with an increasingly desperate situation, while politicians—many of whom don't have a clue or hope infrastructure problems will just go away—allocate limited funding.

The more I explored the story of Sam Schwartz and the near-collapse of New York City's Williamsburg Bridge, the more I came to view him as a national hero.

Critically valuable research and writing assistance was provided by Dan Penrice, who helped to sort through the many complex federal and state funding mechanisms, used by politicians largely to ensure that federal funding continues to flow to their friends for new projects, as opposed to maintenance of our failing infrastructure. Playing a critical role during this phase of the book, David Tannenwald provided research that helped to trace federal and state funding through its arcane routes to our roads and bridges nationwide. An interview with the historian Owen D. Gutfreund was most helpful in providing a fuller understanding of how the unavailability of funding by states for road maintenance impacted the expansion of our national road system during the twentieth century. My friend and collaborator on *Broken Buildings, Busted Budgets*, Tim Jacobson, came to my assistance by giving valuable editing insights on the late drafts of the book and bringing a fuller sense of order to a seemingly unmanageable topic.

Major assistance in coordinating the vast amount of research generated for each chapter was provided by Marlene Diaz, of LePatner & Associates. Although the data grew each month, she always managed to have the answers to my myriad questions about bridge inspections, FHWA computerized statistics, and the number of structurally deficient bridges in a given state. Providing immeasurable assistance in laying out the various drafts of the book and incorporating graphs and charts was my assistant, Tadhg O'Connor. As with each of my previous books, his patience and calm demeanor kept everything in order throughout.

Special thanks also must be given to Dottie DeHart. From the inception of the project, Dottie provided incredibly insightful direction and always had an encouraging and thoughtful approach to the ideas embodied in this book. As someone immersed in the world of book publication, her experience and friendship kept me moving forward at every phase of the work.

Finally, to the people closest to me I owe the greatest debt. Persevering over two years at any task asks an enormous amount of love and understanding from those who sit and wait and provide the words of support when one is tired, lacking ideas, or at a dead end. To my beloved Marla Tomazin I am enormously grateful for listening to my mutterings on countless occasions, as I worried that I was not striking the right tone or unable to portray the right message that the facts called for. Her inspiration was there at every stage of the process. My son Evan and his wife, Wesley, read the manuscript at several stages and provided helpful insights into the financial sections of the book, as well as advice for me to stay on point at various times. Evan's critiques combined a son's fair acknowledgments of what was right in the manuscript while sparing me no comfort as to what I had gotten wrong. No father could be more blessed than I was by the enthusiastic and cheerful support of my younger son, Mark. My daughter, Karen, remains a true inspiration in the lives of all who have been blessed to know her. To each of those named in this paragraph, this book is warmly dedicated to you.

# Special Comments

HON. JAMES L. OBERSTAR, *Chairman,*

*U.S. House Committee on Transportation and Infrastructure*

There be three things which make a nation great and prosperous: a fertile soil, busy workshops, easy conveyance for men and goods from place to place.

—Sir Francis Bacon (1561–1626)

The U.S. surface transportation network, unmatched by any other in the world, is the backbone of the nation's economy. It has provided American businesses and consumers with enormous economic competitive advantages and access to markets over the course of the past century.

In recent years, however, the commitment to make long-term surface transportation investments has eroded. In the absence of the political will to make these badly needed investments, we continue to watch as the condition and performance of the system deteriorate and our competitive advantage on the world stage slips.

Nearly sixty years after much of the interstate highway system was constructed in the 1950s and 1960s, we are now seeing many facilities become stretched to the limit of their design life and beyond. The world-class surface transportation system passed on by previous generations of Americans has reached the age of obsolescence and now needs to be rebuilt. Mounting costs just to maintain these assets are consuming a growing share of the nation's overall investment in surface transportation infrastructure. Meanwhile, the demands placed on the network and the cost to address new challenges continue to grow more rapidly each year.

In its final report, issued in January 2008, the National Surface Transportation Policy and Revenue Study Commission identified the deterioration from aging and use as "one of the greatest threats to the nation's surface transportation network." Today, nearly half (43 percent) of all vehicle miles traveled are on roadways that are not rated as "good" for ride quality. Over 150,000 bridges—one of every four in the United States—are structurally deficient or functionally obsolete.

We have taken surface transportation infrastructure for granted in the United States, and we are seeing the consequences of that attitude. The American public and our growing economy have demanded a lot from our roads and bridges over the years, and the system can no longer stand the strain. As Barry LePatner writes in this book, "America is always about the next new thing. We build beautifully. But building brings with it responsibility that extends long past the date when a project is completed and put into use. Our record of maintaining what we build is less than beautiful."

According to the U.S. Department of Transportation, the federal government's annual investment is less than two-thirds of what is needed just to maintain our roads and bridges in their present condition, let alone begin making improvements.

Unfortunately, infrastructure is not like fine wine. It does not improve with age. As LePatner points out, we do not save money by deferring maintenance. As infrastructure is allowed to deteriorate, the cost of maintenance and repair climbs, and the longer we wait, the faster and higher it climbs. It is time to take responsibility for these conditions, and to make the needed investments to maintain the system we currently enjoy and to build the twenty-first-century system that America demands.

LePatner's book should sound the alarm for anyone—in and out of government—who uses and values our national transportation assets. We must develop the political will and the sense of urgency to get the job done, or suffer a crippling blow to our economy, our national standing, and our way of life.

# Foreword

ROBERT PUENTES, *Senior Fellow,*
*Metropolitan Policy Program, Brookings Institution*

Few Americans would deny the importance of our nation's infrastructure system. It's how we get around. It's necessary for communication. It's how we get to our jobs each morning. It fosters the movement of people, goods, and ideas. The problem is that our infrastructure system is so prevalent that we often don't even notice it's there.

Americans today are complacent about infrastructure, and unfortunately, it usually takes a tragedy before we even begin to think about the massive investment we need to make in repairing and maintaining our system of roads, bridges, and tunnels. Most Americans expect the system always to be there, functioning safely and efficiently. For example, we tend to assume that we can turn on the faucet and always get clean, safe water for our households. It takes a sewage system failure, such as the one Boston recently experienced, for us to realize otherwise. We assume that the levees will always hold, until they fail as they did in New Orleans after Hurricane Katrina. We assume that our roads and bridges are safe for our daily use, until a bridge collapses as the I-35W Bridge did in Minneapolis in 2007.

And it is precisely this attitude of complacency that impelled Barry LePatner to write *Too Big to Fall* at precisely this critical time. He pulls no punches by describing a neglected system that has become severely broken down. His book is valuable because it serves as a call to action to start finding solutions for fixing the infrastructure system now so that we don't wait for the next big tragedy to strike before we begin tackling the problems.

What sets LePatner's book apart from other works on the national infrastructure is the doable solutions he provides to get the ball rolling—reprioritizing how funds are allocated and spent on projects, placing an emphasis on better leadership, deploying new technology, using public-private partnerships to help fund the transportation program. He also utters the all-important caveat that before solutions to problems can be effective, we must first reform the system itself.

In *Too Big to Fall*, LePatner explains that to understand the severity of the situation, one has to acknowledge that our nation's infrastructure system is not simply a bridge here or a highway system over there. It is a network of networks. And if one aspect of the system suffers, so do all the rest. He hammers home the stark reality that there are security, safety, and economic implications every time a piece of the system fails.

For example, our national security relies on having a robust system of transport options for when a part of the system does break down. Consider what happened on September 11, 2001. On that day, we needed safe alternatives, in addition to roads, for evacuating people from downtown Washington, D.C., and downtown New York City. In New York City ferry boats were available, and in Washington, D.C., the Metro system was used. Our national security hinges on this issue of redundancy and making sure that the system is nimble enough to handle massive disruptions. On September 11, 2001, the system worked the way we needed it to. But, as LePatner points out, our infrastructure system is becoming increasingly less reliable.

A fundamental policy goal must be to make sure people are safe on the transportation system. Here we've reached a critical turning point. It's no longer simply an inconvenience when we experience infrastructure problems. Now, without the necessary repairs and maintenance, our safety is greatly compromised.

When the I-35W Bridge first collapsed, there was a pervasive feeling that a similar tragedy could happen anywhere, at any minute. Many of those within the industry, myself included, felt that the collapse would signify a turning point. Surely, I thought, now we would really begin to take action to solve these critical problems. Shortly after the bridge collapse, a congressional bill was introduced that would have begun to address these infrastructure issues. But time went by, and we escaped other tragedies. The harsh realities of funding needed repairs caused elected officials to put their heads back in the sand. The bill that was introduced went nowhere because it was accompanied by an increase in the Federal gas tax, and politicians didn't want to upset voters with increased taxes.

We Americans returned to our daily lives and settled back into the complacent notion that the system couldn't possibly fail us in such a way again. We began, once again, to ignore the problems with our nation's infrastructure. *Too Big to Fall* makes all too clear that if we allow our infrastructure system to continue down the path it's on, we will do so at our own risk.

The book also emphasizes the economic implications of allowing our infrastructure system to break down. Traffic congestion, unfilled potholes, closed bridges, and the numerous other problems that arise out of our broken system cost our metropolitan economies billions of dollars each year. These problems increase the prices of the goods we purchase. They prevent companies from being able to predict and accurately estimate the costs of their supply chain needs.

At a time when the United States is desperate for an economic boost, President Obama has proposed a plan to double the nation's exports in just a few years' time. Take the proposal at face value, and it is an ambitious plan. But when you look at the significant effect such an increase would have on our nation's infrastructure system, you have to wonder if the system would even be capable of handling such an increase.

LePatner recognizes the critical importance of providing the public with an understanding of the larger connections between the transportation and economic imperatives. He focuses attention on problems that will significantly impact our nation's ability to protect its citizens as well as to grow and prosper in a dynamically changing world economy.

That said, there is no denying that these issues are tough to tackle. Problems are numerous, and the possible solutions are often wrapped tightly in political red tape. LePatner helps readers get a grasp on the enormity of the problem by zeroing in on a specific tragedy. One that undeniably represents our failing system.

The main character in *Too Big to Fall* is the I-35W Bridge collapse. LePatner approaches the events leading to the collapse and what happened in the investigations after the collapse in a manner that I haven't seen done before. What he uncovers is a history of neglect. A lack of maintenance and repairs. A lack of funds to provide them. And government agencies that didn't act fast enough. But most important, he never allows the reader to lose sight of the fact that these issues are not limited to the I-35W collapse. Debates similar to those that went on in the Minnesota Department of Transportation prior to the I-35W collapse are going on now in state DOTs across the country. They are, as LePatner makes clear, issues that affect and stall countless infrastructure repairs and projects today.

In discussing research findings, LePatner does not just recite the typical statistics and big numbers that are so difficult for us to wrap our heads around. He understands that trying to grasp the fact that we need $2.2 trillion to fix existing infrastructure is overwhelming. What he has done here is paint a very vivid picture, using real projects to explain the policies that are responsible for the problems we have today and the policy solutions that are the best candidates for fixing them. This book goes beyond the usual call for a massive investment in infrastructure.

LePatner talks about reforming the system *before* we invest, and that is one of his most important points. He calls out politicians for choosing to fund only those projects that will make them look good on election day. He chastises the overemphasis on new-capacity projects that are initiated in place of much needed, often underfunded routine maintenance and repairs.

The broken system, it's important to note, is a topic that LePatner is all too familiar with. In his previous book *Broken Buildings, Busted Budgets: How to Fix America's Trillion Dollar Construction Industry*, LePatner examines the prevalence of construction cost overruns and missed deadlines within the construction industry itself. These problems only add to those we are experiencing with the nation's infrastructure. Lack of funding is a major reason why our bridges and roads are in the neglected state they are today.

We cannot keep pouring money into a fundamentally broken system. We need a more reliable way of funding these projects, and that will require a reformed construction industry. Contractors on government projects must honor the budgets they are given. We can no longer suffer budgetary disasters on public projects, such as the one experienced with Boston's Big Dig, a project whose cost ballooned billions of dollars over budget.

Pending in the House as these pages are being written is a half-trillion-dollar federal transportation reauthorization. The reauthorization isn't being held up by policy. It's stuck because there is no politically palatable way to pay for it. And when funds are available, they aren't always spent wisely and responsibly. System reform is an imperative. And that begins with changing the conversation in Washington. *Too Big to Fall* belongs on the desk of every transportation official, governor, and member of Congress who wants to work productively toward finding solutions rather than continuing to add to the problems plaguing our nation's infrastructure.

The American people must realize we are going to have to pay to fix this system. We need to make tough decisions regarding increasing the gas tax and creating a national infrastructure bank. We need to put systems in place to ensure that government contracts are given to those construction contractors who provide realistic budgets and timetables. We need to repair our existing system while also planning the projects that will be necessary in order to move the nation toward a low-carbon future.

The prevailing theme in *Too Big to Fall* is that we absolutely must think differently about how we maintain our infrastructure system and build smartly for the future. It's not about finding the cash and building more new projects. It's really about changing the way we do business. We need more transparency in the system. We need accountability. We need to make sure funds are allocated responsibly.

We need to reward those who perform well and penalize those who don't.

One area where we can make huge strides is technology. LePatner devotes a chapter to what he calls the "Technological Imperative." He explains how new technologies can help detect problems earlier, when they will be cheaper to fix. LePatner is 100 percent correct. We need to dramatically ramp up the deployment of advanced technology in our transportation system. Not only will it help us better maintain the current system at a lower cost, but it will create much needed manufacturing jobs.

The United States used to be on the front lines of innovation, and transportation technology should be something that we do tremendously well. But we are falling behind, and neither LePatner nor I can see any valid reason for it.

Now is the time to push for traction on these issues. We've made progress in many other sticky areas of domestic policy, such as health care, education, and welfare. There is no reason why we can't also tackle the critical public policy issue of infrastructure reform. It's time to bring this dialogue out from behind the closed doors of Washington and into the public light.

What does the future hold for the for the nation's infrastructure system? Here again, LePatner and I seem to be in the same camp. We are optimistic because we have to be. I think Americans will get something done. I think it will be painful. But we are inching ever closer to the reality that there is no other alternative. If we can get Congress to move on these issues, and if we can begin incorporating the technologies that are already available to us, the nation could be positioned quite well to compete in a low-carbon, export-oriented, innovation-fueled future. I hope *Too Big to Fall* will serve as the wake-up call that kicks us all—politicians and the public alike—into action.

# Introduction

The history of the United States is integrally linked to the development of its transportation system. Our nation's expansion was fueled by major infrastructure undertakings such as the Erie Canal and the first transcontinental railroad, which enabled commerce to transform sparsely settled areas and created successive waves of economic growth.

From the levees restraining our navigable waterways and the aqueducts providing our drinkable water to the interstate highway system, our infrastructure was essential to our achieving many of our critical national objectives.

Yet we no longer demonstrate a national commitment to assign the massive amounts of funding needed to maintain these important assets. Instead, we prefer to invest in new public infrastructure and fail to address the rapid deterioration of existing roads, bridges, and dams across our country.

In our pursuit of growth, we have forgotten about our existing transportation system, which in many instances dates back over a hundred years and is the connective tissue that enables the movement of our nation's commerce as well as the traveling public. And in the process, we have begun to choke on congestion that ties up our roads and impacts our economy, as it adds untold environmental pressures on a nation struggling to control its addiction to the automobile.

As a measure of how dangerous the condition of these public assets has become, the American Society of Civil Engineers issued a devastating report in 2009, which concluded that the overall condition of our nation's infrastructure—including its dams, wastewater treatment plants, power grid, roads, and bridges—deserves a grade no higher than D.

The purpose of this book is fourfold. First, it takes the reader into the world of our nation's transportation system. Specifically, it looks at our roads and bridges to give the traveling public an understanding of what is needed to maintain our infrastructure facilities after a project's completion. As will be shown, our national and state leaders have failed to recognize the importance of maintenance, exposing us to the dangers posed by an infrastructure system in need of repairs costing trillions of dollars.

The u.s. transportation system includes over 600,000 bridges, of which nearly a quarter are deemed to be either "structurally deficient" or "functionally obsolete."[1] Every day these bridges and the roads that lead to them carry millions of people, including children in school buses; trains and trucks that supply goods and services to our hospitals, supermarkets, and other businesses, as well as our military forces, who need to use these structures to move quickly during an event involving national security.

Second, this book defines the magnitude of the infrastructure problems we face, and the economic imperatives that will eventually make it clear to federal and state leaders that—just as some companies and banks have been deemed too big to fail—our bridges and other critical infrastructure elements are too big to fall.

For too long, politicians have ignored the growing needs of the existing infrastructure in favor of allocating funds for new projects. Over the past twenty years, nearly 600 u.s. bridges are known to have failed, yet our leaders do not see this fact as a critical indictment of our inadequate spending on the repair and maintenance of these structures.

No one should ignore the fact that a bridge failure, even one that is not a tragic collapse, is no small event. When a bridge fails structurally, it must be closed completely or normal traffic across its span must be limited. These events impact communities across our nation and affect commerce throughout the regions involved.

Third, this book lays out the extent of the failures we are currently encountering with these massive transportation facilities. Decades of neglect by our policymakers has led us to believe that we can defer addressing this problem. But the reality is that we are running out of time, and only a handful of our leaders are paying any heed to the frightening statistics being released about the nation's infrastructure.

The tragic collapse of the I-35W Bridge focused national attention on the problems associated with an aging bridge inventory that had not received sufficient funding to keep it in good condition. Despite warnings from engineering consultants that the bridge was beset by myriad maintenance problems—and had what is called fracture-critical design, meaning the failure of one structural member would trigger the collapse of the bridge—in the year preceding the collapse, the Minnesota Department of Transportation (MN/DOT) decided to defer needed bridge redecking owing to a lack of funds.

Yet, within months of the collapse, the federal government provided over $250 million, allowing MN/DOT to build a state-of-the-art bridge with technology that it had been unable to pay for only months earlier. What federal and state transportation authorities have not yet acknowledged to the public as of the date of this writing is that there are 7,980 bridges in our nation today facing the same problems that the I-35W Bridge encountered in the years leading up to its collapse.

Fourth, the book calls on our leaders to reprioritize how they allocate and spend the hundreds of millions of dollars that flow out of Washington each year to state transportation departments. We must demand that funds provided to states are used for projects that minimize widespread metropolitan congestion and for repairs and maintenance to the aging roads and bridges across the country.

Correcting these widespread infrastructure problems while continuing to meet the needs of a growing population—one that is set to grow by 100 million people by 2040—will take an enormous national commitment. Unfortunately, the reality is that our nation as a whole, and our government leaders in particular, do not yet possess the proper mind-set for addressing these problems. In fact, it is clear that our national and state leaders continue to view the allocation of federal transportation funding as choice opportunities for ribbon-cutting ceremonies and for awarding contracts to contributors, who will support politicians' reelection campaigns.

And funding problems aren't going to go away any time soon. Exacerbated by the collapse of the financial world and the slow economic recovery that has followed, even the $787-billion stimulus program has provided little real relief for the massive problems of our declining roads and bridges.

As part of its 2009 job stimulus program, the U.S. Department of Transportation appropriated $48 billion for highways, roads, and bridges. The stimulus plan added another $27.5 billion over a two-year period. However, the challenge currently facing our nation is that we need to focus on the physical neglect that is daily causing our infrastructure to decay, neglect that—according to the American Society of Civil Engineers—will cost approximately $2.2 trillion to redress.

Our outdated and overused road system is falling apart. Vehicular travel on America's roads increased 41 percent between 1990 and 2006, while miles of available road increased by only 4 percent. As a result, congestion has increased enormously. According to the 2009 Texas Urban Mobility Report, prepared by the Texas Transportation Institute,[2] drivers in metropolitan areas spent 4.2 billion hours—nearly a full work week for every traveler—delayed in traffic in 2007.

The mere act of commuting over these congested byways wasted 2.9 billion gallons of gas, enough to fill fifty-eight supertankers. All of this has led to an annual congestion cost for the nation that amounts to a staggering $78 billion! And this cost is not a one-time occurrence, nor is it likely to decrease over time. If we do not give our infrastructure the corrective work it needs, these costs are destined to rise further, pulling down our fragile economy at a time when it can least sustain further losses.

Exacerbating this problem is the fact that our nation lacks an overarching transportation policy that lays out a map to get us out of this crisis. We must overcome outdated congressional funding mechanisms that serve political as opposed to national transportation goals, a lack of vision about how the private sector can work with the government in a constructive partnership to benefit states starved for funding, and an unfathomable reluctance to apply advanced cost-saving technologies to the inspection and remediation of our transportation system. The problem demands leadership that can include all these issues in a cohesive game plan of performance and accountability.

Unless that occurs, the crisis will continue to affect today's traveling public, and we will be leaving future generations to find solutions.

As I began the research for this book, I quickly came to understand that many of the policies behind our national and local transportation programs evolved from perceptions that were rooted in an earlier era, and are no longer relevant. Instead, they represent the political interests of large constituencies that have come to rely on this money as a source of power, without regard to any long-term implications.

Too often, state and local governments have been proposing large-scale transportation projects only after receiving assurances that the federal government would provide a significant portion of the funding to build the project. For example, there would never have been a Big Dig—a project whose cost ballooned from the original $2.4 billion to an eventual $22 billion—had Massachusetts politicians not secured federal guarantees to cover the initial bulk—as well as the growing cost—of the project. But the balance had to be provided from state funding, and the irony of this biggest boondoggle in U.S. transportation history is that Massachusetts is now saddled with paying such amounts to complete and maintain the project that the state is teetering on the edge of bankruptcy.

Any hope that federal and state governments have learned important lessons from this debacle is misplaced. Each year, construction of airports, sports arenas, and other government-subsidized projects prove that such boondoggles are on the rise. In essence, we build new transportation projects while ignoring our aging roads and bridges, which are failing.

Many experts in government and financial circles who have struggled to understand why such formidable obstacles have arisen to prevent the funding of adequate maintenance for our infrastructure believe that the answer lies within the nature of the American political process itself. Gary S. Becker, an economist at the University of Chicago, has argued that "a problem in getting adequate resources to any important government activity [such as infrastructure] is that they must compete with so many other demands on the very liberal overall budgets. In particular, spending on road safety has to compete against spending on medical care, retirement benefits, housing subsidies, public transportation, agricultural subsidies, and numerous other ways to spend government revenues."[3]

I chose to focus this book on our roads and bridges because they are the backbone of our transportation system. These structures play an essential role in our commercial interests at home and overseas, and in our national security. In our nation's cities and rural areas alike, we need to recognize the increasingly dangerous nature of the crisis. The story of how our nation's leaders ignored for decades the importance of our infrastructure to our national well-being, and how we allowed our roads and bridges to deteriorate, is one we need to understand and learn from.

*Too Big to Fall* brings into focus the critical role played by the 600,000 bridges that comprise our National Bridge Inventory. Few Americans understand that bridges are comprised of thousands of moving parts that are in constant need of attention if they are to continue to operate as originally designed. In effect, a bridge is a finely calibrated machine that, much like a car or airplane, has an expected life span, requiring increasing amounts of maintenance if it is to be safely used decades after being put into operation.

This book makes a direct plea to our nation's leaders to rise above the divisiveness of current politics and recognize the peril we find ourselves in. The story of our beleaguered infrastructure transcends political affiliations.

I believe that many of our federal and state leaders are fully aware of the crisis, which has been reported to them by their transportation agencies. Unfortunately, we sorely lack leadership from the federal government. We need leaders who recognize the urgency of developing a coordinated policy that combines federal, state, local, and private interests into a single strategy for rescuing our transportation system. In the absence of such a new national transportation plan, I have no doubt that we will see many more tragedies like the one on I-35W in the years ahead

The origins of *Too Big to Fall* may lie in a congressional subcommittee's request for me to testify before it in 1983, following the publication of *Structural and Foundation Failures*, which I wrote with a professional engineer, Sidney M. Johnson. The subcommittee was investigating recent collapses of major buildings, bridges, and other facilities such as the Hartford Civic Center, and the skyway within the newly opened Hyatt Regency hotel in Kansas City.

In preparing to testify, I gathered extensive evidence to show that major hotels, hospitals, schools, arenas, and other facilities across the nation were being constructed without the active oversight of the very architects and engineers who had designed them. The members of the subcommittee were shocked to learn of this and other details about how we build large, complex structures. The report they issued warned of the perils of failing to ensure that our largest structures be properly designed, constructed, and maintained. Several of the report's findings and recommendations, while still valuable, remain unfulfilled to this day.

Since the issuance of that congressional report, little has improved in the way we build and maintain the nation's public facilities. When it collapsed, the I-35W Bridge in Minneapolis had been rated structurally deficient by its inspectors for the previous sixteen years. It had experienced advanced corrosion, frozen bearings, and poor maintenance, entitling the state to receive federal funding to maintain it.

In the weeks and months following that tragedy, I listened to state transportation leaders and governors tell the media and the public that there was little need to be concerned about their own states' bridges since "just because a bridge is rated 'structurally deficient' does not mean it is in danger." As this book will reveal, those statements were made by public officials who were either naive or intentionally set out to mislead their constituents as to the nature and extent of the hazards facing the traveling public in their states.

In chapter 1, I briefly recount the story of the New York State Thruway's Schoharie Creek Bridge, which collapsed on April 5, 1987, in a flood as a result of rushing waters that swept away the surrounding supports beneath one of its piers, resulting in ten deaths. A commission appointed to investigate the Schoharie Creek Bridge failure concluded that "while the bridge's design and construction may well have been deficient, with proper inspection and maintenance, this bridge would not have collapsed." Twenty years later, after the tragic collapse of the I-35W Bridge, another investigation—this one conducted by a law firm hired by the Minnesota State Legislature—concluded once again that while the bridge's design and construction may well have been deficient, "with proper inspection and maintenance, this bridge would not have collapsed."[4]

A detailed and critical look at the history of the I-35W Bridge and its maintenance as revealed in the documentary record forcefully suggests that this structure—like the Silver Bridge, the Sunshine Skyway Bridge, the Mianus River Bridge, and the Schoharie Creek Bridge before it—was destroyed in large part by the inability of those charged with its care to inspect it, maintain it, and remedy its known defects that threatened the safety of the traveling public.

In a speech before the National Council on Public Works Improvements, Edward V. Regan, a former New York State comptroller, stated: "When highways and bridges are regularly maintained there is no press coverage. When they are rebuilt it is an 'event.' There is a ribbon cutting and plenty of press coverage. The incentives, therefore, are for public officials to purposefully starve the maintenance budget. . . . Until this motivation . . . is acted upon, we will be treated to recurrent infrastructure crises."[5]

As will be discussed in chapter 5, the NTSB findings on the I-35W Bridge collapse were a rush to judgment that failed to address significant factors that led to this unnecessary tragedy. In addition, the findings failed to pass along the lessons that should have been drawn from this horrific event.

We face a crisis of growing proportions as our nation's infrastructure ages without sufficient financial resources to bring it back to acceptable standards. Today, the average bridge in the United States is more than fifty years old. Most bridges in the country were designed for a fifty-year life span, and they have not received the necessary maintenance to ensure their safety during their extended use.

Due to the nation's economic collapse, a more cautious and poorer American population has traveled less, reducing the money collected through fuel taxes and tolls that are supposed to provide most of the funds for maintaining our roads. Politicians have been loath to raise gasoline taxes, while drivers have not been given adequate incentives to purchase more fuel-efficient vehicles. And if they were to do so in large numbers, which would have a great effect on the environment and cause a reduction in the need for imported oil, that too would have an inverse impact on funding for road maintenance, as revenues from gasoline taxes would decline.

Other solutions will need to be identified if we are to escape the consequences of decades of misdirected funding for our transportation system. These solutions might include an overall increase in the number of toll roads to be developed by public and private partnerships. These new vehicles for private investment, widely utilized in other parts of the world, would enable the federal and state governments to shift more of the cost of road and bridge maintenance to private interests, in return for upfront payments.

There will be no easy solutions for the problems discussed in this book. Because state governments lack both the financial resources and the geographic perspective to propose creative alternatives to the morass of the current status quo, national solutions are needed.

In chapter 6, I offer a series of recommendations designed to provide a road map to address these complex issues. It is my hope that these suggestions will initiate a national debate to engage political, transportation, and national policy experts, as well as average citizens, who are daily affected by the current state of our nation's infrastructure.

The risks of continuing to ignore our ill-maintained national infrastructure are almost unimaginable. We can no longer fail to devote massive amounts of money to repair our aging roads and bridges. We must begin to set a national policy that goes beyond the myopic vision of state and local politicians who prefer to use federal transportation funds on pork-barrel projects. We will need to reorganize our priorities for years to come, or risk the lives and well-being of our fellow citizens.

George E. Peterson of the Urban Institute has argued that it is political factors rather than economic issues that are the cause of inadequate infrastructure financing. Peterson found merit in the argument that "infrastructure spending has been unable to compete effectively with other budget claims for political reasons," observing that "budget reductions that trigger employment layoffs, wage freezes, and cancellation of public services meet immediate and vigorous opposition. At least in the past, maintenance deferrals and cancellation of underground capital projects have been much less visible to the electorate." In Peterson's view, the larger reason for inadequate infrastructure investment, including maintenance, reflected "a deliberate budget choice exercised by public officials and by voters," even though "it is possible—indeed, likely—that with better and more plentiful information as to the condition of facilities and the consequences of deferring repair investment, local governments would have chosen to spend more for these purposes."[6]

For those who would seek to dismiss the facts that support the thesis of this book, I ask them to consult the many professional engineers in state transportation departments who face these problems on a daily basis. These professionals understand the physics of bridge and road design, and the real problems of ignoring what happens to steel and concrete when they are exposed to the elements without a strict regimen of ongoing maintenance.

I urge all readers to study the lessons learned from the bridges presented in chapter 1 of *Too Big to Fall* and ask which type of leadership they would wish to have presiding over their own state or local transportation departments in the years ahead.

# 1 A Tale of Two Bridges

Walking through its faded, cramped domestic terminal, I got the feeling of a place that once thought of itself as modern but has had one too many face-lifts and simply can't hide the wrinkles anymore. In some ways, LAX is us. We are the United States of Deferred Maintenance. China is the People's Republic of Deferred Gratification. They save, invest and build. We spend, borrow and patch. —Thomas L. Friedman, A Word From the Wise, *New York Times*, March 2, 2010

Any analysis of our nation's infrastructure in the twenty-first century quickly becomes a classic tale of image versus reality. If we were to listen to the authorities placed in charge of our roads, bridges, and power and other systems critical to maintaining our domestic and global commerce, we would hear of the great need for investment in new projects but little about the need for critical, even emergency, repairs of existing structures. We would be told in conventional public relations language that despite the fact that over 25 percent of the nation's 600,000 bridges were not designed to handle the traffic that currently goes over them, there are no unsafe structures and no need for the traveling public to be concerned.

And while our nation promotes itself at home and abroad as the world leader in technology and education, when it comes to our vital infrastructure, we are a prime example of inefficiency and misinformation, with a top-to-bottom governmental system that chooses to ignore one of our nation's most pressing problems. As Michael Keeley, a former Los Angeles deputy mayor, stated about city administration, we need to think of government "as a big bus" which is "divided into different sections with different constituencies: labor, the city council, the mayor, interest groups, and contractors. Every seat is equipped with a brake, so lots of people can stop the bus anytime. The problem is that this makes the bus undrivable."[1] Those authorities who make such soothing statements about our nation's infrastructure would be hard pressed to provide evidence for them. The fact is that the structural backbone of our nation—upon which we depend for the reliable and efficient delivery of people, goods, and services—is in great peril.

In the final analysis, just as our high-school science teachers taught us, gravity wins. Just as it is not possible for aircraft to stay up in the sky indefinitely, it is not possible for bridges to stand forever. Both are products of human ingenuity, inventiveness, investment, and technology. Both are machines engineered for specific purposes, consisting of hundreds if not thousands of synchronized moving parts that have to withstand human use, the elements, and the challenge of operating efficiently within changing environments. What keeps an airplane aloft is the constant forward motion of a carefully designed machine, fueled by an enormous amount of energy. There must be continuous and carefully coordinated and documented maintenance procedures to ensure that the machine meets the challenges of flight.

A bridge also is a hugely complex machine. If it is to continue to carry travelers across its span, its design must be matched by the quality of its construction and attention must be paid to its maintenance during its intended life span. Airplane manufacturing is a product of standards and controls meticulously adhered to, by virtue of uniform fabrication within a factory setting where quality is controlled. But we do not have the luxury of mass-producing bridges. Rather, they are built to very specific standards and specifications at one-of-a-kind locations. There is no learning curve from prior mistakes in design or fabrication of an exact precursor. But just like airplanes, bridges are not built to last forever. For both, maintenance is mandatory. Without it, gravity wins sooner or later—and sometimes without warning.

This book will tell the story of our nation's failure to provide the mandatory maintenance for our roads and bridges, and why and how that has come to pass. It will also tell a classic American tale about our nation's fascination with building anew and about how—in our desire to build the next new road or bridge or building—we have too often forgotten the importance of maintaining that which is no longer new.

The story begins with two different bridges of different vintages in different parts of the country: the I-35W Bridge over the Mississippi River in Minneapolis and the Williamsburg Bridge traversing the East River in New York City. One fell down and was national news for a considerable period of time; the other nearly fell down and was local news for a matter of days. In each locale, and in fact around the nation, the public never grasped the broader implication of these stories: that these situations were symptomatic of larger issues, and the nation should be deeply concerned about our aging transportation system.

The reasons for these bridges' failures that local officials offered to the public were not the real reasons. Each of these situations reflected decades of deferred maintenance so that transportation funding could be used elsewhere. In each situation, public officials had neglected public safety and betrayed public trust. Few Americans are aware that between 1989 and 2003, 500 bridges failed throughout the United States.[2] These numbers will continue to rise unless we take immediate steps to change the way we manage and maintain our aging infrastructure.

## The I-35W Bridge: Catastrophe

When the I-35W Bridge in Minneapolis shuddered, buckled, and collapsed during the evening rush hour on Wednesday, August 1, 2007, plunging 111 vehicles into the Mississippi River and sending thirteen people to their deaths, the sudden, apparently inexplicable nature of the event at first gave it the appearance of an act of God. "The Bridge collapsed for no apparent reason," stated an investigative report by the law firm Gray Plant Mooty, commissioned by the Minnesota legislature and published nine months after the accident.[3] Yet, bridges do not collapse for "no apparent reason" The public believes that bridges often collapse because they are knocked down by wind, water, or collisions with large objects such as boats or planes, although in fact, even in such circumstances, defects in the structure may be the ultimate cause of collapse.

Bridges are designed to withstand winter weather, hurricanes, and other extreme conditions. When a bridge is struck by a violent external force or collapses under some less extreme form of duress, the cause may be imperfect design or any number of other reasons.[4] For all their sense of solidity and grandeur and their seeming sense of permanence, bridges and their thousands of moving parts are always exposed to the elements. Any recognition of how a bridge fails must start with an understanding that the process begins as soon as the structure is completed, with its exposure to weather and traffic. If its support system rests in a river or a stream, the bridge will experience the effects of corrosion from exposure to the water that flows around it (which is especially a problem if the bridge is located over salt water). Moving the soil around the bridge's foundation, the flowing water may eventually cause scour (loss of designed support) at the foundation.

No two bridges can ever be precisely alike. The variety of conditions under which each bridge is constructed ensures this. Factors such as the size of the span, the nature of the waterway or roadway to be spanned, the amount of traffic anticipated immediately and in the future, the soil at each end of the bridge, and the economic conditions under which the bridge must be designed and built all ensure that the each bridge will be unlike any previous one. Similarly, bridges fail for many reasons. Errors or omissions in the engineering plans and specifications; defective materials or construction; workers' lack of necessary skills to perform critical work; inadequate funding or time to perform the work; inadequate maintenance, which accelerates the degradation of the original materials; and graft and corruption are some of the factors that can lead to a failure. In addition, not all failures lead to the collapse of a bridge. A failure may be defined as an occasion when a necessary function of the bridge cannot be performed, or when a bridge fails to meet defined performance specifications. Although not all failures result in highly publicized collapses, failure often requires the closure of all or part of a bridge.

The I-35W Bridge was ultimately brought down by a long history of inadequate maintenance resulting from managerial and financial shortsightedness. Designed in 1964 by the St. Louis–based firm of Sverdrup & Parcel and opened in 1967, the bridge was built at a time when the bulk of the nation's freight moved by rail and not by massive eighteen-wheel trucks. It was built to carry approximately 60,000 cars per day. The bridge was 1,407 feet long, with three main spans of steel deck-truss construction. The first important point to understand about the design of this bridge is that the structure was designed as fracture-critical, meaning that the failure of any one of its supporting structural members could result in the collapse of the whole bridge.

During the post–World War II boom in bridge building in the United States, fracture-critical steel bridge designs were common as a means of streamlining construction and saving costs. They remained common until the 1980s, when new specifications issued by the American Association of State Highway and Transportation Officials (AASHTO) led to a requirement of greater load-path redundancy—in other words, bridges now had to be designed so that if one structural support failed, the load could be distributed among other supports in order to prevent a sudden, catastrophic collapse. When the I-35W Bridge was built, it was not unusual—in fact, there are 18,857 fracture-critical steel deck-truss bridges still in use in the United States today.[5]

The bridge underwent two modifications over the years. The first of these was an expansion, performed by the Minnesota Department of Transportation (MN/DOT) in 1977, in which the thickness of the concrete overlay on the road deck was increased from six inches to eight and two lanes were added to the original six lanes for traffic, increasing the width of the roadway. The second modification, also undertaken by MN/DOT, took place in 1998, when a concrete median, side barriers, drain systems, and bird guards were added. In the meantime, as car and truck traffic increased and the weight of these vehicles grew over the years, loads on the bridge increased considerably, as suggested by the 1977 expansion project. By 2007, the year the bridge collapsed, approximately 160,000 cars were passing over it every day,[6] and the combination of increased dead load (the weight of the structure itself, heavier after the 1977 and 1998 modifications) and increased live load (owing to higher traffic volume and heavier truck loads) was significantly greater than the structure's design load.[7]

From 1967, when the I-35W Bridge was built, to 1997 a number of prominent national collapses and near misses should have served as clear warnings to federal and state authorities that our infrastructure required immediate attention. More and more money was being funneled into the transportation system but was being spent on new projects instead of needed maintenance. In the same year that the I-35W Bridge opened, the worst bridge disaster in American history to date occurred.

The collapse of the Silver Bridge over the Ohio River between Point Pleasant, West Virginia, and Kanauga, Ohio, during rush hour in the Christmas shopping season, killed forty-six people and shocked the nation. A West Virginia court found clear evidence of shoddy inspection procedures but declined to find the state (which owned the bridge) guilty of negligence.

On May 9, 1980, the Sunshine Skyway Bridge over Tampa Bay collapsed, killing thirty-five people. A freighter veering off course in a storm struck a pier, triggering the collapse. While the disaster initially seemed to be an act of God, investigation disclosed that the ultimate cause of the collapse was the Florida Department of Transportation's failure to care for the bridge and adequately protect the piers from collisions. Nearly two years before the accident, the June 4, 1978, *Floridian*, the Sunday magazine section of the *St. Petersburg Times*, had featured an article titled "What Could Make the Skyway Bridge Fall Down?"[8] The article reported that a key pier was known to be cracked and, in fact, it would turn out that the Florida Department of Transportation (Florida DOT) had known since 1969—eleven years before the bridge collapsed—about significant problems with all the piers of the south span of the bridge but had done nothing in response besides taking palliative measures, creating task forces, and performing studies.

The *Floridian* article also mentioned "a stream of reports detailing the weakening of the structure by corrosion" and included an interview with the chief of bridge maintenance for the Florida DOT, who had been the project engineer on the south span of the Sunshine Skyway. According to the article, the department official admitted that the state had put off the repair of corroded support members while waiting for the bridge to be designated as part of the interstate highway system, which would entitle the state to qualify for an upgrade paid for by the federal government. At a hearing held by the Coast Guard Board of Inquiry within days of the Sunshine Skyway's collapse, the same official who had spoken with the *Floridian* reporter testified that "putting fenders around the pilings of the Skyway Bridge to guard against such collisions had been discussed for some years, but"—in a refrain that would be echoed by other transportation officials over the next few decades—"there was never money in the budget to do it."

In the 1980s, two major bridge collapses became the impetus for further improvements in the art of bridge inspection and maintenance. The 1983 collapse of a major section of the fracture-critical Mianus River Bridge on I-95 in Greenwich, Connecticut, killed three people when their cars fell from the bridge. The cause of the collapse was attributed to corrosion, metal fatigue, and lack of adequate maintenance. As a study for the Transportation Research Board explained: "The [Mianus River] failure precipitated significant research into fatigue behavior of steel connections and existing NBIS [National Bridge Inspection Standards] programs were modified to incorporate more rigorous inspection procedures for fracture-critical bridges. Specialized training programs were also strengthened to increase the bridge inspection community's understanding of fatigue and fracture problems."[9] As a result of one of several recommendations about the bridge inspection process made in the report of the National Transportation Safety Board (NTSB) on the Mianus River Bridge collapse, inspectors were now required by the NBIS to report on a greater number of bridge components and conditions than previously and to "assign condition ratings to critical bridge components."[10]

Then on April 5, 1987, the catastrophic failure of the Schoharie Creek Bridge in upstate New York, attributed to scour and the failure of the New York State Thruway Authority (NYSTA) to take adequate measures to protect the bridge's piers and abutments from it, resulted in the requirement that states "identify bridges that are susceptible to scour and develop special underwater inspection procedures."[11] The NTSB investigation of the Schoharie Creek Bridge collapse also faulted both the NYSTA's inspection program and the oversight of bridge inspection and maintenance on the Thruway by both the NYSTA and the FHWA.[12] What alarmed the NTSB most was that only two years earlier, it had completed an investigation of the collapse of the Chickasawbogue Bridge near Mobile, Alabama,[13] which concluded that underwater inspections by states had not been carried out in a proper manner.

Based on that investigation, the NTSB had recommended that the FHWA "establish criteria for inspecting the underwater elements of bridges . . . as they relate to bridge design and maintenance." Although the FHWA promised the NTSB to prepare new rules for underwater inspections, they were not promulgated until April 1987. What was most revealing were the dire warnings set out in a 1988 NTSB safety recommendation about the failure of not only the FHWA, but also AASHTO to prevent this type of collapse from occurring repeatedly across the nation. The NTSB warned that "the circumstances that led to the collapse of the Schoharie Creek Bridge were not isolated events but may represent conditions that can occur at other bridge sites throughout the country." Noting that the design of the Chickasawbogue Bridge was similar to that of many other bridges constructed in the late 1940s through the 1960s, the NTSB noted that "there is a potential for other similarly designed and constructed bridges to collapse catastrophically from erosion of their foundations."[14]

When the NTSB then asked the FHWA how many bridges across the nation were similar to the Schoharie Creek Bridge, alarmingly, the FHWA was unable to provide that information. A separate request to three states revealed a list of several hundred such bridges over water with similar designs that lacked redundancy—that is, the designs were without structural support to keep the bridge up if one member failed. As a result, another twenty-five bridges were immediately closed for repair.[15] Further investigation by the NTSB revealed that at least 43,000 bridges in the nation had not been inspected within the prior two years, although regulations mandated such inspections.

The story of the I-35W collapse represents a more alarming version of the same story. The most obvious starting point of this disaster must include the failure by MN/DOT to provide needed maintenance for a bridge that was deteriorating for many years. The basic facts, supported by the voluminous record of the bridge's inspection teams, tell a simple tale. In 1991, after numerous reports of deterioration, inspectors downgraded the bridge's previous rating of satisfactory to poor or structurally deficient. Such a drop in rating entitled MN/DOT to receive federal funding for the bridge's remediation. While accepting federal funding for ongoing repairs during the sixteen years until its collapse on August 1, 2007, the state never managed to improve the bridge's rating of poor. Despite repeated warnings from outside consultants from 2001 to 2006 that this fracture-critical bridge needed strengthening to avoid collapse if even one structural member failed, MN/DOT officials continued to treat the bridge as one that was safe for the over 160,000 vehicles that traveled across it every day.

The November 2008 NTSB report, which followed fifteen months of investigation, tellingly ignored the maintenance record for the I-35W Bridge. Pursuing an entirely different course, the report presents a surprisingly different picture. Simply put, the NTSB advised the public and transportation officials around the country that this was a one-time occurrence, caused by a simple design error that had gone undetected at the time of construction. Therefore the NTSB treated the I-35W collapse—which resulted in thirteen deaths, injuries to 145 other people, and massive economic disruption to the Twin Cities metropolitan area (plus $278 million for an entirely new bridge)—as a one-off from which no lessons could be learned to avoid future failures. A careful analysis of the NTSB report shows that it masked far more than it revealed about how the I-35W was maintained, funded, and operated. This failure to address the ongoing deterioration of a forty-year-old fracture-critical bridge—rather than a design failure at the time of construction—brought this structure to its tragic and preventable end. Moreover, the story of the I-35W is not an isolated tale of one state's transportation agency. It is the tale of the culture of neglect that permeates our national transportation system.

Yet the NTSB's final report said that the failure of the bridge was the result of a design error—specifically, the underdesign of the gusset plates (metal plates used to connect structural members of a truss and hold them in position at a joint) at six nodes of the deck truss. Careful analysis showed that these gusset plates should have been an inch thick but instead were only half that thickness, contrary to the original design specification. At the time of its construction, all of the other similar gusset plates were designed and fabricated as being one inch in thickness, thereby complying with the design standards for this type of bridge.

The NTSB concluded that the primary cause of the failure was the error in the design of the gusset plates at the U10 node (near the south end of the bridge's central span) that had gone undetected both before and after construction in 1967. Adding to the stresses on the too-thin gusset plates, the report stated, were "substantial increases in the dead load . . . on the day of the accident, [from] the traffic load and the concentrated loads from the construction materials and equipment."[16] The concentrated loads of the construction materials and equipment over the U10 node, amounting to 578,735 pounds of machinery, sand, and gravel—equivalent to the weight of a 747 airplane[17]—had been placed there by the contractor who was replacing a deck overlay.

According to the NTSB report, had all the gusset plates met design standards at the time of construction, then—even with the increased weight from the bridge additions, the increase in traffic, and the weight of the construction materials and machinery—the collapse would not have occurred.[18] As we will see, this analysis displayed at best a partial picture of the factors involved in the bridge's collapse and presented a misleading conclusion that focused the nation's attention away from other causes that exist today in countless other bridges around the nation.

In the NTSB's account of the I-35W disaster, the concentration of hundreds of tons of construction equipment and material on one relatively small point on the bridge played a role equivalent to that of the freighter that hit the Sunshine Skyway Bridge in 1980. The construction equipment and materials on the I-35W Bridge just happened to be placed at one of its weakest points, directly over one of the nodes where the gusset plates were too thin. By blaming only the bridge's engineers and faulting procedures that failed to detect the poorly designed gusset plates during construction inspections,[19] the safety board implicitly cleared MN/DOT, the contractor who was doing the overlay work at the time of the accident, and all others of any responsibility for the bridge's failure.

Is it true that the I-35W Bridge collapsed in 2007 because of a design flaw that went undetected when the structure was designed, fabricated, and constructed in the mid-1960s? Should standard bridge inspection procedures at the time have detected the design error before the bridge was completed? Why and how did the bridge remain operational for forty years with such a critical design flaw? Were engineers on the staff of MN/DOT wrong to have overlooked the error when two lanes were added to the bridge in 1977, and a median strip constructed in 1994? Do the maintenance and inspection records for the bridge reveal other factors that were minimized or overlooked by the NTSB during its investigation? This book challenges the official findings and offers a far more alarming explanation for the tragic end of the I-35W Bridge.

The NTSB's findings were subjected to criticism even before they were published in November 2008. In January of that year, after NTSB Chairman Mark Rosenker made a preliminary announcement that an error in the design of the gusset plates was the critical factor in the collapse of the bridge, James Oberstar of Minnesota—chairman of the House Committee on Transportation and Infrastructure, who had promptly introduced a bill to overhaul national bridge inspection procedures following the I-35W disaster—angrily accused the NTSB of rushing to judgment. That same month, a member of the Minnesota state senate, who is also a licensed professional engineer, voiced his own doubts in an article in the Minneapolis-St. Paul Star Tribune. "The collapse was not an act of God; it was an error of oversight," wrote Jim Carlson, a member of the Minnesota legislature's joint committee on the I-35W collapse. "Something was missed."[20] Actually, a lot of things had been missed for a very long time.

The NTSB's findings virtually ignored over sixteen years of inspection reports that showed continually deteriorating structural conditions, factors that were highlighted in several outside engineering reports commissioned by MN/DOT. These reports, which detailed the frailties of this fracture-critical bridge, made a series of recommendations—which went largely unheeded—for addressing the problems resulting from neglected maintenance.

In 1967, the year the I-35W Bridge opened, the collapse of the Silver Bridge in West Virginia spurred the creation of the National Bridge Inspection Program, the first in the nation's history. In 1971, the U.S. Department of Transportation developed the NBIS, which mandated routine inspections at least once every two years of bridges that were a part of the federal-aid highway system (highways supported by federal funds).[21] Federal standards for inspections of bridges call for regular observations and measurements that capture the physical and functional state of a bridge. These standards, set out in AASHTO's *Manual for Condition Evaluation of Bridges*, have been adopted by all state transportation agencies. The inspections, largely close-up visual examinations, are performed by individuals who have met certain qualifications—often as the result of a three-week course under the purview of the FHWA. All inspections include examination of a bridge's major components: the bridge deck, superstructure, and substructure. Certain bridge components are impacted by weather and use and thus require careful inspection on a regular basis. As shown in Figure 1, each area of a bridge must be inspected to ascertain its

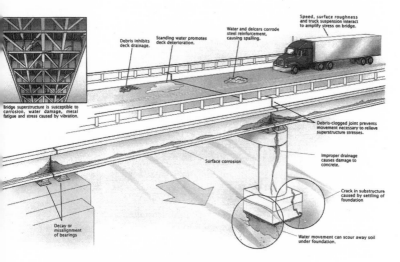

**Figure 1. Areas of a bridge most impacted
by continued lack of maintenance.**

Kenneth F. Dunker and Basile G. Rabbat, "Why America's Bridges Are Crumbling:
Inadequate maintenance has piled up a repair bill that will take decades to pay.
Indeed, the scope of the problem is only now becoming clear," *Scientific American*,
Volume 266 Number 3 (March 1993) 66–72.

condition, so that inspection reports can document any progressive
deterioration over time.

Not coincidentally, the increased inspections mandated for all
bridges in the NBIS revealed cracking on steel highway bridges.[22] Because the I-35W Bridge was designed as a fracture-critical bridge, it was
required to be inspected annually starting in 1971. By 1993, in addition
to its annual inspection, it began receiving annual, in-depth fracture-
critical inspections under new requirements in the federal Surface
Transportation and Uniform Relocation Assistance Act of 1987.

The first noteworthy event in the inspection history of the I-35W

Bridge occurred in 1991. Until that year, the rating for its superstructure in the numerical system stipulated by the NBIS had ranged from 7 to 8 (good) for the years 1983 to 1990. However, it dropped abruptly in 1991 to 4 (poor) and remained in this condition until the Bridge collapsed sixteen years later. Bridge ratings range from a high of 10 for newly built bridges to a low of zero. A drop of three rating levels from good to poor represented the I-35W Bridge's accelerating structural deterioration. According to MN/DOT's *Bridge Inspection Manual*, a rating of 4 means that the "superstructure has advanced deterioration. Members may be significantly bent or misaligned. Connection failure may be imminent. Bearings may be severely restricted."[23] Such a rating reflects corrosion in critical stress areas as well as the existence of fatigue cracks, which form as the result of excessive vibrations.[24] This downgrade pushed the bridge into a category of structurally deficient bridges, a category containing tens of thousands of bridges evincing continual deterioration throughout the United States.

While the NTSB findings on the cause of the collapse made no reference to the condition of the bridge bearings, reports of highly regarded consultants found that these bearings, frozen by years of rust, may have played a contributory cause in the collapse. MN/DOT's inspection reports acknowledged that the I-35W Bridge's members were bent or misaligned and that critical bearings had been rusted and frozen in place preventing movement. All of these signs of deterioration should have required close scrutiny, but that never happened. The NTSB ignored the significance of these reports.

In June 2006, at the last regularly scheduled state inspection of the I-35W Bridge prior to the collapse, inspectors gave the superstructure a rating of 4, noting surface rust corrosion and pack rust connected with the unsound condition of 15 percent of the paint; numerous problems with the main truss members, including poor weld details, section loss, and flaking rust; and a variety of problems with the floor beam trusses, stringers, truss bearing assemblies, and other components.

Naturally one wonders what the inspection reports on the bridge were saying about its condition during this period, and in fact one of the answers to this question is especially revealing. As required by MN/DOT's *Bridge Inspection Manual*,[25] the annual fracture-critical inspections that the agency began performing on the I-35W Bridge in 1994 were supposed to be in-depth, but reviews of the reports resulting from these inspections reveal significant lapses in documenting ongoing corrosion. As a recent article on bridge safety in a National Academy of Engineering journal explains, one of the causes of bridge collapse is "decay from cracking or corrosion, often indicating improper maintenance and inspection," while "one of the major responsibilities of bridge inspectors is to watch for such deterioration."[26]

The AASHTO fracture-critical inspection guidelines require that inspection reports identify the precise amount of corrosion and section loss so that future annual inspections can chart any growth of deterioration. Inspectors are required to visually analyze build-ups of rust and, if necessary, to measure rusted areas using tools or ultrasonic thickness meters. The purpose for such precision is quite clear: to allow the evaluation of the effect of the losses on support member capacity from year to year.[27] Only by documenting the ongoing corrosion with precision is it possible to evaluate the loss of member capacity over a period of time.

In the case of the I-35W Bridge, the inspection report for 1993 identified and measured section loss on certain trusses, but the 1994 fracture-critical inspection report—as well as those for every year between 1995 and 2007, except for 1996—merely reported "section loss at gusset plate, bottom chord, truss #2."[28] The reports do not quantify the amount of observable loss, as required.[29] Thus, the inspection reports covering fourteen of the sixteen years during which the I-35W Bridge was rated in poor condition provided no documentation of the extent of ongoing corrosion on fracture-critical members of the bridge.

While MN/DOT was failing to document how rapidly corrosion was progressing on the I-35W Bridge, and allowing the other conditions noted in the June 2006 inspection report to proliferate, it *was* paying attention to another problem: fatigue cracks, to which steel bridges are prone. In 1998, the same year that the concrete center median, side barriers, drain systems, and bird guards were added to the bridge, an inspection discovered "numerous cracks in beams supporting both the north and south approach spans," a condition that was termed a "'critical finding,' although not one that required closing of the Bridge."[30] MN/DOT made necessary repairs and increased the frequency of inspections from once to twice annually until, in 2000, it reinstated the annual inspection schedule after additional testing was performed on the approach spans and no new cracking was found.[31]

Meanwhile, concerned about the possibility of fatigue cracking on the deck truss, MN/DOT hired the University of Minnesota to, as the Gray Plant Mooty report put it, "evaluate the potential for fatigue cracking in the deck truss, and estimate the remaining life if fatigue cracking was a potential," as well as to "recommend increased inspection or retrofitting, if necessary." The university's report, issued in March 2001, provided good news: fatigue cracking on the deck truss was not to be expected during the remaining life of the bridge.[32] The University of Minnesota researchers recommended that certain areas of the main truss and floor trusses be frequently inspected, sounding a cautionary—and prescient—note in the report's concluding comments about the fragility of the bridge's fracture-critical design: "Concern about fatigue cracking in the deck truss is heightened by a lack of redundancy in the main truss system. Only two planes of the main trusses support the eight lanes of traffic. . . . Therefore, if one member were severed by a fatigue crack, that plane of the main truss would, theoretically, collapse."[33] The key finding of these consultants was that if any one crack severed a critical member, the entire fracture-critical bridge was at risk.

In light of such concerns, late in 1998 or early in 1999, MN/DOT discussed with HNTB Corporation, a nationally recognized expert in the design and maintenance of bridges, possible ways of adding redundancy—i.e., removing the risks posed by the bridge's fracture-critical design. Discussions between MN/DOT and HNTB—which included a proposal from the latter in May 2000 listing "a set of proposed tasks to evaluate and increase the redundancy of the Bridge" and renderings of "supplemental plates" as well as a "new oversize gusset"[34]—lasted until the end of 2001 without the company's receiving any compensation. Then in March 2003, instead of pursuing this work with HNTB, MN/DOT issued a request for interest (RFI). HNTB responded to the request, but so did URS Corporation, another large engineering firm, which was awarded a pair of contracts later that year. Why, after spending three years in consultations with HNTB, did MN/DOT issue the RFI and hire URS for this job? URS, it turned out, had recently hired Don Flemming, a former head of MN/DOT's central bridge division who had also been state bridge engineer from 1986 to 2000. While Flemming was still at MN/DOT, he had spoken to his colleagues about the need to add redundancy to the I-35W Bridge.[35] At URS, not surprisingly, Flemming became "a primary contact for MN/DOT."[36]

URS's two contracts—one entailing evaluation of the condition of key superstructure components, and the second the performance of the remedial work—addressed three main areas: identifying those main superstructure truss members highly susceptible to fatigue cracking, and the implications if such members failed; identifying methods to repair present and future fatigue cracks; and developing a method to replace the deck as a means of reducing known stresses on the bridge. URS agreed with the University of Minnesota report that had found that fatigue cracks were not expected to develop in the deck truss, but the company concluded that "fatigue concern should not be completely discounted," for reasons including that "access to the fatigue susceptible details inside the truss sections is very limited for crack inspection . . . and therefore a timely discovery is unlikely to happen should a crack occur for some unusual causes."[37] In essence, URS highlighted the major shortcoming of an inspection process that relied almost exclusively on visual investigation to detect what was largely invisible. Significantly, the URS contract omitted one task that HNTB had included as part of its proposal: an analysis of the gusset plate connections.[38]

Despite the work outlined in the URS contracts, over the course of the more than four years between the signing of the first contract in June 2003 and the collapse of the bridge in August 2007, no steps to add redundancy were ever taken. Nor were any steps taken to inspect and analyze the gusset plates, despite the fact that a 2003 URS report contained photographs of the bowed gusset plates.

URS began work on its second contract with MN/DOT on the I-35W Bridge in January 2004. The work took longer than expected, and the date for its completion was extended several times owing to circumstances "arising in part from the unique complexity of the project."[39] By spring 2006, however, MN/DOT was evaluating three recommendations that URS would present in a preliminary report in July 2006. These recommendations were that MN/DOT: (1) completely redeck the bridge in order to add structural redundancy; (2) retrofit fracture-critical truss members with steel plating to add redundancy, most notably "five of the eight critical members [that] are fracture-critical," such that a failure of any one of them would cause instability of the structural system; and (3) continue to inspect the bridge regularly.

In an August 2006 response to the URS preliminary report, MN/DOT staff supported the company's recommendations and seemed to show every intention of following up on them, asking for advice, for example, on how the recommended redecking should be staged. Don Flemming's successor as state bridge engineer, Dan Dorgan, also asked for an important clarification of URS's recommendation about how to retrofit the eight critical members identified by the URS report. He cited a section of the report that highlighted the instability of the bridge's structural system and, as the Gray Plant Mooty report noted, Dorgan wanted URS to make explicit to "others in MN/DOT that are not knowledgeable in structures" that the following phrase in the URS report must not be misunderstood: "*If the conclusion is the instability would likely lead to collapse of the bridge that should be state* [sic] *clearly.*"[40]

In effect, what Dorgan was instructing URS to make clear was that when dealing with a fracture-critical bridge such as I-35W, every government official involved in decision making must be capable of fully understanding that an instability that "would likely lead to collapse" is merely a euphemism, and that any report likely to become a part of the public record must state clearly that a failure of a critical structural member would automatically result in a total collapse of the bridge.

But there was a clear reluctance on the part of MN/DOT to address these long-standing problems despite the sense of urgency reflected in the reports by the consultants. MN/DOT asked URS for a detailed analysis to determine the number of lanes that could be kept open to traffic during the redecking, and where and how much construction material, vehicles, and equipment could be stored on the bridge.[41] Precisely how URS answered these questions is not known. What is known is that these concerns about asymmetric loading—i.e., the need to avoid an imbalanced loading of a fracture-critical bridge—would, one year later, prove to have been critical indeed. Whether or not URS's response was correct, the contract and specifications provided by MN/DOT to the redecking contractor in 2007 failed to include clear instructions to avoid an asymmetric overload of materials being used for the repaving, thus ignoring the fragility of the structure.

Regardless of the support from MN/DOT's engineers for pursuing URS's recommendations, or the engineers' recognition of the potential gravity of the issues at hand, there would be plenty of reservations expressed at MN/DOT when it came to budgeting funds to carry the recommendations out. In fact, by the time that an investment strategy meeting was held in July 2006, MN/DOT officials had decided that any complete redecking of the bridge would not occur until 2022. The decision to postpone deck replacement—which was estimated to cost a financially unobtainable $15 million—sixteen years into the future was a major decision that contributed to the bridge disaster in August 2007. Despite MN/DOT's clear recognition that adding redundancy to the I-35W Bridge was a critical step in ensuring its safety, as well as URS's determination, as expressed in the Gray Plant Mooty report, that "replacing the existing deck with one that was continuous throughout would decrease live stress loads by 20 percent in some of the critical fatigue-prone members and improve the structural redundancy of the Bridge,"[42] that option was pushed sixteen years into the future even before it was formally presented.

The financially unobtainable option of completely redecking the bridge, however, was not the only one that was discussed, and deferred, by MN/DOT officials at the July 2006 meeting. Also under discussion was URS's second, much less expensive, recommendation for retrofitting steel members. Judging from the meeting minutes, MN/DOT officials clearly understood that such retrofitting would significantly reduce the risk of further fatigue cracking until the bridge could be redecked, no later than 2022. They were reluctant to take even this step as a result of the cost. The officials also understood the risks entailed in opting for nothing more than conducting further inspections, even though their worst-case scenario turned out to fall far short of the real danger. If a crack were to be found after a decision to forgo retrofitting, it would take months to order steel for the reinforcement, and the bridge would have to be closed for the duration of the remedial work. An even bigger problem would be if the bridge were so badly compromised that it had to be condemned and closed until a replacement was rebuilt. In effect, by 2006 MN/DOT officials had been fully briefed by their bosses that their principal job was to come up with a transportation budget that put building new projects ahead of repairing existing ones, and that gave priority to addressing the most projects, rather than the most necessary ones.

In October 2006, MN/DOT finally did budget the money for a retrofitting that was scheduled to go out for bids in the fall of 2007. But that work would never be performed, owing to a series of additional decisions involving both budget considerations and an apparent reluctance on URS's part to speak more directly about the perceived risks detailed in its reports. That December, URS presented MN/DOT with new recommendations for retrofitting the bridge. Specifically, URS determined that acoustical or magnetic testing was sufficient to detect fatigue cracks of a size necessary to give cause for concern. URS recommended that MN/DOT: (1) retrofit all fifty-two fracture-critical tension members to add redundancy; (2) conduct nondestructive examination testing (NDE) of all fifty-two members with the use of technological sensors; or (3) implement a combination of those two recommendations. URS even obtained bids from testing companies, informing the state that a complete examination of the bridge with what appeared to be the latest available technology would cost less than $200,000.

On December 6, MN/DOT staff members met to begin planning the preparatory work entailed in retrofitting the bridge. Then in a January 17, 2007, conference call, URS surprisingly warned MN/DOT that drilling for the retrofit that URS itself had recommended could weaken the bridge. The same day, MN/DOT decided that, instead of hiring out this work to consultants as URS had recommended, it would rely on visual inspections performed by MN/DOT personnel (combined, if necessary, with ultrasound technology) to determine whether there were any cracks in the bridge large enough to justify a retrofitting. However, once again MN/DOT failed to show a sense of urgency about addressing a known series of problems that threatened the structural integrity of the bridge. When inspection efforts were initiated in May 2007, only half the bridge was inspected, and no URS personnel were asked to participate. MN/DOT employees who were assigned to the job later acknowledged that not only did they have different understandings of their work's purpose, but they had not even consulted with URS prior to performing their inspection.

Following the May inspection of half the bridge, MN/DOT scheduled a meeting with URS that would never take place—it was slated for August 20, nearly three weeks after the bridge collapsed—to discuss the inspection results. As a result, at the time of the I-35W collapse, MN/DOT had been working for eight years with teams of consultants seeking information on fatigue cracks and securing recommendations for repairing a seriously deteriorated bridge. After detailed studies by the University of Minnesota, HNTB, and URS, the net result was a tentative plan to address the serious issues presented by the consultants a decade hence, and the authorization to proceed with a cosmetic paving project. Any action to add critical redundancy was either deferred or rejected.[43]

Even the simple project to provide new paving for the bridge was riddled with errors. In February 2006, while MN/DOT was working with URS on a proposal for redecking the entire bridge to add structural redundancy, its central bridge construction unit was preparing the paperwork for approval of another, previously budgeted project that would replace the top two inches of concrete on the bridge's deck, a largely nonstructural, cosmetic operation. Shortly thereafter, the central bridge engineer called URS to express concern that MN/DOT was planning for deck and joint repairs without considering recommendations for a more permanent repair. The URS representative responded: "Personally, I would defer the proposed deck work and plan for a deck replacement and strengthening project."[44]

The proposed deck overlay would have improved drivability but would have done nothing to improve the superstructure rating.[45] In contrast, the deck replacement that URS was recommending would have gone a long way to improve the integrity of the bridge's structural support system. It would have decreased the live stress loads in some of the critical fatigue-prone members of the superstructure and improved the structural redundancy. In April 2006, MN/DOT officials met to discuss these two options. A third option—replacing the entire bridge—was also discussed but immediately ruled out at this time, owing to the prohibitively high estimated cost of $75 million, although it is unclear from MN/DOT records how this sum was computed or whether it merely reflected the state's portion after anticipated federal funding.

Several conclusions can be drawn from MN/DOT's internal conversations involving funding for this work. First, MN/DOT ruled out any project for the short term that required a commitment in excess of $3.5 million. This limited MN/DOT's choices to the nonstructural deck overlay option promoted by central bridge. Acknowledging the financial handcuffs that constrained its choice of options for remediation, officials noted that the two chief benefits for the overlay scenario were that "it delays bridge replacement the most" and "allows time to acquire the funds needed for the deck replacement [structural redundancy] and the bridge replacement."[46] Officials used the term "budget-buster," an internal phrase that referred to projects for which there was no short-term likelihood of finding sufficient funding. The option of replacing the entire deck at an anticipated cost of $15 million was deferred to the period between 2017 and 2022, notwithstanding the fact that this option incorporated the strengthening of members in this fracture-critical bridge. Finally, although the officials acknowledged that the bridge needed to be replaced altogether (at an estimated cost of more than $75 million), they put off that project to the distant future—between 2057 and 2062.[47]

In order to choose between these two options—the more provisional, though less expensive, deck overlay and the deck replacement, which would have partially fulfilled the objective of adding redundancy to the bridge, as contemplated since 1999—MN/DOT decided that it needed to perform a surface-penetrating radar survey, at an estimated cost of $40,000. This cost was comparable to a previous survey performed in 1999 and used to determine the rate at which the deck was deteriorating. The radar survey was scheduled for August 2006, but then—in a penny-wise decision comparable to the one the following winter to forgo high-technology testing to determine the extent of fatigue cracking on the bridge—it was "not completed due to funding."[48] In July, MN/DOT made the decision to go ahead with the nonstructural deck overlay and postpone the redecking until 2022.

The decision to forgo a surface-penetrating radar survey would have further implications for the cosmetic overlay project. By choosing a different, inferior method to use in preparation for the deck overlay, it would not be until the top two inches of concrete were removed from the deck of the bridge that MN/DOT would discover that the inner portion of the deck was so badly deteriorated that more than the top two inches would have to be replaced in several locations.[49] That decision is important less for its literal consequences than for its illustration of the corner cutting—in both large and small ways—

that characterized MN/DOT's maintenance of the bridge over much of its life.

Like the later decision to rely primarily on visual inspections to determine the extent of the fatigue cracking on the bridge's superstructure, MN/DOT left in place a bridge that had been identified as lacking needed redundancy in the event of the failure of a structural member. It did not act on any of the recommendations made by a series of consultants. It ignored photographic evidence from 1999 and 2003 showing that several gusset plates had bowed from excessive pressures, indicative of incipient failure that went unattended for forty years. It failed to act on the information provided by its consultants to make decisions crucial to the safety of the traveling public. Finally, without including the services of URS, which studied the bridge for over four years, it pursued a largely nonstructural interim repair in lieu of longer-term remediation. Finally, MN/DOT permitted a contractor to load 578,735 pounds of construction material atop a structurally deficient fracture-critical bridge that was fully understood to be unable to carry this additional load.[50]

The NTSB would later dismiss any connection between the bridge's collapse and MN/DOT's maintenance of the bridge, or its poor condition for sixteen years prior to its failure. The report said nothing about MN/DOT's decision-making process or whether MN/DOT had acted prudently in light of the URS recommendations to protect the well-documented fragility of the bridge.

The story of the I-35W Bridge raises a number of "what ifs." What if MN/DOT had tackled the problem of the bridge's lack of load-path redundancy head-on, instead of avoiding the issue for eight years? What if it had undertaken the high-tech testing that URS recommended and discovered that the condition of the deck truss required either retrofitting or deck replacement to be performed as soon as possible, and that some lanes—if not the bridge itself—should be closed to reduce the likelihood of failure? What if MN/DOT had agreed to retain HNTB, which had offered to furnish an analysis of the fatefully misdesigned gusset plates? What if HNTB had identified the bowed gusset plates as a critical deficiency, which would have led to an immediate closing of at least some lanes on the bridge and a decision to immediately prepare for deck replacement? And what if the engineers and managers at MN/DOT, who clearly understood the technical analyses and warnings of the various consultants' reports they had commissioned, had heeded a directive a year earlier, which called for immediate action on "critical deficiencies" and sounded the alarm? Finally, what if the engineers at URS had stated their findings about the bridge's condition more plainly and had demanded, as professionals sworn to protect the interests of the public above all else, that MN/DOT officials find the funding necessary to address the critical structural problems they had identified or close the bridge to protect the public?

Only ten days after the I-35W Bridge fell down, the Minneapolis-St. Paul *Star Tribune* ran an article describing the decrepit state of another bridge in the Twin Cities metropolitan area, the Highway 36 Bridge over the St. Croix River, near the town of Stillwater. That bridge was then being crossed by nearly 10,000 vehicles per day, although federal officials had termed its condition "basically intolerable." In fact, the article stated, the Highway 36 Bridge was but one of many in Minnesota "considered to be in worse shape" than the I-35W span had been. "While the public finds federal labels such as 'intolerable' and 'deficient' alarming," the *Star Tribune* writers observed, "experts downplay the public's perception of such terms and say they don't necessarily translate into a bridge being unsafe. 'It is not a safety issue where the public needs to be concerned,' said Dan Dorgan, the state's top bridge engineer." Yet the article also reported that in 1984, a former Minnesota transportation commissioner, Richard Braun, had closed a bridge in St. Paul that he suspected had become unsafe for travelers. "To this day I have no idea how I had the guts to do this all by myself," Braun told the *Star Tribune* reporters. "I had no backing from anyone."[51]

Since the I-35W Bridge collapse, MN/DOT has increased the number of bridge inspectors and crews to oversee its 14,000 state, city, and county bridges. And while the state has added 281 new maintenance workers, critics point out that the state legislature transferred $35 million from MN/DOT operations to reserves that cover construction cost overruns for new projects. Most importantly, MN/DOT closed several other major bridges because of similar deterioration, which may have avoided other failures. Much of this was accomplished as the result of the state legislature's override of Governor Tim Pawlenty's veto of a badly needed transportation funding bill.

### The Williamsburg Bridge: Close Call

Taking measures to protect the public from an endangered bridge can be unpopular. Occasionally, however, there are individuals with both the sense of urgency and the courage to do just that. As another illustration of how rare it is for engineers and transportation officials to withstand the pressures to place the interests of political budget balancing over the those of the traveling public, the Star Tribune article cited a case from another American city in the 1980s: "Samuel Schwartz faced scorn from merchants, commuters and the mayor, when, as chief engineer overseeing bridges in New York City in 1988, he closed the Williamsburg Bridge between Manhattan and Brooklyn." "You have to have a lot of backbone," the reporters quoted the former New York City transportation official as saying. "You're gonna catch both political heat and public heat."[52] The story of Sam Schwartz and the Williamsburg Bridge is a story of both rare personal courage and of how the state of our infrastructure has left American transportation officials today with nothing but difficult choices.

Sam Schwartz, then deputy commissioner and chief engineer of the New York City Department of Transportation (NYCDOT), recalls a sunny weekend afternoon in April 1987, when he sat in the backyard of his Brooklyn home reading a consultant's report on the Williamsburg Bridge, one of three historic suspension bridges that connect the New York City boroughs of Brooklyn and Manhattan. As the operational head of the agency charged with the care of most of New York City's 2,027 bridges,[53] Schwartz had been in a high state of vigilance that month, not simply because of the condition of the bridges in his own portfolio. On the first Sunday in April that year, two spans of the Schoharie Creek Bridge (located far upstate, near the junction of Schoharie Creek and the Mohawk River, northwest of Schenectady and part of the New York State Thruway) had collapsed and fallen into the creek, plunging five cars into the water and killing ten people.

New York State bridge engineers had already known about the particular dangers threatening the integrity of the Schoharie Creek Bridge, owing to the widely publicized lessons of the failure of the similarly designed Chickasawbogue Bridge near Mobile, Alabama, in April 1985. In November of that year, seven months after the Chicka- sawbogue Bridge fell, the Thruway had been directed by the NTSB to inspect the Schoharie Creek Bridge for scour (the underwater erosion of the supportive material around a bridge pier) within six months, since the bridge had not been inspected at all during the previous five years. In March 1986, Thruway authorities had finally arranged to contract for an underwater inspection of the bridge, but the contract's implementation was delayed. The New York State Department of Transportation had proposed to fold the Thruway's inspections into the department's next round of inspections. This might have yielded a savings to the Thruway of approximately $5,000. But such a change adds time, which in government terms is rarely months and often a year or longer, as was the case here. There was no venality involved— neither was there any sense of urgency. Even in the absence of a tangle of competing interests like the one that paralyzed MN/DOT and its consultants on the I-35W Bridge, there appeared to be no compelling need for anyone at the Thruway to act promptly. No one viewed this inspection as anything more than routine. But within months, the Schoharie Creek Bridge went down.

Schwartz didn't actually need the example of the recent disaster on the New York State Thruway to focus his most careful attention on the bridges in his own charge. On becoming NYCDOT's chief engineer in 1986, he had inherited a collection of bridges—including such ma- jor waterway bridges as the Manhattan Bridge and the Williamsburg Bridge, both of which crossed the East River—that had been badly neglected for forty years. Part of the problem was organizational. Responsibility for New York's waterway bridges—once centralized and given highest priority in a Department of Bridges created when the five boroughs of New York City were consolidated in 1898—had, beginning in the Depression, been turned over to increasingly larger, more politicized municipal entities: the Department of Public Works, the Transportation Administration, and finally the Department of Transportation. By the time Schwartz had assumed his responsibilities, his department had been pushed far down into the bowels of the bureaucracy.

In 1972, Congress established the federal bridge inspection program to improve the quality of bridge inspection and maintenance nationwide. Within a year after the establishment of the program, however, New York City was plunged into a financial crisis that brought it to the verge of bankruptcy, a fate that Mayor Abe Beame spent nearly his entire term trying to combat. Needless to say, the city was able to do little in this period to address its growing backlog of deferred bridge maintenance. In the late 1970s, with the city on the road to financial recovery, the administration of Mayor Ed Koch (whose first term began in 1978) launched a ten-year bridge rehabilitation program as part of a larger capital spending program for the city. The bridge program had a budget of $8.6 million in 1978; by 1986, it had risen to $13.5 million.

Yet as Schwartz and Transportation Commissioner Ross Sandler noted in their 1988 report: "If maintenance had been performed adequately over the past several decades, capital expenses would not be for wholesale reconstruction, but rather for periodic replacements of certain bridge elements or material upgrading."[54] Moreover, amid increasing city budgets for bridge rehabilitation during Koch's first two terms, cuts in the city payroll had reduced the number of bridge painters and other workers—who were critical to keeping the bridges operational—employed by NYCDOT from 40 to 26 and from 184 to 111, respectively, between 1978 and 1986.[55] To make matters even worse, from the late 1970s to the mid-1980s, NYCDOT had been badly managed under the leadership of Anthony Ameruso—a protégé of Brooklyn borough president Meade Esposito whom Koch had appointed as transportation commissioner in 1978, although Ameruso was widely regarded as unqualified for the job. Soon after Koch was sworn in for his third term in January 1986, his administration was engulfed in the biggest political scandal in New York City since the days of Boss Tweed—centered on NYCDOT and its various mob-connected political patrons.[56]

Sam Schwartz owed his promotion to chief engineer and first deputy commissioner at NYCDOT in 1986 to the fallout from this scandal. A traffic engineer by training, Schwartz had joined the department in 1971 and risen through the ranks to become head of the Traffic Bureau in 1982, the only bureau head at NYCDOT untainted by political connections when the transportation-related scandals came to light four years later. Koch appointed Ross Sandler, a former assistant U.S. attorney for Manhattan who had been a special advisor to the mayor since 1981, his new commissioner of transportation, and Schwartz became Sandler's second in command, running the day-to-day operations of NYCDOT while the new commissioner spent much of his time dealing with city hall and the city's Office of Management and Budget.

As chief engineer, Schwartz found that one of his top priorities was to monitor the progress of the city's program for the rehabilitation of nearly 300 of its bridges. Among the oldest and most historically significant of these were the four East River bridges—the Brooklyn, Manhattan, Williamsburg, and Queensboro—all erected between 1870 and 1909 and dubbed by one NYCDOT engineer "New York City's red carpets."[57] A program for the rehabilitation of all four bridges had begun in 1980, and none too soon—in 1981, a pedestrian was killed when a broken diagonal stay cable snapped on the Brooklyn Bridge. Of the East River bridges, however, the one known to be most in need of repair was the Williamsburg, which carried nearly a quarter of a million drivers, bus and train riders, and pedestrians per day.

The Williamsburg Bridge was the second suspension bridge erected in New York City and the first and the longest cable bridge in the world to be built entirely of steel. After the opening of the Brooklyn Bridge, the city's first suspension bridge, in 1883, civic leaders in the Williamsburg section of Brooklyn began to demand a bridge to Manhattan of their own, albeit one that would be cheaper and more quickly constructed than its predecessor. The new, 7,300-foot bridge had a span of 1,600 feet. Designed by Leffert Lefferts Buck and completed in 1903, it would take over its rival's title as the longest suspension bridge in the world (a distinction it would keep until the erection of the Delaware River Bridge between Philadelphia and Camden, New Jersey, in 1926). It had double the load capacity of the Brooklyn Bridge, due to the strength of its cables (spun by the John A. Roebling's Sons Company) and its record-setting width, and it was built in only half the time.

At the beginning of the twentieth century, precise quantitative analysis was impossible to attain. As a result, engineers overdesigned structures by safety factors of four or more. Bridges were built like battleships. Moreover, the Williamsburg was conceived and designed prior to the automobile revolution. The bridge's patrons on the New East River Bridge Commission failed to meet their goal of building the Williamsburg Bridge for less than the $15 million that the Brooklyn Bridge had cost, as the final price tag for the Williamsburg—$24.2 million—was three and a half times the original estimate of $7 million. Yet this was not for lack of frugality on the designer's part. One way in which Buck achieved the economies required of him was by using ungalvanized wire for the Williamsburg's four massive cables. While inspectors found evidence of cable corrosion and broken wires less than a dozen years after the bridge was completed, the cables continued to perform under loads that the original design never contemplated. Despite efforts through the years to protect the cables, by the late 1980s, they were thought to have only five to ten years of remaining life, and NYCDOT was trying to determine how to strengthen or replace them.

In 1979–80, the Williamsburg Bridge had undergone the first complete inspection in its history, with inspectors from the engineering firm of Ammann & Whitney. Their investigation disclosed heavy corrosion in some of the steel members and deteriorated concrete, along with inadequate lane alignment, roadway width, and curb and railing details. The main concern arising from the 1979–80 inspection, however, had to do with the condition of the cables. But it was not until five years later that NYCDOT hired Stanford Research Institute International (SRI) to perform a focused study of the cables, and it was SRI's report that Sam Schwartz was reading in his Brooklyn backyard that afternoon in April 1987.

Since he was not himself a bridge engineer, during his first few months as chief engineer, Schwartz had to rely mostly on what he had been told by others about the state of the cables on the Williamsburg, although he soon began reading everything he could lay his hands on about the subject. Perusing the 1985 SRI report, he came upon some sentences that riveted his attention. He read that the Williamsburg Bridge was built with a safety factor of 4.0 in 1903. The safety factor of 4.0 was indicative of the overdesign in the best practices of the period. Schwartz remembered one particularly arresting sentence: "At this corrosion rate, we estimate the present safety factor of the cable is 2.5 and will drop to 1.7 by the year 2005." He went on to read that when the safety factor reached 2.0, the bridge should be shut down, and that the most conservative approach would be to assume that the current safety factor of the bridge was 2.5 or less. This told Schwartz that he should close the bridge when the safety factor reached 2.0, an event that was assumed to have occurred two years earlier, with the numbers declining steeply in the meantime.[58] To Schwartz, this meant he had to shut the bridge, once he confirmed that the safety factor had reached its critical point.

Alarmed, Schwartz summoned the SRI consultants to New York to explain the "or less" and to estimate the probability that the safety factor was now below 2.0. The figure the consultants came up with was one in twenty. Schwartz had also come to learn of a second design flaw in the Williamsburg. By virtue of the bridge's design, all four of the cables (two on either side) were wrapped around the truss. As a result, Schwartz knew that the failure of a single cable would cause the deck to twist violently to the side, pitching perhaps 6,000 drivers, subway riders, and pedestrians into the East River. To complicate matters further, the consultants advised him that the failure of a single cable could happen without warning. Schwartz did not have to be a bridge engineer to know that a 5 percent chance of 6,000 people being killed was not one he could consider taking.

The next question Schwartz asked the consultants was how he could buy time to sort all these problems out and get some better scientific data on the condition of the cables. Since the safety factor is a mathematical calculation that assumes the bridge is fully loaded—in this case, with bumper-to-bumper traffic and one train after another—Schwartz thought that he could lighten the load by reducing the number of lanes on the bridge. Instead of eight lanes, he proposed leaving five lanes open, with the other three made to look like a work zone. He could order the transit authority to allow only one train on the suspended span (only the middle span is suspended) at a time. The consultants and city engineers all agreed that at least an additional six months could be bought this way. Schwartz then ordered the shutdown of three lanes and issued orders to the transit authority.

On May 10, only a few weeks after Schwartz's emergency meeting with the SRI consultants, to the consternation of Schwartz and NYCDOT, the whole city of New York became aware of problems with the Williamsburg Bridge. Somehow, the bridge had been rated safe after state inspections in 1985 and 1986 failed to identify any potentially hazardous flaws. Thus, when the news media reported that two thirty-pound support bars from the bridge's eastbound outer roadway had fallen into the East River on May 8, the true nature of the bridge's condition became public news for the first time.

The bridge was closed on the evening of May 8, after the police noticed a ten-foot-long hole in the grating and whisked Schwartz and his wife away from a concert at the Brooklyn Academy of Music to show him what they had found. The inspection that followed turned up three instances of loose or cracked grating in other sections of the same roadway (which had undergone repair work as recently as 1982). The extent of unremediated bridge deterioration for decades had rendered these types of problems routine for a bridge of this age. Schwartz and his inspectors determined that there was no danger that the roadway would collapse, and emergency repairs were completed on May 11. From Schwartz's point of view this amounted to a distraction, for he still had to decide how to respond to the SRI consultants' estimate of a 5 percent chance that one of the bridge's cables could break at virtually any moment.

The city's existing plan for the Williamsburg Bridge called for a recabling by 1995, a procedure that had never before been tried on a suspension bridge as big as the Williamsburg. The project was estimated to cost the astounding sum of $250 million, with another $250 million for rehabilitating the bridge's roadways and supporting structures. Meanwhile, with word circulating through the bridge engineering community about the studies being done on the Williamsburg's cables, six unsolicited proposals for replacing the bridge had been received by transportation officials of New York State and City, all claiming that a new bridge could be built for essentially the same amount of money it would take to rehabilitate the current one.

The state and city Departments of Transportation both preferred the rehabilitation option and applied for funding assistance from the FHWA. The engineering firms that wanted to replace the bridge, however, took their case directly to Elizabeth Dole, then U.S. Secretary of Transportation. When Dole agreed with the firms and the FHWA (citing the Williamsburg's narrow roadways and low clearances for trucks and buses) blocked the allocation of any federal money for rehabilitation, Schwartz decided to fight back. For one thing, NYCDOT's plan for rehabilitating the bridge called for minimal disruption to traffic while the work was taking place. Could an entirely new bridge really be built at an acceptable cost without greatly disrupting traffic and the surrounding environment? Just as importantly, in Schwartz's mind, was the historic character of the Williamsburg Bridge and its cultural significance for generations of New Yorkers. Should a bridge like this be torn down just because the federal government preferred funding construction of a new bridge to paying for the old one's rehabilitation? Schwartz's question highlighted a decades-long governmental attitude that would lead the nation's infrastructure to even greater depths of disrepair.

Registering his objections, Schwartz succeeded in negotiating a deal with the federal and state governments to form a commission to study the condition of the bridge, assess the relative costs of repair and replacement, and make binding recommendations as to how the city, state, and federal governments would proceed. Appointed by Governor Mario Cuomo and Mayor Koch and chaired by Schwartz and Foster J. Beach III, Regional Director of the New York State Department of Transportation, the Williamsburg Bridge Technical Advisory Committee (TAC) included nine of the top bridge engineers in the United States, with representatives from the federal government as observers. To determine what the cost of a new bridge would be, the TAC launched a competition that brought in twenty-five proposals from around the world. The TAC's own estimates reached a far different conclusion, which was that a new bridge would cost an estimated $800 million.[59]

In the meantime, Schwartz remained extremely worried about what the SRI consultants had said about the perilous state of the Williamsburg's cables. Feeling that he was in over his head, Schwartz called in the eighty-year-old Blair Birdsall, a celebrated bridge engineer who had worked for John A. Roebling and Sons on the Golden Gate Bridge and the Chesapeake Bay Bridge, performed cable repair and maintenance on the East River bridges, and was now a partner in the consulting firm of Steinman, Boynton, Gronquist & Birdsall.[60] Schwartz told Birdsall about the SRI consultants' estimate of 5 percent and showed him the 1985 SRI report. "This is hogwash," Birdsall replied, flinging the report across the table. "I'll get back to you." A week later, Birdsall returned to Schwartz's office to announce his discovery that, owing to a simple arithmetical error that was repeated mistakenly in a computer model, SRI's report had overestimated the number of broken wires in the cables by a factor of seven. To Schwartz's relief, the SRI report, when corrected for this error, actually showed that the safety factor for the cables was well above the stated estimate of 2.5—the normal safety factor for a newly constructed suspension bridge.

While this was certainly good news about the cables, Schwartz now turned his attention to what the SRI consultants had told him about the Williamsburg's anchorages. It was there that each of the bridge's four 1,200-ton, $18^{3}/_{4}$-inch cables were splayed into thirty-seven strands of 208 wires each, then wrapped around eyebars embedded in concrete. SRI had found broken wires that suggested fragile cables. Outside of the anchorages, however, SRI had taken samples from only one small section of the bridge's cables and confined its inspection to wires on the surface or very near it. Schwartz and his colleagues on the TAC wanted to go (literally) deeper, inspecting the cables' interiors and subjecting them to every test of their integrity and strength that then existed. Once again, they turned to Steinman, Boynton, Gronquist & Birdsall, this time to perform an extensive series of mechanical, chemical, metallurgical, and fractographic tests.

In what Schwartz now says was the most frightening moment of the entire, painstaking inspection, he ordered all cars and workers off the bridge while the consulting engineers opened up the splay castings that held the cables together just before they entered their anchorages—a procedure that had never been tried before. Schwartz's fears were well-founded: some of his advisors had expressed concerns to him that this procedure would cause the cables themselves to unravel. But the results were as reassuring as they could be. The Williamsburg's cables were indeed damaged, but mostly near the surface, with little breakage or weakening of the interior wires, yielding a safety factor of over 3.0. With splicing of broken wires and rehabilitation and protection of the entire cable, which the TAC estimated would cost less than $50 million, followed by careful maintenance, Schwartz learned that the cables could be made to last indefinitely.

With this verdict in hand, some might have been tempted to do only a quick inspection of the rest of the bridge. It was already winter when the cable studies were finished, and the TAC had been given a mandate to complete its work by June 1988. The engineers on the TAC, however, urged Schwartz to accelerate inspection of the rest of the bridge. Schwartz, his boss, Ross Sandler (representing New York City), and Foster Beach (representing New York State) finally succeeded in convincing their respective budget offices to each contribute $1 million for this work. The $2 million enabled the TAC to take the next step and retain consultants for inspection services. To keep costs down, they used city and state inspecting engineers working side by side with outside consultants. The inspection team now began an inspection of all of the Williamsburg's structural members.

Schwartz had previously learned the importance of being aggressive in inspecting another old steel bridge, the Manhattan Bridge. In 1986, just after he and Ross Sandler had assumed the top posts at NYCDOT, a veteran bridge engineer had marched into Sandler's office and told him that he had to immediately take all the trains and cars off the north half of the Manhattan Bridge. Schwartz went to the bridge and was shown the problem: blasting performed to clean the eyebars around which the cables were wrapped in the anchorages had revealed that up to half the eyebars' steel had corroded away. The remnants of the corroded eyebars could have snapped, and one or more cables—having nothing left to anchor them—would no longer have been able to support the bridge deck.

Recalling this experience with the Manhattan Bridge, Schwartz ordered the entire Williamsburg Bridge to be blasted. The blasting turned up approximately 400 holes in the steel, mostly the result of salt damage—although water leakage and inadequate painting were factors as well. Salt, used widely to lower the freezing point of snow and ice during New York's brutally cold winters, and poor drainage were also found to have caused significant disintegration of the approach slabs of the bridge's roadways.

The most dramatic discovery came on April 12. Schwartz was summoned from his office and driven in his NYCDOT car, its siren sounding, to the Manhattan approach to the Williamsburg. There he was shown a steel column—one that supported the roadway on one side and train tracks on the other—split down the middle, the resulting gap wide enough for a person's hand to be wedged into it. There was no way of telling how long the column had been cracked, or how the damage had been missed in prior inspections. Schwartz gave instructions for police to be stationed at both ends of the bridge and for all vehicles, trains, and pedestrians to be ordered off the structure. Then Ross Sandler, with Schwartz at his side, got on the phone and broke the news of the bridge's closing to a very unhappy Mayor Koch.

The Williamsburg Bridge would remain closed for two months—the first time that a bridge in New York City had ever been closed completely. In the meantime, the *New York Times* revealed that, as early as 1971, NYCDOT had been warned by a consultant about severe corrosion under the bridge's approaches, but that "despite repeated inspections since then, the deterioration continued, festering virtually unchecked during three city administrations and the tenure of five transportation commissioners." In 1978, a report from the New York City comptroller stated that there was a "strong possibility of structural failure" on many city bridges, and that on the Williamsburg (as the *Times* story paraphrased the report), "steel rivets were sheared in the center, a sign that the bridge was no longer able to expand and contract." As Schwartz describes it, "a bridge is a machine. It sways back and forth with the wind, rises and falls with the traffic load and expands and contracts with changes in temperature. Bridge engineers strategically place bearing plates and rocker arms to allow the bridge to move in multiple directions. These plates and arms must be cleaned and lubricated periodically to allow for the sliding and twisting."[61] Over decades and through repeated budget cycles, all New York City's oilers, the men who had cleaned and lubricated the city's more than 2,000 bridges, were let go or reassigned. There was no outcry from the public; in fact, no one seemed to notice. But the bridges continued to obey the laws of physics. They expanded, twisted, and swayed in ways their design engineers had not planned, once the oilers stopped working. The steel and concrete supports began to crack. Without immediate action by Ross and Sandler, gravity would soon win out.

Schwartz grasped the magnitude of the problem when he learned that all traffic on the Williamsburg Bridge had been halted on March 28. The bridge was being jacked up to slide a load-bearing pedestal back into place. The bearing plate, which is designed to slide and accommodate movement due to temperature changes, had frozen due to dirt accumulation and lack of lubrication.[62] The pedestal was cracked and, half of it had moved a few inches each winter as the cold steel contracted. It was now just inches from total collapse. The Times story also reported that parts of the bridge had been painted often while other sections went neglected.[63]

The closure of the Williamsburg Bridge caused a furor in the city. Commuters, neighborhood business owners, politicians, and budget officials directed their ire not toward those who had been responsible for neglecting the city's bridges for so many years, but rather toward Schwartz, Sandler, and the current staff at NYCDOT. Demonstrators took to the streets at the ends of the bridge, carrying signs with slogans such as "Save Our Businesses & Jobs" and "Fix It Fast." A photo of Koch on an inspection tour, wearing a hard hat and an expression of utter chagrin, captures the mayor's response to the revelation that one of the city's major bridges had become an intolerable threat to the public's safety. Not that Koch and the city's other politicians exactly adopted this view.

Schwartz had to rely mainly on the media, which he courted assiduously, to document for New Yorkers the appalling condition of the bridge and explain the degree of negligence that had led to major remediation. When the New York Times published an article praising him and Sandler for their political courage in closing the Williamsburg,[64] one of thirty-two New York City bridges that would be at least partially closed during Schwartz's tenure at NYCDOT, Schwartz feared that he was finished. He spent part of one day watching the same scene from To Kill a Mockingbird over and over—the one in which Atticus Finch (played by Gregory Peck) is spat upon and wipes the spit off his face rather than fight back against his attacker. Schwartz summoned the courage to ask for a meeting with the mayor, and won a reprieve. What saved Schwartz from being fired was the political immunity he and Sandler enjoyed in the aftermath of the NYCDOT scandals, and the efficiency with which the earlier repairs to the Williamsburg Bridge had been made.

Schwartz still faced the major challenge of repairing the bridge and restoring service on it. The repairs that were now required were greater than any in the past—reinforcing critical members, installing supplemental deck beams at the most important locations, and attaching over 400 steel plates to corroded beams. Nevertheless, Schwartz was able to restore partial service on the bridge by the last week in May and full service by August, three and a half months after the bridge's closing.

By taking the actions that he did, Schwartz exhibited a clear sense of urgency. He understood the value of seeking out the best consultant engineers, challenging and weighing their findings, and acting decisively to address critical remediation needs. He understood how and where to secure needed funding despite dire economic times for his city and state. And he placed his own moral and ethical obligation as a professional engineer and protector of the public welfare above short-term solutions and political expedience. Schwartz not only prevented whatever tragic consequences might have occurred as a result of decades of neglect, but he also saved the Williamsburg Bridge itself, along with hundreds of millions of taxpayers' dollars.

Every bridge is unique, as is the history of its design, construction, and maintenance, so it is not possible to make a point-for-point comparison between the stories of the I-35W Bridge in Minneapolis and the Williamsburg Bridge in New York. Yet this tale of two bridges does highlight themes central to any understanding of how America's roads and bridges—indeed, all of our nation's infrastructure—have fallen into the neglected and dangerous state that exists today. Both the I-35W Bridge and the Williamsburg Bridge received inadequate inspection and maintenance over the course of many years, to the point where dealing with the consequences of this neglect entailed political costs as well as capital expenditures far in excess of what preventive maintenance would have cost over the same period. In both cases, those charged with the responsibility of caring for the bridge—and the safety of the public it served—were faced with difficult choices framed by considerations of money, politics, and professional and moral responsibility. Though the particular set of choices was different in each case, both called for a sense of urgency that was lacking in the actions taken by MN/DOT officials and their consultants, but clearly present in the conduct of Schwartz's Williamsburg Bridge team.

Unfortunately, one can only speculate about whether the I-35W Bridge—and the thirteen people who lost their lives on it—might have been saved had anyone at MN/DOT been as dogged in pursuit of the truth about that bridge's condition as was Sam Schwartz in the case of the Williamsburg Bridge. But the instances of heroic action by transportation officials in these times of shortchanged transportation budgets are few and far between. Sam Schwartz must be viewed as a rare exception. Sadly, the I-35W Bridge story represents the norm in this country today. We cannot simply hope for more Sam Schwartzes to bail us out of similar tragedies. Ultimately, the significance of what happened, and what failed to happen, in Minnesota transcends the story of one particular bridge.

For much of the last twenty-five years, Americans have been averting their eyes from the condition of the roads and bridges that provide the vital transportation lifelines of our nation. Filling potholes and hoping for the best will no longer do. Politicians who learn of the need to remediate deteriorated bridges in their communities can no longer continue to allocate most of the limited transportation funding to contracts for election campaign contributors who build new roads. Our collective failure is systemic, not individual, and expresses itself in a historic reluctance to pay for maintenance, as opposed to new construction. The first step in understanding how we have arrived at the present state of our roads and bridges is to trace the history of how Americans have paid, and declined to pay, for their upkeep. And it is to this history that we must now turn.

# 2 Following the Money

## Road and Bridge Funding and
## the Maintenance Deficit

In the wake of the collapse of the I-35W Bridge in Minneapolis, attention quickly focused on the straitened financial condition of the Minnesota Department of Transportation (MN/DOT). Within months, reports began to circulate about how political and financial considerations may have affected decisions made in the months leading up to the disaster. MN/DOT officials issued predictable, and doubtless sincere, denials that they would never have compromised the safety of a bridge out of financial considerations. "No, we would never do that because of money," said a MN/DOT engineer, for example, when asked if financial constraints had played a role in the decision not to reinforce steel members deemed particularly susceptible to cracking.[1]

Yet there should be no doubt that inadequate funding was a key factor in MN/DOT's decisions not only to call off the planned retrofitting of the bridge but also to forgo nondestructive testing that would have revealed the full extent of fatigue cracking on the bridge. And it was inadequate resources for remediation that led to the decision to put off until 2022 the deck replacement that would have added redundancy to the bridge. Moreover, it was not until after the I-35W Bridge fell into the Mississippi and killed thirteen people that Minnesota Governor Tim Pawlenty gave up his previously unshakable opposition to raising the state's gasoline tax, thus providing needed revenues for the financially starved MN/DOT. "This isn't a bridge that failed. This is government that failed," concluded a Minnesota state legislator.[2] The same could be said of New York City when, owing to short-sighted budget cuts, NYCDOT stopped lubricating its bridges, with the eventual result that the Williamsburg Bridge became separated from its abutment at one end—a defect that could easily have led to disaster.

The same can be said, in fact, of the United States as a whole, which—according to the 2009 *Report Card for America's Infrastructure*, issued by the American Society of Civil Engineers (ASCE)—faces a five-year investment shortfall for its roads and bridges of $549.5 billion.[3] How did the nation get into this mess? It did not happen overnight and, viewed in historical perspective, represents the failure not just of government but of the entire American polity to come to terms with the true cost of a highway infrastructure that was once the best in the world but that now stands in need of extensive, and expensive, remediation.

### The Creation of the American Highway System and the Origins of the Maintenance Deficit

Our nation has a long history of neglecting the maintenance of its roads and bridges. In colonial times, the upkeep of a post road was the responsibility of the local government, and local residents were required to provide the labor for the maintenance. After the revolution, traffic on what was still a small network of roads began to increase, and existing maintenance efforts proved ineffective. To deal with heightened demand, state governments chartered private turnpike companies that were given the right to build roads and charge tolls for their use; in the absence of government standards, the quality of the turnpikes varied considerably from place to place. These early examples of public-private partnerships acknowledged the inability of local governments to build roads as efficiently as private enterprise could.

After 1800, many states used tolls to pay for the upkeep of major roads while continuing to use state labor to maintain local ones. As the country expanded in the first half of the nineteenth century, much debate centered on the need for federal funding for road construction and improvement. Congress, immersed in its efforts to address serious postrevolutionary deficits, provided only very limited amounts of support. In 1822, President James Monroe vetoed a bill authorizing federal imposition of tolls to raise money on national roads for maintenance as not authorized by the Constitution.[4] This set a precedent for states to assume the responsibility for maintaining roads, which would survive until well into the twentieth century.

After the Civil War, with road construction as well as maintenance firmly established as a state and local responsibility, local wagon roads remained an important part of the transportation infrastructure even as railroads became the favored means of long-distance transportation. Property taxes, poll taxes, and state labor supported most road construction and maintenance in the second half of the nineteenth century. As a consequence, rural areas, with their smaller tax bases, had fewer and lower-quality roads than did towns and cities. Urban roads, however, were often very poorly maintained.[5]

At the dawn of the automobile age, the Federal-Aid Highway Act of 1916—which provided federal assistance for the improvement of rural post roads and was the first federal highway legislation enacted in the United States—gave states the responsibility for designing, building, and maintaining roads in the new national system, while federal officials set and enforced standards. The Federal-Aid Highway Act of 1921 offered federal matching funds to cover half the construction by states of primary roads. This sharing arrangement included the requirement that state highway departments maintain roads built with federal assistance and stipulated that states that failed to keep these roads in good repair would forfeit further federal assistance. The act echoed Congress's adamant prohibition of the use of federal funds for maintenance and repair of state roads.

This division of labor made sense given the tradition of local responsibility for road maintenance, the importance of new and improved roads to local economies, the priority placed on building new roads and improving existing ones at a time when automobiles were first coming into widespread use and pavement was replacing dirt and gravel. It also inaugurated a system of what the transportation historian Owen Gutfreund has called "highway-finance federalism," which survives to this day. This expanded role for the federal government immediately began to have important consequences for the nation's ability and willingness to maintain its system of roads and bridges. One key feature of the system described by Gutfreund was the mechanism by which federal highway aid was "distributed through an independent bureaucracy controlled by 'expert' engineers in the Bureau of Public Roads [created by the 1921 federal transportation act] and in the newly formulated state highway departments."[6] The ever-higher standards developed and enforced by the Bureau of Public Roads (BPR) steadily drove up the costs of road construction and maintenance from the 1920s until World War II. As the nation's road-building spree continued into the 1940s, the increase in the number of roads began to tax the ability of state and local governments to carry out their responsibilities for maintenance.

The 1920s and 1930s saw a boom in road construction in the United States as private interests (the automobile, petroleum, and rubber industries prominent among them) joined forces with the new federal BPR and the recently formed American Association of State Highway Officials (AASHO; later the American Association of State Highway and Transportation Officials) to push for the creation of a national highway network. In 1919, Oregon's need for new revenues to fund road construction led to the introduction of the first gasoline tax in the nation. By 1929, every other state in the country had followed suit, although states funded highway construction from general revenues as well as from the gasoline tax. The first federal gasoline tax was not enacted until 1932, and revenues from the tax went into the federal government's general fund, to the great consternation of the automobile lobby. "By 1925," the historian Kenneth Jackson has written, "the value of highway construction projects exceeded $1 billion for the first time; thereafter, it fell below that figure only during a few years of the Great Depression and World War II. Even during the troubled thirties, . . . state and federal funds were made available for roads because they employed many workers and could be planned quickly."[7]

Amid this much desired expansion of the nation's system of roads, however, state and local governments quickly began falling behind in their maintenance obligations, as local demand for roads and the incentives for new construction provided by the 50 percent federal contribution caused state funds to be devoted to construction at the expense of maintenance. Gutfreund examines how this phenomenon unfolded in one state, Vermont, which in the 1920s undertook a massive expansion of its road system. Eventually supported by federal funds as well as the gas tax the state enacted in 1923 and other state revenues, highway programs accounted for one-fourth of the state's budget by 1921. Although, according to the terms of the Federal-Aid Highway Act of 1921, federal funds could not be spent on maintenance, Vermont heavily favored construction over maintenance in the expenditure of its own funds as well, even assessing municipalities a fee for maintaining highways within their borders.

By the 1940s, the backlog of deferred maintenance had grown to significant proportions. Gutfreund explains: "According to congressional testimony from 1949, [state] highway engineers estimated that Vermont would have to spend over $150 million ($1.1 billion in 2000 dollars) on highway repairs just to maintain the prewar status quo." The minimal funding the state received to address its maintenance needs were such that "total federal highway grants to Vermont each year averaged less than $1.5 million between 1946 and 1950, enough to pay for 1 percent of the backlog." In order for state officials to fill the shortfall that existed between what they needed to spend on highway maintenance and what they could expect from available overall revenues that were allocated to the highway budget, "state officials deferred maintenance and forced more costs down onto cities, towns, and villages. By 1946, state maintenance appropriations had been cut so much that they were no longer sufficient to take care of normal yearly requirements, without any regard to the accumulation of deferred maintenance." To make matters worse, current revenues could not even match federal aid for new construction, let alone pay for maintenance and projects that received no federal aid.[8]

The problem of deferred maintenance of the nation's roads and bridges, already well established by the 1940s, would be considerably exacerbated by the creation of the interstate highway system in the mid-1950s and during the forty-year boom in road and bridge construction that it launched. When the Federal-Aid Highway Act of 1956 made the federal highway system that had first been planned twelve years earlier a reality, it was estimated that the interstate system would be completed in another twelve years. Providing for its maintenance was not a pressing concern for either the federal government or the states, which eagerly took the federal funds (90 percent of the cost of new construction, paid for out of the new Highway Trust Fund that was funded by dedicated revenues from the federal gas tax) that the interstate system made available. The expansion of the national highway system—which according to President Dwight D. Eisenhower's Secretary of Commerce Sinclair Weeks[9] represented the "greatest public-works program in the history of the world"—quickly fed on itself, as demand for new roads only increased in response to a number of related phenomena: greater numbers of vehicles and miles driven; growing congestion in metropolitan areas (a problem that had begun before the end of World War II); taxation, housing, and land-use policies that subsidized sprawl; and the by now well-established policy of undercharging motorists and truckers for their use of the roads.

The rapid proliferation of highways in the postwar era that was a boon to the economy and the personal mobility of Americans only aggravated the problem of deferred maintenance on the nation's older roads. As Gutfreund has shown, the creation of the interstate system placed huge additional burdens on Vermont's state highway budget, even with the federal government paying 90 percent of construction costs. The sheer size and expense of the interstate program made even a state's 10 percent contribution a burden it could not bear without continuing to shortchange maintenance. This problem was shared by other states, as Gutfreund notes: "In the first year after the 1956 Act went into effect, the aggregate matching requirements for all the states was $954 million, 30 percent higher than for the previous year."[10]

The construction of the national highway system without serious attention to how it would be maintained over time bears some resemblance to what, in a later historical context, would be called the domed stadium (or convention center) syndrome in public works, an approach characterized by public officials' "thinking about the publicity involved and the community support engendered by spectacular projects, groundbreakings, and dedications, rather than [facing] the future costs of operating such facilities."[11] As the American highway system expanded, and the infrastructure built in the first flush of the postwar era began to age, the nation's capacity for addressing this looming problem was undermined by another feature of the political arrangements that had brought the system into being: a system of highway finance that disguised the true costs of the nation's roads and bridges from motorists and undercharged them for their use of the structures.

In his history of suburbanization in the United States—a process in which the automobile has obviously played a central role—Jackson succinctly stated the fundamental political question posed by the advent of the automobile as a popular, affordable mode of transportation for increasing numbers of Americans in the first quarter of the twentieth century, and how this question was resolved: "Although the motorcar was the quintessential private instrument, its owners had to operate it over public spaces. What would be the reaction of government?" One solution would have been to levy heavy user fees to reimburse local treasuries in full for the cost of streets, traffic maintenance, and police services. Another possibility was to rely on general taxation to support private transportation. That the latter course was adopted is testimony both to the public perception of the benefits of mobility and to the intervention of the growing power of special interest groups.[12]

The first of the special interest groups that were mostly responsible for persuading government to begin investing in highways in the early decades of the twentieth century was the Good Roads Movement, founded in the 1880s by cycling enthusiasts and eventually expanded to include farmers interested in the improvement of farm-to-market roads, automobile manufacturers, highway contractors, manufacturers of road construction equipment, and civil engineers. While the Good Roads Movement ultimately failed to transcend its rural origins and could not form a durable coalition among the disparate groups it attracted, by the 1920s a true highway lobby had emerged. This powerful new group included not only such business interests as "tire manufacturers and dealers, parts suppliers, oil companies, service-station owners, road builders, and land developers" but also urban merchants and, eventually, city planners.[13]

Yet another interest group—although not explicitly a political one—consisted of engineers in state highway departments who, in 1914, founded AASHO. Along with the engineers in the federal BPR with whom they made highway policy decisions, state highway officials constituted a group of what Gutfreund calls "unelected engineers" who were "largely oblivious to the broader political or social dimensions of the issues at hand." As a result, Gutfreund states, "road building was debated and discussed as a set of narrowly conceived technical concerns. Among the most important consequences of this approach was a lack of substantive discussion, at the outset, of an essential question: *Who will pay for the new road-building programs?*"[14] Out of a desire to build what they deemed necessary for the national progress and well-being, the engineers in the BPR and AASHO became key figures in what developed into a sustained campaign to foist the cost of highway construction (and maintenance, to the extent that it was considered at all) onto the public in general rather than highway users in particular. What this created has proven to be a persistent, and damaging, illusion on the public's part as to the real costs of owning and maintaining a highway system.

When it came to the financing of road construction and maintenance, two essential decisions that were made in the 1920s, at the dawn of the era of modern road construction, governed the trajectory of the nation's ground transportation system. First, as we have seen, the federal government offered the states financial assistance for road construction but not for maintenance. Second, the ultimate cost for building and maintaining highways would be shared between motorists (through the state gas taxes that began to be levied between 1919 and 1929) and federal and state taxpayers generally.[15] The ensuing battle over whether user fees more direct than gasoline taxes should be imposed on the motorists (including truckers) who would benefit most directly from new road construction was a contentious one.

The battle flared up when, at the beginning of the 1940s, the states of Pennsylvania and Connecticut—along with Robert Moses, chairman of the New York State Council of Parks[16]—imposed user fees in the form of toll roads. In doing so, they faced opposition from the BPR, which wanted to preserve what Gutfreund calls the "established paradigm" of "free roads, planned and administered by the bureaucracy created by the 1916 Act."[17] Following the creation of these toll roads, an intense debate took place over whether the new nationwide system of highways, already being planned, should include (as President Franklin D. Roosevelt proposed) six toll roads or should be free, with organizations including AASHO, the American Trucking Association, and the National Association of Bus Operators supporting a broad range of toll-free roads.

The opponents of toll roads would not prevail until after a battle that lasted through the 1940s and into the mid-1950s. Impressed by the financial success of the Pennsylvania Turnpike, states and private operators in many locations around the country began in the late 1940s and early 1950s to build or plan for toll roads. The prospect of securing new, lucrative sources of revenue for general and transportation needs was too enticing for most states to pass up. This development, in turn, caused the nation's three largest auto manufacturers to join in 1951 with the oil industry, the AAA, and the trucking industry to start Project Adequate Roads (PAR), in an effort to promote "free" highways through a coordinated nationwide lobbying campaign.[18] Despite some splintering among the various anti-toll interest groups, these forces finally triumphed when the legislation creating the interstate highway system in 1956 ensured that no new toll roads would be built as part of the interstate.[19]

Meanwhile, the successful fight against further expansion of toll roads, combined with the incentives for road construction (and pressures on state highway maintenance budgets) created by what was already a forty-year-old system of highway-finance federalism, established a modus operandi that, in Gutfreund's words, "undercharged motorists by a wide margin."[20] To put it another way, American motorists, a group that would eventually come to include almost all but an underprivileged minority, were furnished with an extensive system of roads whose true costs—particularly when it came to operations and maintenance—were to a great degree hidden.

Along with gasoline taxes, state and local bond issues (for the portion of road construction projects not paid for by federal funds) imposed costs on all taxpayers specifically tied to the provision of transportation infrastructure. Only gasoline taxes, obviously, were paid by motorists alone. And as gasoline taxes were kept relatively low (and assessed as a fixed number of cents per gallon rather than as a percentage of the retail price that would raise the tax in step with inflation) and, with license and registration fees, were the only public assessments on drivers (except on publicly owned toll roads) linked specifically to automobile use, Americans were ready to accept the illusion that the operation and maintenance of their roads and bridges were essentially free. All the while, the costs of neglecting the maintenance of these roads and bridges began to mount until, in the 1970s, the federal government took notice and attempted to set a new direction in highway policy.

### The Federal Government Steps In

Even as the building boom inaugurated by the creation of the interstate highway system in the mid-1950s continued, age and heavy use began taking a visible toll not only on the older infrastructure that had been neglected for decades—the East River bridges in New York City, for example—but also on the nation's newer roads and bridges, including the interstate highway system itself. "By the 1970s," as a Federal Highway Administration (FHWA) historian has noted, "the Interstate System was showing signs of wear and tear. Part of the problem was that pavements built in the 1950s and early 1960s were reaching their design life (the number of years a pavement is expected to last, with proper maintenance, based on estimates of the loadings it will absorb during that time, particularly truck loadings). Because the Interstates were carrying more and heavier traffic than predicted, many segments absorbed 20 years of wear and tear in far fewer years than expected."[21] With construction of the interstate highway system well advanced, and recognizing the need to protect the federal taxpayers' sizable investment in that system, the federal government began to shift the emphasis in its funding for roads and bridges from construction to maintenance and repair.

Provision for bridge maintenance and repair came first, as the Federal-Aid Highway Act of 1970, enacted three years after the stunning collapse of the Silver Bridge at Point Pleasant, West Virginia, created the National Bridge Inspection Program and the Special Bridge Replacement Program (SBRP). The SBRP required the U.S. Department of Transportation (DOT) to "inventory all bridges located on the Federal-aid system . . . classify these bridges, and prioritize the bridges by need of replacement."[22] DOT would then use this inventory and classification to evaluate and approve states' applications for bridge replacement funds, which could be used to cover a major percentage of the cost of bridge replacements. Six years later, in another significant departure from the previous policy of leaving maintenance and repair to the states, the Federal-Aid Highway Act of 1976 provided $175 million annually for the repair, rehabilitation, and replacement (the "3Rs") of highways in the federal system, for which the federal government would pay 90 percent of the cost. The net result of this transformed policy was summed up in a report in 1988 from the Congressional Budget Office (CBO), which found that "this expanded federal role [in providing for maintenance on the federal highway system] was paid for out of reduced spending on construction elements of the federal program and by additional spending from federal funds."[23]

The new legislation reflected both the declining condition of the national highway system and the perilous financial condition of the states. In an assessment of road conditions around the country initiated by the federal government, forty-four states had reported a decline in the quality of their highways between 1970 and 1975, while as of 1975, according to an article in U.S. *News & World Report*, "42 percent of all paved highways and 27 percent of the interstate pavement were rated either 'fair' or 'poor.' " (This article also noted: "Pavement classified as fair may seem as smooth to many motorists as a brand-new highway. But engineers warn that a highway can hide its defects for years as it deteriorates—and then seem to collapse overnight.") The same article reported that a "recent government inventory" had found that nearly one-fifth of the country's 564,000 highway bridges were "inadequate or unsafe."[24] Meanwhile, a report to Congress mandated by the 1976 federal highway legislation concluded: "The backlog of R-R-R work on approximately 8,000 miles of older Interstate segments is estimated to cost $2.6 billion (1975 dollars). Thereafter, the continuing annual need for R-R-R work is estimated to be $950 million (excluding inflation)."[25] These findings, it is important to note, came at a time when the oil shock of the early 1970s had resulted in reduced revenues for both federal and state governments from gasoline taxes, while a combination of higher oil prices and the overall inflation of the period had significantly raised the costs of road construction and repair.

The Surface Transportation Assistance Act of 1978 made the "3R" program permanent, although it also reduced the federal share of 3R work from 90 percent to 75 percent. The 1978 law also expanded the SBRP (which it renamed the Highway Bridge Replacement and Rehabilitation Program) to make bridge repair and rehabilitation, as well as replacement, eligible for federal funding. (The Federal Highway Act of 1981, which "established early completion and preservation of the Interstate system as the highest priority highway program,"[26] would extend federal funding to cover a fourth "R"—reconstruction, for which it committed the federal government to paying 90 percent of costs—although this was essentially a technical adjustment following from a decision to remove certain still incomplete segments of the interstate from the system.)

The federal government's continuing attention to the need for restoring the nation's roads and bridges came in the midst of growing alarm about the state of this infrastructure—and the sums of money required to address it—in the press and the public. The 1978 U.S. *News & World Report* article quoted above not only reported on the deteriorated state of American roads and bridges but also noted that "the cost of upkeep and renovation [for highways and bridges], estimated at $329 billion between now and 1990, is so enormous that nobody knows where enough money can be found."[27] In 1982, a *Newsweek* article titled "The Decaying of America" cited more alarming statistics. "Today one-quarter of the interstate-highway system is worn out and needs resurfacing," the *Newsweek* authors reported. "Nationwide, 248,500 bridges—45 percent of the total—are structurally deficient or functionally obsolete. . . . One-fifth of the nation's bridges are so dangerously deficient they are either restricted or closed. . . . But DOT estimates that needed repairs could cost as much as $47.6 billion." As for the nation's roads, "still 1,500 miles short of completion, the once proud 40,500-mile interstate-highway system will need $33 billion worth of repairs in the next decade." Conditions on the larger network of primary and secondary roads were even more ominous. According to DOT estimates, the article reported, it would cost "more than $500 billion over the next ten years—more than Federal, state and local governments combined spent on all public works in the 1970s."[28]

Amid the sense of urgency expressed by these and similar stories in the national press, the CBO issued a report in June of 1982 that reviewed the history of the interstate highway system—then over 97 percent complete[29]—the perils it now faced, and possible courses of action. Identifying "mounting repair needs," "escalating completion costs," and "declining financial resources" as the critical challenges facing the system, the CBO report reviewed the rationale for the federal government's traditional policy of funding road construction but not maintenance and repair (i.e., the much higher cost of construction, and the common-law tradition of local responsibility for road maintenance). Making a useful distinction between ordinary maintenance (which the federal government continued to view as a state and local responsibility) and the "3R" activities of resurfacing, restoration, and rehabilitation, the CBO cited two reasons for the federal government's decision to begin providing financial assistance for 3R work: first, "the mix of traffic using some roads has become increasingly nonlocal," so that "state priorities for road repair are increasingly diverging from federal priorities"; and second, although "road repair was once a relatively inexpensive activity . . . , with the emergence of more intercity vehicular travel and the use of increasingly heavy vehicles, the cost of rebuilding worn out pavements can be nearly as much as building new roads." It also noted that many older interstate routes were nearing the end of their design life and that "virtually no major repairs were made during the first 15 years," finally estimating that approximately $16 billion would be needed for repairs between 1980 and 1990 yet less than half the amount was made available under then-current federal authorizations.[30]

So broad was the recognition in the early 1980s that the federal government needed to act to protect its $176 billion dollar investment in the interstate highway system that, in January 1983, President Ronald Reagan signed the Surface Transportation Assistance Act of 1982, which raised the federal gas tax from four cents to nine cents per gallon (the first increase in this tax since 1961) in order to provide funds for the rehabilitation of interstate highways and bridges, the federal share for which was now returned to 90 percent. Four cents of the nickel increase was designated for what became the Highway Account in the Highway Trust Fund (HTF), while the remaining cent was to go into a new Transit Account within the HTF. The law provided $10.3 billion over four years for 4R work on the interstate system—a level of funding that would be increased even further by the Surface Transportation and Uniform Relocation Assistance Act of 1987.

The 1982 legislation also significantly increased funding for bridge replacement and rehabilitation, the need for which was now widely recognized. In 1983, the year of the Mianus River Bridge collapse in Connecticut, a report from the U.S. General Accounting Office noted

that the FHWA had just estimated the cost of replacing or rehabilitating the nation's bridges at $49 billion, and stated: "The threat to
safety, the inconvenience, and the financial burden of deficient
bridges have become concerns to the public and all levels of government."[31] But as we shall see, these words went unheeded as the level
of ignored infrastructure maintenance soared to new heights over the
ensuing two decades.

The next and, ultimately, most important step in the effort to shift
federal highway aid from construction to maintenance and repair
came in 1991 with the passage of the Intermodal Surface Transportation Efficiency Act of 1991 (ISTEA, pronounced "ice tea"). A 1988 report from the Congressional Budget Office had found that the "most
important" of the infrastructure challenges facing the nation might
be "the transition from an era of construction to an era of management," noting that "the rate of return on maintaining the condition of
the federal-aid highway system is on the order of 30 percent to 40 percent, while the rate of return on new construction, save in certain urban areas, is very low."[32] ISTEA created a new Interstate Maintenance
(IM) program—for which it authorized $17 billion over six years—as
well as a new funding category, the National Highway System (NHS),
that included both the interstate system and other highways deemed
to be of national importance. It permitted IM funds to be used for 3R
work on the interstate system and for the reconstruction of bridges,
interchanges, and overpasses on existing interstate routes (although
not for "new travel lanes other than high occupancy vehicle lanes or
auxiliary lanes"), and, for the first time, made preventive maintenance
on federal-aid highways eligible for federal funding (through the IM
program).[33]

ISTEA also continued the Highway Bridge Replacement and Rehabilitation Program (HBRRP), which it funded at $16.1 billion over the
six-year period covered by the law (although it would not be until 2002
that the FHWA would determine that a change to federal-aid highway law made by Congress in 1995 authorized use of HBRRP funds,
in limited circumstances, for preventive maintenance on federal-

aid highway bridges[34]). In a set of provisions that would ultimately weaken the effectiveness of the law, a complicated set of formulas was designed to give states flexibility in spending their federal transportation funds. But in what would prove to be a virtual boondoggle for state politicians across the country, the law also permitted them to transfer money in and out of various FHWA programs, including not only a surface transportation program covering roads and bridges, but also other programs, as long as they addressed such issues such as safety and "congestion mitigation and air quality improvement."[35] Even with such provisos, however, ISTEA and the legislation that followed it represented a hugely significant reorientation of federal policy away from construction and toward maintenance of the nation's major highways and bridges. An FHWA official noted on the tenth anniversary of the law's enactment: "Before ISTEA, funding for maintenance was an anathema."[36]

By 1995, as a result of the changes in federal policy culminating with the passage of ISTEA, approximately half of all federal highway spending was for rehabilitation and reconstruction.[37] The Transportation Equity Act for the 21st Century (TEA-21), enacted in 1998, guaranteed $23.8 billion for highways and bridges through 2003. But, in another indication that Congress was losing its focus on repairing and maintaining the national highway system, TEA-21 also acceded to state demands by expanding the IM program for uses including "new interchanges, new rest areas, additional noise walls, etc."[38]

The trend of permitting almost any project within the ambit of IM flexibility was further extended by the cumbersomely named 2005 federal transportation legislation, the Safe, Accountable, Flexible, Efficient Transportation Equity Act: A Legacy for Users (SAFETEA-LU),[39] which authorized $25 billion for the IM program over five years and $21.6 billion for bridge program funding. The new law allowed the use of federal funds for preventive maintenance for bridges on both federal-aid and non–federal-aid highways but also enunciated the principle that, with respect to highway spending, the federal government "shall in no way infringe on the sovereign rights of the states to determine which projects shall be federally financed."[40] Shortly thereafter, a new word began to creep into the political lexicon. Critics noted that SAFETEA-LU contained over 5,000 earmarks—formerly categorized under the rubric of pork barrel politics—representing a sharp escalation of state officials' use of federal transportation funding for purely political purposes. As many Americans were beginning to suspect, the by now long-standing effort of the federal government to direct more funding for road and bridge maintenance and repair was losing its focus and coming up against some unexpected obstacles.

## Unintended Consequences:
## Policy Failures in the "Era of Management"

The escalation in federal funding for road and bridge repair and maintenance since the early 1980s and especially the early 1990s, combined with the efforts and expenditures of the states, has brought about significant improvements in the overall condition of the nation's automotive transportation infrastructure, albeit with significant exceptions. For roads, improvement is evident in five of the six functional classifications the FHWA uses to categorize federal-aid highways. Whereas, in the early 1980s, one-quarter of the interstate highway system was "worn out," by 1995, according to FHWA data, only 6.3 percent of rural interstate miles and 10.4 percent of urban interstate miles were rated in "poor" condition. By 2006 those numbers had fallen to 2.0 percent and 5.2 percent, respectively. Rural "principal arterials" other than the interstates went from 12.0 percent to 3.3 percent of miles in poor condition from 1995 to 2006, and rural minor arterials from 12.7 percent to 5.9 percent. Urban freeways and expressways other than interstates also showed improvement, going from 14.6 percent to 6.5 percent in poor condition. Only urban principal arterials (major roads other than interstates and other freeways and expressways), which were egregiously bad to begin with, failed to improve significantly from 1995 to 2006, going from 27.1 percent to 25.6 percent in poor condition.

Meanwhile, although 11.9 percent of the approximately 600,000 bridges in the National Bridge Inventory (NBI)—and 13.5 percent of those not in the NHS—were classified as "structurally deficient," this number was down from 20.7 percent in 1992, the year after the passage of ISTEA, and would have been 12.5 percent even if more than 29,000 bridges had not been added to the inventory since 1992. The percentage of functionally obsolete bridges in the NBI improved only marginally over this same period, from 14.0 percent in 1992 to 13.3 percent in 2008, for an overall deficiency rate that year of 25.2 percent as compared with 34.8 percent in 1992.[41]

However, the growing gap between needs and resources for the maintenance and repair of the nation's roads and bridges makes it clear that, in spite of more than thirty years of efforts, the federal government has largely failed to address this problem. Both the federal government and the states are implicated in this failure, for which four factors have been principally responsible. First, the expectation in the late 1980s and early 1990s that the nation's automotive transportation system was about to undergo a transition from "an era of construction to an era of management"[42] proved to be ill founded, as the United States dealt with continued growth in demand for mobility by continuing to build new roads and bridges. Second, states have shown a tendency to substitute federal transportation funds for their own, thus reducing their overall transportation spending to below the level where they could provide adequately for the growing problem of maintenance and repair. Third, states have taken advantage of the flexibility in federal funding formulas to transfer money out of programs intended for road and bridge maintenance and repair. Finally, states have responded to certain perverse incentives in federal funding formulas to defer maintenance until infrastructure deteriorates to the point at which it qualifies for federal funding for reconstruction and replacement. (As we will see, some state departments of transportation respond to criticism on the third score by citing these incentives for the neglect of maintenance).

Although definitive, comprehensive data on state spending on new construction versus maintenance and remediation are hard to come by, the incentives for states to invest in the former at the expense of the latter are powerful and stem from a number of sources. The politics of ribbon cutting (closely related to the domed stadium or convention center syndrome), in which state and local politicians prefer spending for visible, splashy, new public works to investing in such humdrum activities as maintenance and minor repair, is an easily observable phenomenon. It is also one that is encouraged, in part, by the fact that the federal government, since the creation of the interstate highway system, has shouldered 90 percent of the cost of new construction of roads and bridges. As the 1982 CBO report noted, "The 90 percent federal contribution provides a substantial incentive for states to expand their participation independent of their actual transportation needs." In addition, construction generates employment, which leads to retail and other tax-generating revenue: "This occurs because construction activities themselves generate jobs, which, in turn, generate additional retail and other economic activity, and ultimately result in increased state tax revenues by virtue of the enhanced employment, both direct and indirect." As a result, "apart from the value of the roads itself, the Interstate program provides significant economic returns through its stimulation of local construction activity and indirect increases in related economic activity." Thus, the predominant incentive for states to undertake construction projects of this nature is that the major subsidy by the federal government throws off a number of economic benefits that all start with the construction process.[43]

Needless to say, this account of how the "stimulation of local construction activity and indirect increases in related economic activity" caused by new road and bridge projects tells only part of the story of the political incentives involved.

As noted above, the first highway construction boom of the twentieth century received impetus in the 1920s from a powerful coalition of business interests that joined with the BPR and AASHO in promoting road building at the federal and state levels. By the dawn of the interstate era, this coalition had expanded considerably. The American Road Builders Association (ARBA), to which General Motors was the largest contributor, formed what Kenneth Jackson calls "a lobbying enterprise second only to that of the munitions industry." "By the mid-1950s," he writes, the ARBA "had become one of the most broad-based of all pressure groups, consisting of the oil, rubber, asphalt, and construction industries; the car dealers and renters; the trucking and bus concerns; the banks and advertising agencies that depended upon the companies involved; and the labor unions." Real estate professionals and home builders also joined the lobbying effort for construction of the interstate highway system, hoping to benefit from a boom in suburban home construction like the one that had been fueled by the surge in road building and automobile sales in the 1920s.[44] Today the ARBA, now called the American Road & Transportation Building Association, has divisions for contractors, manufacturers, materials and service providers, planning and design professionals, and public-private venture entities, among others—all rich sources of political campaign contributions that, for the most part, have replaced the forms of so-called honest graft prevalent in an earlier era of city and state political machines.[45]

It is not only the expanded highway lobby that has kept up the pressure for new construction, however, but also the practice of undercharging motorists that the original collection of interest groups behind early road construction put in place in the 1920s. In the 1988 report in which it proclaimed the need for a "transition from an era of construction to an era of management" on the federal-aid highway system, the CBO spelled out the fundamental problem—familiar to any economist—with concealing the true costs of automobile infrastructure and undercharging those who use it. "As currently structured," the CBO wrote, "federal infrastructure programs fail to provide either infrastructure users or state and local managers with incentives to make efficient choices. Since the benefits of using facilities are not tied to the costs of providing them, federal programs lead to inflated perceptions of the demand for infrastructure."[46]

The same problem has been described more recently by the National Surface Transportation Infrastructure Financing Commission, which wrote in its February 2009 final report that the problem was not caused merely by the failure to invest sufficient funding. It recognized that "our system is underpriced. Basic economic theory tells us that when something valuable—in this case roadway space—is provided for [at] less than its true cost, demand increases and shortages result. Shortages in our road system are manifested as congestion." If the cost of using a transportation system is structured to be substantially less than it costs to provide the services the public uses, not to mention any social costs of congestion and pollution, "this underpayment contributes to less efficient use of the system, increased pavement damage, capacity shortages, and congestion."[47]

The growing problems of capacity shortages and congestion have become an unofficial rationale for those urging the construction of still more roads and undercharging motorists for their use. Each of these, in turn, leads to the need for even more new roads requiring maintenance—and leaving the nation with more roads whose maintenance may be neglected.[48] Today our outdated and overused road system is crumbling.

Moreover, the problem goes beyond congestion in big cities. Potholes are accumulating on rural highways and in small towns' roads. The people of Maine spend $250 million a year fixing cars damaged by poor roads in the state. Poor road conditions cost American motorists $54 billion every year in repairs and operating expenses—$275 per motorist. Decaying roads are dangerous as well as inconvenient. The AAA estimated that in 2006, traffic crashes killed 42,642 people in the United States—roughly one death every twelve minutes. An additional 2.6 million people were injured—nearly one per second.[49] There is every reason why this situation will continue to get worse. In our troubled economic times, state and local governments are cutting back on services and deferring even more maintenance. With gas prices historically higher over the past five to fifteen years, politicians are not inclined to raise gasoline taxes, a major source of revenue for roads. With the advent of the nation's financial crisis in 2008, manufacturers are turning their attention to more fuel-efficient vehicles while the federal government is offering greater incentives to auto manufacturers to produce engines that do not rely on oil, such as hybrids and diesel and electric vehicles. If that trend continues, over time it will reduce revenues from gas taxes.

This new initiative is expected to continue but there remains little prospect for Congress to raise the gasoline tax at a time when all politicians deem such an action to be tantamount to removal from office.

### The Substitution of Federal for State Funds

A recent study from the U.S. Government Accountability Office (GAO) has found another reason for inadequate spending on road and bridge maintenance and repair during what was supposed to be an era of management, beginning with the passage of ISTEA in the early 1990s. In an August 2004 report, the GAO found that, during the previous twenty years, although state and local investment in highways had "outstripped" federal highway investment, federal investment had increased at double the rate of state and local investment (47 percent versus 23 percent) in the 1990s. It further found that in the four years after the passage of TEA-21 (1998–2002), state and local investment had *decreased* by 4 percent in real terms, while federal investment had increased by 40 percent. The GAO concluded from its examination of funding and spending patterns that federal-aid highway grants had "influenced state and local governments to substitute federal funds for state and local funds that otherwise would have been spent on highways," and that "substitution [of federal for state and local highway funding] may be limiting the effectiveness of the strategies Congress has put into place to meet the federal-aid highway program's overall goals."[50]

By the GAO's "conservative estimate," approximately half of the increase in federal highway funds for the states since 1982 had been "used to reduce states' level of highway spending effort," and the rate of this substitution had increased significantly in the 1990s—i.e., after the passage of ISTEA. Indeed, the GAO further concluded, "the [federal-aid highway] program is to some extent functioning as a cash transfer, general purpose grant program" in which, despite DOT's development of "performance measures and outcomes. . . . currently there is no link between the achievement of these measures and outcomes and federal funding provided to the states."[51] This finding provoked little reaction in Congress, DOT, state legislatures, or state or local transportation agencies, and for good reason. While infrastructure assets at all levels of government were deteriorating with increasing frequency, it had become a habit to disregard the growing signs of horrible consequences to come, when the bill for repairing or replacing the nation's roads, bridges, levees, and other structures came due. With preservation and remediation of the nation's roads and bridges, as we have seen, having been a major stated goal of federal highway policy at least since the passage of ISTEA, the GAO report provided more evidence of unintended consequences flowing from federal highway funding policy, to the detriment of the condition of the nation's roads and bridges. Yet leaders throughout the nation exhibited no new sense of urgency to change existing policies.

### Transfers of Federal Road and Bridge Funds

The flexibility given to states under ISTEA and subsequent federal highway legislation that made federal funding available for maintenance and remediation was intended, in the spirit of federalism, to allow the states to address their needs in their own unique ways. Yet this approach also undermined important goals behind federal highway policy in what was supposed to be a new era of management.

How states spend their federal maintenance and repair funds in relation to the specific needs for which those funds are provided was the subject of a 2003 report from the nationwide coalition known as the Surface Transportation Policy Project (STPP). The study—titled "The $300 Billion Question: Are We Buying a Better Transportation System?"—examined data from 1992–2001 in four areas, including "road pavement conditions and road repair spending" and "bridge conditions and bridge repair spending." (The other two categories—

traffic safety and air quality—are ones for which states are allowed to transfer Highway Bridge Program funds under the terms of TEA-21.) The report concluded that "conditions and performance have improved in areas where targeted funding exists" and that "much of the credit for these repairs and improvements rests with specific funding provided through the Bridge Repair and Interstate Maintenance programs in the federal surface transportation laws—ISTEA and TEA-21."[52] For example, the percentage of major U.S. roadways rated in less than good condition had dropped from 70.1 percent in 1994 to 49.9 percent in 2001, while the proportion of interstate highways in the same condition had improved from 60 percent to 34 percent over the same period, owing to the federal IM program created by ISTEA. Meanwhile, the structural deficiency rate for the nation's overall bridge inventory dropped from 20.7 percent in 1992 to 14.2 percent in 2001, a development that the STPP attributed to "dedicated bridge repair funding in ISTEA and TEA-21 through the federal Bridge repair program."[53]

However significant these achievements might be, the STPP report went on to state, all the areas of transportation studied "could have seen far more dramatic improvements had Congress closed accounting loopholes in the current law that allow states to shift funds out of road and bridge repair . . . into more traditional highway construction programs."[54] Citing pavement conditions as an example, the report noted that the nation could have expected even greater improvement "had states and Congress adopted a stronger 'fix it first' policy and closed accounting loopholes in the current law." Despite an overall improvement, "there was tremendous variation among the states and among different types of roadways," with interstate highways improving the most while "urban and suburban roads off the Interstate system improved the least," with "68.4 percent of roadway miles in poor, mediocre, or fair condition."[55]

For bridges, the STPP found, the problem of states' transferring federal funds out of the programs for which they were apportioned was even worse: "Of the five core funding programs under ISTEA and TEA-21, the federal Bridge repair program has been by far the most neglected: states collectively have invested less than three of four dollars that were available (a 73% obligation rate) under the federal Bridge program. This means that states left $7.9 billion in Bridge money on the table, over ten years, in favor of funding other programs." For both roads and bridges, the STPP concluded, "spending on repairs decreased as a share of all spending in 25 states. In another five states, the absolute dollars spent annually on road and bridge repair actually *decreased* during the first four years of TEA-21, relative to ISTEA spending—despite the influx of new money."[56]

The effects of the leeway enjoyed by the states in spending federal transportation funds may be one factor in the performance of both states that have done the best job of maintaining their infrastructure and those that have done the worst. The wide gap between the two groups is evident in state rankings for both road and bridge conditions. For example, the STPP report on the state of American roads as of 2001 revealed an extremely large spread between the states at the top and those at the bottom: Georgia, with only 2.8 percent of its roads rated as not in good condition, and Nevada, with 8 percent, topped the list, while the six lowest-ranked states (Oregon, California, Rhode Island, Massachusetts, Missouri, and Hawaii, in descending order) all had over 80 percent of their roads rated in only fair, mediocre, or poor condition.[57]

State rankings by percentage of bridges rated structurally deficient also show a significant gap between the top and bottom performers: in the FHWA's National Bridge Inventory for 2008, the five states with the lowest proportion of structurally deficient bridges (Florida, Delaware, Nevada, Arizona, and Texas) all had structural deficiency rates of less than 4 percent, while the five worst states (South Dakota, Iowa, Rhode Island, Oklahoma, and Pennsylvania, in descending order) all had 20 percent or more of their bridges rated structurally deficient. The ten worst states—which included relatively small ones such as Rhode Island, Vermont, New Hampshire, and North Dakota—together accounted for 38 percent of all the structurally deficient bridges in the United States, while the five worst accounted for 25 percent.[58]

Although a variety of factors doubtless accounts for the disparity in performance between high-ranking and low-ranking states in the maintenance of roads and bridges, it is notable, in light of the STPP report's findings, that low-performing states show a tendency to leave federal money designated for road or bridge repair on the table. For roads, the STPP report, which covers the crucial ten years (1992–2001) following the enactment of ISTEA, shows that three of the ten states with the highest percentage of roadway miles in less than good condition in 2001 (Massachusetts, Connecticut, and New Jersey) were also among the ten with the "lowest percentage of federal funds (excl[uding] planning and engineering) on road repair."[59] Massachusetts—87 percent of whose roads were in less than good condition in 2001, and which had embarked in 1991 on its massive Central Artery/Tunnel Project, better known as the Big Dig—spent a meager 12 percent of its federal highway funds on road repair over this period, and another five of the ten states with the worst roads in the country (Hawaii, California, Connecticut, Arkansas, and New Jersey) spent less than the national average of 33 percent. Of the remaining states among the worst ten, three (Missouri, Rhode Island, and Oregon) were essentially at the national average, and only one (South Dakota) was spending substantially more (74 percent). Meanwhile, of the ten states whose roads were in the best condition in 2001, only three—Georgia, Nevada, and Florida—spent less than the national average of 33 percent of federal highway funds on road repair, and those three states ranked first, second, and fourth in the country, respectively, for the condition of their roads.[60]

The data on bridges reveal a comparable situation. Three of the ten states that had the most structurally deficient bridges in the country in 2008 (Pennsylvania, Rhode Island, and Vermont) were also among the ten states that had the lowest ratios of Highway Bridge Program (HBP) obligations to apportionments (i.e., money contractually obligated for bridge work as a percentage of the amount apportioned to a state by federal formulas) over the period 2003–7 (58 percent, 71 percent, and 63 percent, respectively), and five of those ten states (the three mentioned above along with Missouri and New Hampshire) obligated less than 100 percent of their HBP apportionments over this period and were all below the national average of 89 percent. Pennsylvania (which had the highest percentage of structurally deficient bridges in the country—27 percent—in 2008) and Vermont also allowed their percentages of structurally deficient bridges to increase from 2001 to 2008, a period during which the nationwide structural deficiency rate dropped by slightly more than two percentage points. Meanwhile, of the ten states with the lowest percentages of structurally deficient bridges in 2008, all but one (Arizona, which had the fourth-best record in the country) obligated at least 90 percent of their HBP apportionments over the period 2003–7.[61]

Some state and federal transportation officials argue, however, that HBP obligation-to-apportionment ratios are misleading indicators of how well states are maintaining their bridge stocks. They point to another factor that has hindered the effectiveness of federal efforts to direct spending to road and bridge maintenance: the perverse effects of federal funding formulas that actually create incentives for states to allow their infrastructure to deteriorate.

### Perverse Incentives

When the Williamsburg Bridge Technical Advisory Committee was formed in the late 1980s to assess whether that historic but seriously deteriorated structure should be repaired or replaced, it found that the cost of replacing the bridge's approach structures and rehabilitating the main and side spans, towers, and cables would come to only $400 million, as compared with the $800 million it would have taken to construct a new bridge. Yet Sam Schwartz of NYCDOT had to fight for the opportunity to save the bridge, after the U.S. Department of Transportation blocked an allocation of federal funds for its rehabilitation (see chapter 1).

What ultimately proved a successful effort to save the Williamsburg revealed a further absurdity. In the aftermath of the decision to repair rather than replace the bridge, Schwartz calculated that "if New York had spent $2 million annually (in 1992 dollars) for 89 years, the bridge could have been properly maintained and its steel could have lasted more than 200 years. In the past 89 years, instead of spending $178 million, we probably spent closer to $20 million on maintenance, so the $400 million the city will spend to rebuild the bridge represents a waste of more than $200 million." Meanwhile, a study of the city's bridge program that Schwartz and NYCDOT's commissioner, Ross Sandler, wrote in 1988 found that New York—which was then spending over $400 million per year on its bridges, more than half of which were structurally deficient—ought to be spending only $154 million annually: $100 million for capital improvements and replacement, and $54 million for preventive maintenance. "But the city," Schwartz later explained, "was spending only $5 million per year on preventive maintenance, requiring over $400 million per year in capital replacement to keep most of our inventory of bridges open. The study found that if we had doubled our annual maintenance level from $5 to $10 million, our capital needs would have dropped by $100 million. In other words, a $5 million investment would have yielded a $100 million benefit—a twenty-to-one-payoff!"[62] To Schwartz, the caretaker for one of the nation's largest bridge inventories, the numbers tell a story that is difficult to ignore.

How could the city have been, as Schwartz put, "so stupid" as pass up the opportunity for nearly $100 million annually in savings in its bridge program? He went on to explain how the rules of the federal Highway Bridge Program encouraged such waste: "A well-maintained bridge is regularly cleaned, painted, and lubricated, and minor parts are repaired as needed. These items are typically funded out of a city's expense budget, which is also used for police officers, teachers, and hospital workers." However, requests from a transportation agency for funding for bridge painters will always lose out to other budgetary demands for fire or police needs. "In fact, preventive maintenance historically could not be paid from city capital funds, state bond money, or myriad federal sources." But under the funding mechanisms that state transportation agencies operate, if you have "a deficient bridge, with rusting steel and crumbling concrete, [it] was eligible for just about every city, state, and federal program. If repairs are federally funded, the city may end up spending only a fraction of the total cost. Thus there is incentive to let a bridge deteriorate."[63]

Sam Schwartz recalls predicting in 1992 that the flexibility given to states in ISTEA would not translate into more than a small percent of federal bridge funds being used for anything besides "major rehabilitation, replacement, or new facilities" in coming years. Schwartz was still lamenting this situation fifteen years, later when the I-35W Bridge collapsed after being rated in poor condition since 1991. In 2007 he observed: "When it comes to infrastructure we have become junkies for other people's money."[64]

In testimony before Congress just over a month after the I-35W Bridge collapsed, another transportation official lamented the perverse incentives provided by the rules that govern spending of federal bridge funds by state and local governments. Appearing before the House Transportation and Infrastructure Committee in September 2007, Kirk Steudle, director and chief executive officer of the Michigan Department of Transportation (MDOT), argued that "federal road and bridge funding programs have not kept pace with the state of the practice of asset management, and the rules that govern use of those funds are not always compatible with asset management." Steudle stated that in the two preceding years, his department had "spent less than 90 percent of its federal bridge funds, not because we weren't investing in bridges, but because the rules for those funds are too restrictive." Michigan, he testified, inspected its bridges "more thoroughly and more often than required by federal law," established a set of strategic goals for its road and bridge preservation program, and employed preventive maintenance to slow the deterioration of its bridges. In order to achieve its goals, however, Michigan had to "look outside the Federal Highway Bridge Program," for reasons Steudle explained with the following example:

> Today, States are not allowed to use Federal bridge funds to improve a structurally deficient bridge deck if other elements, such as the superstructure or the substructure, are still in good condition.

Let me give you a specific example. In Michigan, we have 608 structurally deficient bridges. 223 of those bridges are because the bridge decks are poor. The superstructure and substructure are rated in fair or good condition. Those 223 bridges are not eligible for the Highway Bridge Program funding right now. 43 of those are serious. They are rated at a 3 going back to that rating scale. So we are using the State funds to replace those bridge decks. From an asset management standpoint, this simply does not make sense because the structurally deficient bridge deck actually accelerates the deterioration of other bridge elements. It is like saying you will not replace the shingles on your leaky roof until the moisture has destroyed the drywall or cracked the foundation.[65]

The conflict between sound asset management practices and the incentives offered by federal policy for allowing roads and bridges to deteriorate that Steudle describes can no longer be ignored by federal and state transportation officials. This dilemma has been made particularly acute by the perfect storm of a combination of factors. On the one hand, we have experienced decades of increasing demand for maintenance and repair due to the aging of infrastructure and the consequences of past neglect. On the other hand, we face a steady decline in state revenues that can be used for road and bridge maintenance and repair. This mismatch between needs and resources hampers the efforts of states that have recognized the need to dramatically improve the condition of their transportation infrastructure while facing significant political and economic impediments.

### Stuck in the Mud:
### The Disparity between Needs and Resources

The United States as a whole is not spending nearly enough on its roads and bridges. In its 2009 *Report Card for America's Infrastructure*, the ASCE estimates the gap between need and current spending for bridges and highways separately and in the aggregate, and the shortfalls are dramatic. According to the ASCE, the country needs to be spending

$17 billion per year to "substantially improve current bridge conditions" but is now spending only $10.5 billion on bridge construction and maintenance.[66] The ASCE figures include sums for both structurally deficient and functionally obsolete bridges. However, a breakdown given by the American Association of State Highway and Transportation Officials (AASHTO) in its own recent report on transportation funding needs shows that because 34 percent of total bridge needs are accounted for by structurally deficient bridges,[67] current needs would be approximately $5.8 billion per year while current spending is approximately $3.6 billion. For highways, the ASCE *Report Card* states: "Current spending of $70.3 billion per year for highway capital improvements is well below the estimated $186 billion needed annually to substantially improve conditions." Over the next five years, the ASCE calculates, the nation needs to spend $930 billion on its roads and bridges (including, again, both structurally deficient and functionally obsolete bridges) but will actually spend only $380.5 billion (including $27.5 billion in stimulus funds), for a five-year shortfall of $549.5 billion.[68] The staggering shortfall represented by these studies should make it even clearer that infrastructure assets will reach a critical turning point if we fail to address these issues.

State governments—besides having limited resources for a variety of needs, among which infrastructure investment is easily short-changed[69]—have faced stiff challenges in recent years in their efforts to fund even minimal transportation efforts. One significant factor has been construction costs, especially because in 2003–8 the price of key materials rose anywhere from 36 percent (for concrete) to 306 percent (for diesel fuel), as shown in figure 2.

Declining revenues from gasoline taxes owing to the greater fuel efficiency of vehicles has been another significant challenge for states, as it has been for the federal government's Highway Trust Fund. This is true despite the fact that politicians at the state level have shown a surprising willingness to increase their gasoline taxes for the better part of the last thirty years.[70] As a result—in a particularly stark illustration of how highway users in America continue to be under-

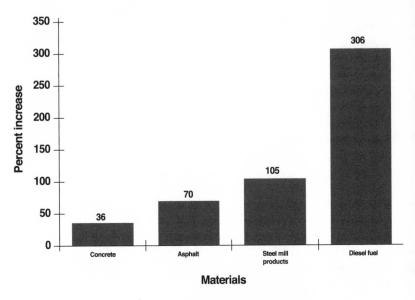

**Figure 2. Construction costs, 2003–2008.**

American Association of State Highway and Transportation Officials,

*Bridging the Gap: Restoring and Rebuilding the Nation's Bridges*, July 2008 (http://

www.transportation1.org/BridgeReport/scarce.html, accessed August 6, 2009).

charged for the upkeep of roads and bridges—the costs to motorists have dropped sharply since the dawn of the interstate era.[71]

The convergence of deferred and neglected maintenance costs with declining revenues, exacerbated by the dilemmas for state transportation officials described by the head of MDOT, is well illustrated by the case of Michigan, a state that has done a poor job of maintaining its roads and bridges for many years but is now making a serious effort to overcome this legacy. Michigan's roads and bridges are in poor condition compared with those of many other states. In 2006, the state ranked in the bottom third of all states for the condition of its rural and urban interstates and rural principal arterials.[72] Of its urban principal arterials, 36.3 percent were rated poor in FHWA data for the same year—almost eleven percentage points higher than the national average, which put the state eighth worst in the country—and the condition of these roads had actually gotten considerably worse in the years between 1995 (when they were rated 25.6 percent poor) and 2006. However, the condition of Michigan's state trunk line highways generally improved significantly from the mid-1990s to the mid-2000s, going from 64 percent in good condition in 1994 to 81 percent in 2004.[73] Meanwhile, with 13 percent of its bridges rated structurally deficient in 2008, the state ranks thirty-third in the country in that category, although its record is only slightly worse than the national average and has improved significantly since 1992 (when 23.4 percent of its bridges were rated structurally deficient).[74]

MDOT's determination to deal with its infrastructure remediation needs is also reflected in its budget priorities. The department's current highway investment plan calls for spending, on average, only 5.8 percent of its annual budgets in 2009–13 for capacity improvement and new roads, and its average annual spending for routine maintenance over this period is set to nearly double the amount spent for that purpose in 1997. MDOT will face severe challenges in implementing its plans in coming years. As it reported in the preliminary draft of its five-year transportation program for fiscal years 2009–13, a combination of declining revenues from the state gas tax (which at 19 cents per gallon in 2007 was almost exactly at the national average of 19.25 cents per gallon for that year[75]) and vehicle registration fees and increased costs for raw materials such as asphalt and steel means that "MDOT will not be able to match all federal-aid dollars beginning in 2010."[76]

Projecting state revenue shortfalls of $354 million that will result in a loss of over $2 billion in federal matching funds in 2010–13, MDOT has adopted a reduced investment strategy for its highway program. Under this strategy, the state will spend $660 million less on repairing and rebuilding roads, $316 million less on repairing and rebuilding bridges, and $88 million less on routine maintenance in 2009–13 than it would have done ordinarily. As a consequence, MDOT also projects that the percentage of the state's highways rated in good condition—already expected to fall from over 90 percent in 2008 to just over 70 percent in 2013 under a scenario of full funding—will decline to less than 70 percent in 2013; by 2020, when even under a full funding scenario barely 50 percent of the state's highways will be in good condition, the number will fall to just over 40 percent with reduced funding.[77] Meanwhile, the percentage of Michigan bridges in good or fair condition, projected to rise slightly between 2009 and 2017 with full funding, will decline by over five percentage points over the same period (from 90 percent in 2009 to 85 percent in 2017).

Michigan has been affected more severely than most other states by the current recession, but the fiscal plight of MDOT is similar to that of transportation departments in other states with particularly acute needs for infrastructure remediation. New Jersey is another state ranking in the bottom third of all states for the condition of its rural and urban interstates and rural principal arterials.[78] Between 1992 and 2008, New Jersey cut its percentage of structurally deficient bridges from 24.8 percent to 11 percent, but the percentage of poor pavement miles on its major urban roads increased between 1995 and 2006—markedly so in the case of urban "other principal arterials," which went from 18.8 percent in poor condition in 1995 to 47.3 percent in 2006. Recognizing that it is on an unsustainable course, the New Jersey Department of Transportation (NJDOT) is projecting that annual spending on new roadway capacity will never exceed $250 million through 2030, while the annual need for maintenance, renewal, and operations will come to $6 billion by that year. Meanwhile, according to its planning document, "NJDOT estimates the cumulative capital costs of this plan to be $118 billion (in year-of-expenditure [YOE] dollars), and the cumulative operating and maintenance costs to be about $4 billion (YOE) through 2030."[79] Rhode Island, yet another state that consistently ranks near the bottom for the condition of its roads and bridges (49.7 percent of its nonexpressway urban principal arterials were in poor condition as of 2006, and 22.3 of its bridges structurally deficient in 2008, with both figures representing a decline in conditions since the early 1990s), must close a projected annual shortfall for its highway program of $285 million between now and 2018 by finding new revenues amounting to 80 percent of currently projected ones.

These three states are not alone: funding deficits for infrastructure maintenance are a nationwide problem. Yet even if those deficits were filled tomorrow, the crisis of neglect that has overcome our nation's infrastructure would not disappear. We need more than money alone. How states use, or choose not to use, the limited resources that are currently available reflects on the culture of the state transportation agencies entrusted with caring for our infrastructure assets. The decline in our nation's transportation infrastructure is directly correlated to the denigration of the role of the individuals who were largely responsible for the design and construction of these facilities. As we shall see below, we must begin to recognize the significance of the declining influence of professional engineers in state transportation agencies. This new reality compounds the challenge of money and is explored in the next chapter.

# 3 No Sense of Urgency
## The Politics and Culture of Road and Bridge Maintenance

America is always about the next new thing. We build beautifully. But building brings with it responsibility that extends long past the date when a project is completed and put into use. Our record of maintaining what we build is less than beautiful. Examples abound. One is the neglect of New York City's bridges over several decades following World War II. Another is the 100-year-old Longfellow Bridge connecting Boston and Cambridge, which has deteriorated badly despite rehabilitation work performed in 1959 and 2002. These and countless other examples conclusively establish why it is extraordinarily important to start maintaining a bridge from the moment it is built. Maintenance cannot wait until there is a problem. Keeping up is much easier and less costly than catching up.

If a bridge or other transportation facility is operated without attention to its ongoing needs—that is, if required maintenance is deferred—the government or other organization that owns it will unquestionably face higher capital costs for eventual replacement. U.S. bridge owners have failed to learn this lesson, and it is costing our nation dearly. State transportation agencies have come to recognize that funding for any failure of an infrastructure facility will not come out of their own budgets; capital funds, usually provided by state or federal governments, will meet such emergency needs. From the agency's point of view, therefore, it makes financial sense to let the facility decline to the point where other agencies will pay to fix it. Today, transportation agencies lack the resources to bring up to acceptable standards our aging infrastructure, which has gone without upkeep for too long. Requests to politicians go unheeded, as these agencies lack any political clout given the prefer-

## Effect of Maintenance on Aging Infrastructure Assets

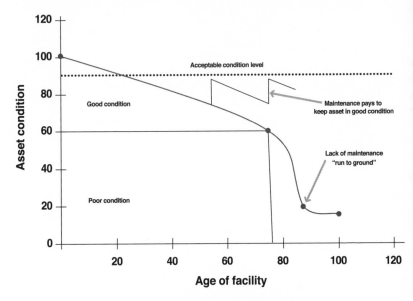

**Figure 3. Condition vs. age curve and impact
of maintenance or lack thereof.**

American Association of State Highway and Transportation Officials (AASHTO),
*Bridging the Gap: Restoring and Rebuilding the Nation's Bridges*, Washington, D.C.:
AASHTO, 2008, 3 (http://www.transportation1.org/BridgeReport/docs/
BridgingtheGap.pdf), accessed March 26, 2010.

ence for spending on new roads, tunnels, bridges, and high-speed
rail lines.

Using a mathematical model developed by a group of Dutch engineers, the Pioneer Institute, citing the costs for the historic and very
deteriorated Longfellow Bridge in Massachusetts, calculated that an
annual investment in routine maintenance, over the bridge's life span
to date, of one percent of its capital cost would have yielded savings
of just over $80 million compared to the current estimate for return-
ing it to a state of good repair. Using this same model, interestingly,
the institute's report also found that a 1 percent annual investment

in maintenance would have yielded three times more savings than a 2.5 percent annual investment. This calculation illustrates the general principle that there is a clear correlation between the eventual cost resulting from deferred maintenance and how much is actually spent annually on maintenance over a bridge's lifetime: "In general, maintenance investments are more cost effective early in the life of the asset. For any asset, it is expected that there is a 40 percent drop in quality over 75 percent of its lifetime, followed by a more precipitous drop in the final quarter of the asset's life. Since deferred maintenance is the compounded effect of deferring maintenance from one year to the next, the cost of deferred maintenance in year one will increase significantly in every subsequent year."[1] The authors cite W. R. De Sitter's "law of fives" estimates that when maintenance is neglected, repairs when they become essential will generally equal five times maintenance costs; if repairs are not made even then, rehabilitation costs will be five times repair costs. The bottom line of overlooking maintenance on a regular basis makes clear the dramatic compounding consequence of deferring maintenance.[2]

As shown in figure 3, the American Society of Civil Engineers (ASCE) and the U.S. Army Corps of Engineers developed a condition versus age curve that identifies the critical importance of providing ongoing maintenance to an asset beginning soon after its completion. At a defined point in the asset's life span, performing deferred maintenance will do little to return the asset to good condition.

The long-standing, widespread practice among states and municipalities of neglecting maintenance is penny wise and pound foolish in more ways than one. Underbudgeting for maintenance and repair increases the backlog of problems that must eventually be addressed. It has also led to major reductions in the numbers of engineers employed in departments of transportation around the nation. Unfortunately, it is often the engineers who provide the institutional memory of how a state's bridges were designed and must be maintained if they are to remain safe for public use.

In Minnesota, in the five years leading up to the I-35W Bridge

collapse, MN/DOT lost 16 percent of its professional and parapro-
fessional engineering staff. In part, this was due to the fact that the
number of engineers nationally has declined, and the competition
for engineers among engineering consulting firms is increasing.
MN/DOT and other transportation departments around the country
have lost engineers to more lucrative or interesting positions in the
private sector.[3]

The other explanation for the loss of engineers in state departments of transportation is that the departments have relinquished
control of bridge designs and design processes to the American Association of State Highway and Transportation Officials (AASHTO). The
reason given for this is that maintaining individual design standards
on a state-by-state basis is too costly, as even before the losses began,
state agencies lacked a sufficient number of experienced engineers to
warrant in-house control over design. As a result, standardization of
bridge and road design has been ceded to national organizations such
as AASHTO and federal funders such as the Federal Highway Administration (FHWA). According to one engineer who has worked with
many state departments of transportation, the result has been that
many good engineers left for more challenging work, "leaving the ap-
prentices to cook dinner."[4]

The flight of engineers is just one symptom of various organizational shortcomings within these departments. After the collapse of
the I-35W Bridge in Minneapolis, the Gray Plant Mooty report commissioned by the Minnesota legislature pointed to various organizational weaknesses within MN/DOT that compromised the safety of
the bridge: a poor flow of information; bad use of expert advice; and
an organizational structure that impeded the maintenance process.[5]
The inadequate flow of information within MN/DOT was related to
the loss of engineering personnel and MN/DOT's largely oral culture.
Information passed poorly if at all between different offices within
the agency, and the lack of consistent written documentation was routinely tolerated.[6]

In January 2003, that weak organization found itself with a commissioner who was a politician, not an engineer, when Governor Tim Pawlenty appointed his lieutenant governor, Carol Molnau, to hold both offices concurrently. This had cascading deleterious effects, as professional staff grew reluctant to express professional judgments and generally "hunkered down" to avoid political controversy.[7] Whether intentional or not, the net effect of this appointment was to politicize the jobs of professional public servants, who were overseeing an aging and deteriorating bridge system with not nearly enough funding to keep it operational. One can only imagine what would have happened to the Williamsburg and Manhattan Bridges in New York City had Mayor Koch appointed his deputy mayor to be transportation commissioner, thus hampering Sam Schwartz's ability to oversee those bridges.

Infrastructure and public works represent a major portion of the projects that keep the construction industry's nearly seven million workers employed annually. As a result, lobbyists for the various trade groups that seek to garner valuable contracts for large infrastructure projects work assiduously in state capitals across the nation. Needless to say, government officials at all levels look to the construction industry for generous support of their election and reelection campaigns. These supporters, in turn, hope to have some impact on legislation as well as allocations of funding for projects that will ensure the future livelihoods of their constituents. This symbiotic partnership extends to service providers such as engineering consultants, architects, and others whose client base is derived from the public transportation sector, and who welcome into their midst retired transportation officials who enjoy the higher pay that the private sector can offer them.

The value assigned to infrastructure maintenance creates unresolved tensions between administrative and managerial interests (who are forced to recognize the need to limit transportation funding for maintenance) and the technical and professional recommendations of civil engineers (who must walk a fine line between reporting the actual extent of deterioration that a lack of maintenance has caused and the recognition that there is no financial wherewithal to fund needed remedial work). This is an old and far-ranging problem, and it makes the job of professional engineers more difficult. Were any of these facts otherwise, there would be numerous states in which the number of structurally deficient and functionally obsolete bridges (nationwide, 25 percent of all bridges) would be less than the national average.

Engineers in America were not always regarded as the colorless technocrats that most people view them as today; in fact, engineers were once a type of American cultural hero. Bridge engineers were particularly celebrated during the great era of u.s. bridge building for feats of construction like the Eads Bridge (1874) across the Mississippi River in St. Louis, the Brooklyn Bridge (1883), New York's George Washington Bridge (1931), and the Golden Gate Bridge in San Francisco (1937). The hero of Willa Cather's first novel, *Alexander's Bridge* (1912), is a bridge engineer named Bartley Alexander: "There were other bridge-builders in the world, certainly, but it was always Alexander's picture that the Sunday Supplement men wanted, because he looked as a tamer of rivers ought to look. Under his tumbled sandy hair his head seemed as hard and powerful as a catapult, and his shoulders looked strong enough in themselves to support a span of any one of his ten great bridges that cut the air above as many rivers."[8] In the 1920s, the poet Hart Crane—who once lived in the same rooms from which Washington Roebling had supervised the construction of the Brooklyn Bridge—made that great structure the central symbol of his long poem *The Bridge* (1930), while his lyric "To Brooklyn Bridge" apotheosizes the work of its bridge engineers: "How could mere toil align thy choiring strings!"[9]

But it was not all poetry: real expertise undergirded the romantic view of engineers. In an era when society regarded engineers as "leading efficiency experts,"[10] Herbert Hoover, originally a mining engineer, ascended to the presidency. Hoover enjoyed immense popularity during and after World War I, and a stint as secretary of commerce in the Harding and Coolidge administrations, on the strength of his organization of European famine-relief efforts[11] and his creation of programs for improved highway safety, motor vehicle standards, and urban traffic control.

From the 1920s through the 1950s, engineers' reputations and self-image continued to rise. They were seen as objective experts who would not be swayed by political and economic interests. In his brilliant biography of Robert Moses, the master planner who remade New York City and its environs according to his own vision, Robert Caro shows that Moses placed high value on his engineering team. As one of Moses' chief engineers explained to Caro, they were doing exactly what they had been trained to do: "He [Moses] made you feel that what we were doing together was tremendously important for the public, for the welfare of people."[12] But engineers' high level of responsibility in the decision-making hierarchy of transportation agencies did not last.

In the 1960s—with the rise of the environmental movement and the urban activism inspired by critics of the automobile such as Jane Jacobs, who challenged indiscriminate highway construction and expansion[13]—political actors began to wrest power away from engineers in highway policymaking. But it was a slow decline. Throughout the building of the interstate highway system, engineers regarded their mission as serving the public, and continued to think of themselves in noble terms.[14] This was exactly the way that Moses felt about his engineers and their purpose.

But as new American thinking reshaped policies dealing with cities and the economy, and as perceptions of neighborhood and environmental integrity evolved, a new type of nonengineering expertise intruded into the sacrosanct world of the professional engineer. Trained management and budget professionals found ample opportunities to gain the ears of political leaders and influence the budgeting process. Much as Moses had learned the critical importance of controlling the tolls he collected from the bridges he built and using those funds to build his own empire, politicians now turned to management and budget experts to find new and creative ways for accessing funding resources at the federal, state, and local levels. At the same time, the veteran engineers who had built the interstate system began to retire, while their younger colleagues who remained on the job found themselves in a vastly changed and more difficult working environment.[15]

The departure of the professional engineer from senior government positions had a lasting impact on policies affecting local transportation agencies. In New York City, according to Sam Schwartz, the eclipse of the engineers in city government came after World War II, when business schools successfully promoted the idea that management was a science independent of any knowledge of particular industries or disciplines. In contrast to the 1930s, when all the major city agencies involved in construction were headed by Cooper Union–educated engineers, today, according to Schwartz, "it is rare to find an engineer as chief of any agency, including transportation, environmental protection, and school construction." City governments across America sprouted offices of management and budget, whose directors had direct access to the mayor while city engineers could only plead with the MBAs who passed through their agencies to make their case for more funding to the new offices. "Flunkies out of Wharton, still wet behind the ears, would stand up and tell a fifty-year-old engineer with twenty to thirty years of experience building and maintaining bridges what to do," Schwartz says.[16]

Schwartz described the choice faced by engineers occupying leadership positions in government transportation agencies as one between serving the public or serving "whoever is the elected official at that time." He cites the oath taken by members of the Order of the Engineer (a graduate and professional association that exists "to foster a spirit of pride and responsibility in the engineering profession, to bridge the gap between training and experience, and to present to the public a visible symbol identifying the engineer") to support the proposition that a professional engineer's first obligation is always to the public. The oath reads in part: "I am an Engineer, in my profession I take deep pride. To it I owe solemn obligations. . . . As an Engineer, I pledge to practice integrity and fair dealing, tolerance and respect, and to uphold devotion to the standards and the dignity of my profession. . . . When needed, my skill and knowledge shall be given without reservation for the public good."[17]

As Schwartz came to learn, engineers in government service across the nation were realizing that their influence and stature within government had become increasingly marginalized. Professional engineers in departments of transportation had to come to grips with the imperatives of infrastructure management and how to address the complex engineering problems that were presented by infrastructure both new and old, which was now being managed by nonengineers. No longer was it the professional engineer who had direct contact with budget directors and other wielders of political authority. This conflict normally takes much less dramatic forms than it often did in New York City in the late 1980s and early 1990s, when Sam Schwartz dealt with these issues. According to one of the most influential works in the extensive historical and sociological literature on the engineering profession in America and its absorption into large organizations, "the engineer's problem has centered on a conflict between professional independence and bureaucratic loyalty"; indeed, "engineers in government have experienced . . . conflicts, if anything more severe than those of privately employed engineers."[18]

The professional engineer in the public sector wrestles endlessly with the competing interests of meeting his or her professional obligations while carrying out projects under political and economic constraints. When transportation politics poses the question of how to direct traffic at the crowded intersection of professional responsibility, political power, and financial feasibility, it is not always possible for engineers embedded in government agencies to respond as suggested in the 1920s by the legendary bridge engineer Gustav Lindenthal: "Engineers are sometimes under the authority of laymen with whom financial considerations may seem more important than safety. If the pressure for cheapness comes from them, then the engineer should decline responsibility for the work."[19] As the actions of

Sam Schwartz in New York suggest, everything depends on the leadership and management of the agency and the larger principles that now inform its decision making.

As a sign of how the engineer's role in current times has been marginalized, it is instructive to examine how engineers were addressed in the report prepared by the National Transportation Safety Board (NTSB) following the collapse of the I-35W Bridge. The report blamed the failure on a forty-year-old engineering error. Could it be true that a simple design error was the primary cause of the bridge's disastrous collapse? Placing the primary blame for a failure of this magnitude on engineers was an attack on the profession as a whole. Yet the silence of the profession has been deafening. The ASCE, the largest professional engineering association in the country, has marshaled no protests and has conducted no investigations of its own to challenge this indictment of individual engineers who are no longer around to defend themselves.

If the NTSB report is to be accepted, it must withstand a close scrutiny of the history of the bridge's maintenance record as well as of how it was designed and built. Any discussion of an aging bridge that fails in this country cannot take place in a vacuum: it must recognize the fact that nearly every state transportation agency is having trouble funding maintenance and the challenges this poses for the upkeep of such bridges. Should the NTSB have evaluated, for example, how MN/DOT's leadership dealt with the conflicting advice received from its engineers and the information received from the state's accountants and managers, who were responsible for allocating transportation funds for all roads and bridges on a statewide basis? Why were the engineering consultants' reports highlighting the perilous state of the I-35W Bridge totally ignored by MN/DOT and the state government, which led to the decision to defer needed replacement for the bridge deck for more than a decade? Did all of MN/DOT's professional engineers agree with these decisions, or did they accede to a bureaucratic mandate to minimize repairs in order to keep their jobs? And if any of these factors were valid concerns, why did the NTSB not deem them worth including in its report, so that other state transportation agencies could learn from what went wrong in Minnesota?

Any infrastructure maintenance program must be carried out within organizational and financial parameters of some kind. It is always the responsibility of engineers to satisfy the requirements of utility, safety, *and* economy in their work.[20] And when engineers assume management and leadership positions in transportation agencies, they must operate as managers as well as engineers. Nevertheless—and even if one factors out political pressures and loyalties as something from which transportation management ought to be isolated[21]—it is possible to identify the differences between managerial judgment and engineering judgment and to ask why the former should be allowed to override the latter where public safety is at issue.

It might have been highly instructive if the authors of the NTSB report—as well as the decision makers at MN/DOT, before the I-35W Bridge collapse—had read the Rogers Commission report on the causes of the January 1986 explosion of the space shuttle *Challenger*. They might have learned a number of useful lessons. One member of the commission, the Nobel Prize–winning physicist Richard P. Feynman, lambasted the management of the National Aeronautics and Space Administration (NASA) for its part in the explosion. What he had to say regarding the management decisions that led to that disaster has great relevance to how we should be managing the 72,000 structurally deficient bridges in our nation today.

In an appendix to the commission's final report titled "Personal Observations on the Reliability of the Shuttle," Feynman zeroed in on a significant divergence of opinion between NASA managers and project engineers on the probability of failure of the shuttle's solid rocket boosters. As readers will recall, it was the failure of the rubber O-rings on one of the spacecraft's two solid rocket boosters—attributed to a design flaw—that the Rogers Commission identified as the cause of the *Challenger* disaster. Whereas NASA management had estimated the probability of failure at one in 100,000, NASA engineers disputed that assessment and put the likelihood of a catastrophic failure at one in 100. The Rogers Commission, with the exception of Feynman, accepted management's judgment that the shuttle was safe. Feynman alone disputed this finding and proved that the engineers' judgment was more accurate and that they had better understood the risks of the mission.

How to account for such an enormous disparity? NASA managers, Feynman charged, had made fallacious, unwarranted inferences from the shuttle's record of successful manned missions prior to the *Challenger* explosion. Validating the estimate of one in 100,000 experimentally was deemed impossible for "it would take an inordinate number of tests to determine it." But Feynman argued that if the real probability were not so small, "flights would show troubles, near failures, and possible actual failures with a reasonable number of trials, and standard statistical methods could give a reasonable estimate." Indeed, "previous NASA experience had shown, on occasion, just such difficulties, near accidents, and accidents, all giving warning that the probability of flight failure was not so very small."[22] Such incidents, in fact, had included observed defects in the O-rings in the form of erosion and blow-by—the very phenomena that would result in the explosion of the *Challenger*. Yet NASA management fell back on the false assurance offered by the fact that no full-fledged failure had occurred in any previous shuttle mission. In a discourse analogous to the one that should be used to address the arguments of transportation officials who have permitted bridges in a terrible state of decay to continue to carry the traveling public, Feynman excoriated this faulty reliance on past performance as a guarantee of future performance:

> [Management's] acceptance and success of these flights is taken as evidence of safety. But erosion and blow-by are not what the design expected. They are warnings that something is wrong. The equipment is not operating as expected, and therefore there is a danger that it can operate with even wider deviations in this unexpected and not thoroughly understood way. The fact that this danger did

not lead to a catastrophe before is no guarantee that it will not the next time, unless it is completely understood. When playing Russian roulette the fact that the first shot got off safely is little comfort for the next. The origin and consequences of the erosion and blow-by were not understood. They did not occur equally on all flights and all joints; sometimes more, and sometimes less. Why not sometime, when whatever conditions determined it were right, still more leading to catastrophe?[23]

NASA managers viewed the project through a different prism, circumscribed by political and financial circumstances. As a result, managers ignored crucial information that the engineers possessed on how O-rings worked. In spite of the variations from one shuttle flight to another, managers behaved as if they understood the engineering and provided the Rogers Commission with seemingly logical arguments based on the success of previous flights as evidence of continued reliability. For example, managers cited prior flights where the O-ring had not failed, despite exhibiting a $^1/_3$ erosion of its radius. Managers deemed this flight a success and rated the O-rings with a "safety factor of three."[24] Feynman thought this was an unusual use of the engineer's term, "safety factor." Safety factor refers to the capacity to withstand or carry excess load, unforeseen extra load, or unexpected flaws and weaknesses in the material. Feynman cited the example of a bridge that, with a safety factor of three, would withstand its full design load times three, without exhibiting any signs of failure. He recognized that failure did not necessarily mean collapse; it could simply mean the appearance of cracks in beams, or in the case of the *Challenger*, erosion in the O-rings. Failure, he urged his fellow commission members, occurs before catastrophe. Feynman knew that the O-rings were designed not to erode at all. But they did erode, and at that moment, they failed. From partially eroded but still performing O-rings, managers inferred safety. Feynman saw failure in the same O-rings and the connection to catastrophe.

In the five years before collapse of the I-35W Bridge, from 2001 to

2006, MN/DOT consulting engineers delivered to MN/DOT managers a list of flawed structural components on that fracture-critical bridge. Everyone associated with the I-35W Bridge was well aware that the failure of any one critical component would lead to a total collapse of the structure. In this sense, the bridge was a far more fragile machine than the *Challenger*. Managers continued to rate the bridge as safe for the traveling public when, by engineering standards, it was well on the road to failure.

In his concluding remarks, Feynman speculated that everything from budget constraints to scheduled launch dates had been deemed greater priorities by NASA managers than best engineering practices dictated. He noted: "If a reasonable launch schedule is to be maintained, engineering often cannot be done fast enough to keep up with the expectations of originally conservative certification criteria designed to guarantee a very safe vehicle. In these situations, subtly, and often with apparently logical arguments, the criteria are altered so that flights may still be certified in time. They therefore fly in a relatively unsafe condition." He pointed out that NASA managers downplayed the significance of the previously damaged O-rings so as not to jeopardize the flow of funding to the program. While he noted that the managers may have actually believed there was no ongoing problem, if so, it demonstrated "an almost incredible lack of communication between themselves and their working engineers."[25]

Given his insistence on including in the Rogers Commission report a much more strongly worded opinion about the failures of NASA management leading up to the *Challenger* disaster than his colleagues on the commission were prepared to deliver, it would be fascinating to know what Feynman, had he lived long enough, would have made of the report of another federal agency—the NTSB's report on the collapse of the I-35W Bridge, released in November 2008. During the sixteen years that elapsed between the bridge's first receiving a rating of poor and its collapse into the Mississippi River, MN/DOT, working with the civil engineering department at the University of Minnesota and two engineering firms, had uncovered widespread corrosion, fatigue cracks, and frozen bearings on the bridge, as well as a recognized need to add redundancy as the ultimate protection against anticipated disaster. Henry Petroski, who has written extensively on engineering failures, asserts: "Successful designs do not necessarily tell us very much about how close to failure they are. Sometimes cracks develop, which signal problems, but they can be attributed to settlement and interpreted to be the wrinkles of age. Any failure, however, is incontrovertible evidence that weaknesses existed—in the design, the workmanship, the materials, the maintenance, or the defense against terrorists."[26] Or, as Feynman wrote about the evidence of design defects in the O-rings on the *Challenger* booster rockets— evidence that NASA management had ignored in the push to launch the shuttle on schedule—such occurrences provide warnings of problems that can lead to disaster.

The Rogers Commission report on the *Challenger* chose to gloss over the managerial lapses and errors of judgment that resulted in catastrophe, attributing the accident to an isolated, original design flaw. The managerial mistakes included the salient fact that the NASA officials who authorized the launch had not known about recent problems the program had experienced with defective O-rings, or about a "written recommendation of the contractor advising against the launch at temperatures below 53 degrees Fahrenheit and the continuing opposition of the engineers at [the contractor] after the management reversed its position." The report added: "If the decision makers had known all of the facts, it is highly unlikely that they would have decided to launch [the *Challenger*] on January 28, 1986."[27] After reviewing the facts and the testimony taken from those closely involved in the process leading up to launch of the shuttle, the report concluded that the evidence "reveals failures in communication that resulted in a decision to launch . . . based on incomplete and sometimes misleading information, a conflict between engineering data and management judgments, and a NASA management structure that permitted internal flight safety problems to bypass key Shuttle managers."[28]

There is little in the NTSB final report on the I-35W Bridge collapse that addresses equivalent "failures in communication . . . incomplete and sometimes misleading information, [or] conflict between engineering data and management judgments," all of which were well-documented aspects of the history of that MN/DOT-managed bridge. In a haunting echo of the main twenty-year-old Rogers Commission report, and not of Feynman's dissent, the report of the NTSB on the collapse of the I-35W Bridge concluded that the "probable cause" of the bridge's failure "was the inadequate load capacity, due to a design error by [the bridge's designer] Sverdrup & Parcel and Associates, Inc., of the gusset plates at the U10 nodes, which failed under a combination of (1) substantial increases in the weight of the bridge, which resulted from previous bridge modifications, and (2) the traffic and concentrated construction loads on the bridge on the day of the collapse." Also "contributing to the design error," the NTSB report stated, "was the failure of Sverdrup & Parcel's quality control procedures to ensure that the appropriate main truss gusset plate calculations were performed for the I-35W bridge and the inadequate design review by Federal and State transportation officials," as well as "the generally accepted practice among Federal and State transportation officials of giving inadequate attention to gusset plates during inspections for conditions of distortion, such as bowing, and of excluding gusset plates in load rating analyses."[29]

In short, the NTSB focused predominantly on the failure of the design engineers—who probably could no longer be held legally responsible, forty years after the fact, given the statute of limitations. Moreover, the design firm had become part of a much larger firm.[30] According to the NTSB, there was no likelihood of discovering this error throughout the forty-year history of the bridge, from the time of its construction until its collapse in 2007. Despite the fact that the bridge was downgraded in 1991 to a structurally deficient status that triggered federal remediation funding, despite its well-known status as a fracture-critical bridge, and despite its record of numerous fatigue cracks, corrosion on gusset plates, frozen bearings, photographs of bowed gusset plates, and consultants' reports stating that the bridge's load capacity safety factor had been seriously eroded, no MN/DOT official, in-house engineering professional, or any consulting engineer retained to analyze the bridge raised a warning flag to alert the agency or the public of the possibility of collapse.

The NTSB report and accompanying analysis contains significant flaws, especially its primary attribution of the bridge's collapse to the failure of one of its component parts. A careful review of the bridge's history in the sixteen years before the collapse highlights significant warning signs that, due to officials' overcautiousness, misjudgment, or refusal to provide funding to make needed repairs placed this bridge on the certain path to eventual failure. Any fair reading of the record must lead to the conclusion that no one associated with the I-35W Bridge ever exhibited the sense of urgency over its critical condition required to prevent this disaster from occurring.

In 1999 and in 2003—when URS Corporation was performing its initial evaluation—photographs were taken of almost every structural element of the I-35W Bridge. Following the bridge's collapse, as the NTSB report noted, "Safety Board investigators reviewed photographs from both of these evaluations that show visible bowing in all four gusset plates at the two U10 nodes," the location of the collapse according to the NTSB. Citing the Gray Plant Mooty investigative report, the NTSB also reported that a MN/DOT bridge engineer recalled observing the bowing of these gusset plates during inspections beginning in the late 1990s, after which he consulted with a fellow engineer and concluded "that's fit-up, that's construction, that's original construction." The NTSB itself accepted this conclusion—that the gusset plates probably were bowed from excessive forces that occurred during construction in 1967—as well as the validity of the inspecting engineer's assumption that "gusset plates are overdesigned" (and therefore could be assumed to have a safety factor of 2.0 or 3.0). The board also accepted the following explanation of why the bowing was not noted on MN/DOT inspection reports, which it quoted in its own report: "Our inspections are to find deterioration or findings of deterioration on maintenance. We do not note or describe construction or design problems."[31] This explanation would strain the credulity of even a novice engineering professional.

Even if the bowing of the gusset plates at the U10 node was never observed prior to the late 1990s, no evidence was provided by either the NTSB or any other documented source to support the supposition that the bowing dated from the time of the bridge's construction in the late 1960s. Thus, it is necessary to consider the possibility that this phenomenon was caused at a later point by forces acting upon the underdesigned gusset plates during the first thirty years of the bridge's service. Yet, an out-of-plane force—i.e., one exerted in a direction not parallel to the plane formed by the gusset plate and the truss member to which it is attached—is required to bend a gusset plate, and gusset plates are not designed to handle out-of-plane forces. If an out-of-plane force was responsible for the bowing of the U10 gusset plates, the bridge was not behaving as it was designed to—and that sort of behavior, as Feynman and Petroski point out, is an indication of potential failure.

Moreover, as bridge engineers other than those at Wiss, Janney, Elstner Associates (WJE)—the firm that was retained by MN/DOT following the I-35W collapse—have postulated, the collapse of the bridge may likely have been caused not by a failure of the gusset plates but by the fracturing of a lower chord truss member that failed, leading to the bursting of the U10 gusset plates that NTSB investigators found after the collapse of the bridge.[32] Thus, there is evidence to conclude that it was not the misdesigned gusset plates that brought the I-35W Bridge down. Subsequent analysis of all the bridge's structural elements indicate that the collapse was triggered by the failure of one or more of the bridge's fracture-critical members, under duress from the asymmetric (unbalanced) loading of 578,735 pounds of construction equipment and materials.

The placement of this assortment of construction material and trucks for the deck overlay project initiated by MN/DOT in lieu of addressing the structural problems of the bridge raises the further problems in MN/DOT's stewardship of the bridge. This unexpected concentrated load somehow slipped under the radar screen at MN/DOT, which had failed to prohibit overloading of the fracture-critical bridge in the overlay construction contract. Prior to this work, two bridge expansion projects had already added significant dead weight to the bridge. Even NTSB Chairman Mark Rosenker acknowledged this in a statement when he concluded: "When they added the weight they didn't realize they were bringing the margins of safety down to where they didn't exist anymore."[33] Add in corroded and frozen bearings— first observed to be functioning improperly as early as 1991, when the bridge was first rated as structurally deficient—and one can understand why some experts have theorized that the bridge did not fail as a result of poorly designed gusset plates.[34]

It is difficult to understand how the NTSB failed to find any fault with MN/DOT's stewardship, based upon the documented history of this bridge. The NTSB missed a critical opportunity to use the lessons that should have been learned from this tragedy to ensure that similar conditions at bridges all across the nation do not lead to similar disasters. On August 14, 2007, the Minnesota legislature appointed a Joint Committee to Investigate the Bridge Collapse, which hired the law firm Gray Plant Mooty to produce its own report. That report, which did not opine on any technical rationale for the collapse, correctly stated: "When a bridge collapses, so does public faith in government." The Joint Committee's charge to Gray Plant Mooty was "to conduct a comprehensive review of all decisions made by MN/DOT that might be relevant to the collapse of the Bridge."[35]

One possible factor in the Minnesota legislature's decision to launch its own investigation was the suspicion aroused by the NTSB's announcement, only a week after the I-35W Bridge fell, that WJE engineers had discovered a possible design flaw in the bridge's gusset plates. Within a week after the collapse, NTSB spokesmen hinted at the prospect that the collapse might have been triggered by defective gusset plates. At a MN/DOT news conference held on August 8, 2007,

Liz Benjamin, a construction engineer, confirmed that workers had dumped large sand and gravel piles on top of the bridge the day of the collapse, but a MN/DOT spokesman refused to confirm the accuracy of the preliminary gusset plate finding.[36]

Suspicion that the supposedly independent NTSB had latched too soon onto a theory that exonerated MN/DOT's maintenance of the bridge was further heightened when, at the beginning of November, U.S. Secretary of Transportation Mary Peters commented at a White House Transportation Legislative Leaders Summit that "a finding of fault was not going to be lack of inspection or lack of maintenance"[37]— prompting Minnesota state senator Steve Murphy to remark, "I think [this statement] taints the findings."[38] Two and a half months later, NTSB Chairman Rosenker appeared at a press conference to announce an NTSB safety recommendation that "for all non-load-path-redundant steel truss bridges within the National Bridge Inventory," the FHWA should "require that bridge owners conduct load capacity calculations to verify that the stress levels on all structural elements, including gusset plates, remain within applicable design requirements, whenever planned modifications or operational changes may significantly increase stresses."[39] Although Rosenker, in his opening statement, was careful to state that "we have not yet determined the probable cause of the accident" and "we do not yet know what caused the I-35W Bridge to collapse,"[40] he went on to call sixteen underdesigned gusset plates the "critical factor that began the process of this collapse."[41]

Rosenker's statements earned him a sharp rebuke from Representative James Oberstar of Minnesota, a Democrat and chairman of the House Committee on Transportation and Infrastructure, who wrote in a letter to the NTSB chairman that "such announcements undermine the process and create the potential for committing the Board to conclusions which will be difficult to change if the subsequent investigation suggests other possible conclusions."[42] Although Rosenker retracted his remarks in a reply to Oberstar's letter, he found himself at loggerheads with the congressman again after the NTSB announced, in late March, that it would not hold an interim public hearing on the I-35W Bridge collapse. The three NTSB board members—all Republicans—who voted against holding an interim public hearing explained their decision by stating that NTSB staff feared that holding such a hearing would take time and resources away from their investigation.[43] Oberstar and the two Democratic members of the NTSB board (who issued a dissent from the majority's decision) replied by arguing that performing a thorough and trustworthy investigation was more important than speed.

Other critics, meanwhile, pointed not only to the partisan nature of the vote against holding an interim hearing but also to Rosenker's history as a political operative who had been active in almost every Republican presidential campaign since Richard Nixon's run in 1972.[44] Not surprisingly, few, if any, of the NTSB's critics were mollified when the board issued its final report in November 2008, confirming all the essential conclusions that had been hinted at for at least a year or more.[45] Nor did the follow-up finding by MN/DOT's consultant, WJE, which confirmed that the gusset plate design error was the cause of the collapse, appear to silence the many voices challenging the NTSB's conclusions.[46]

Although the politics surrounding the NTSB investigation have provided much fodder for speculation as to the possible political motivation of the board's leadership and findings, it does not require a political orientation to observe that the NTSB report has significant flaws, including errors of apparent neglect or omission as well as of technical understanding.[47] Analysis of these flaws, in light of what is known about the maintenance of the I-35W Bridge over its forty-year life span, inevitably raises the question of why the NTSB made no significant criticisms of MN/DOT's maintenance record. This omission is not without precedent. For instance, in its 1970 report on the collapse of the Silver Bridge, the NTSB stated the probable cause was a cleavage fracture in an eyebar that resulted from the joint action of stress corrosion and corrosion fatigue. Contributing causes were the facts that in 1927, when the bridge was designed, the phenomena of stress corrosion and corrosion fatigue were not known to occur in rural areas;

the location of the flaw was inaccessible to visual inspection; and the flaw could not have been detected by any inspection method known today without disassembly of the eyebar joint.[48]

Like its I-35W counterpart, the NTSB's report on the Silver Bridge collapse in 1967 attributed the collapse to a design flaw that inspections allegedly could not have been expected to detect; and, as in the I-35W report, the Silver Bridge report contradicted other extant accounts of how the bridge failed, specifically the finding in a court case that it had been inadequately inspected.

The forty years since the collapse of the Silver Bridge have seen progress in how our infrastructure is maintained. But few who are knowledgeable about how we design, build, and maintain our bridges can be sanguine about the prospects of avoiding future failures as our nation's aging bridge inventory passes its intended life span. When we look at the bridge specifications promulgated in the 1920s by the predecessor of AASHTO, it is clear that today's standards are extraordinarily more complex and demanding in terms of the lessons learned and the needs for the modern engineer to ensure the safety of the traveling public. Charles Seim, a consulting bridge engineer, stated in a recent article: "No longer can one person, like the master builder of old, retain all of the requisite, complex details of today's major project in his or her head. Can the multidisciplinary teams of the future, drawing on the knowledge and expertise of many talented people, be managed seamlessly to create excellent, flawless projects? This indeed is the engineering challenge of the future."[49]

As our bridges age, are we prepared to act quickly enough and to pour billions of dollars into maintenance, rather than building even more expensive replacements? Will our federal and state officials acknowledge that sophisticated technology will be needed by bridge inspectors and engineers, so they can make more accurate condition ratings, needed for more accurate estimates of repair costs? Will politicians continue to favor new road and bridge projects, while neglecting existing structures in serious need of remediation?

Since the collapse of the I-35W Bridge, the federal government has dedicated more funds for use by the states to improve the condition of their infrastructure. But the effects of decades of neglect have saddled the public with enormous costs for repairing what still needs to be fixed. Institutions are not perfect and errors will always occur, but leaving responsibility for allocating transportation funding to local and state politicians risks giving special interests too much influence, while dooming us to increasing costs and a deficit of innovation.

Through public-private partnerships (PPPs), the private sector has sought to provide a much-needed alternative to governmental control of our nation's infrastructure. As we will see in chapter 4, private investment in our infrastructure is an important and attractive alternative in a financially constrained world, where states have literally run out of money to address significant shortfalls in their capital budgets. But we should not rush to adopt PPPs as the single solution to these ills. Instead, we need to carefully review the number of risks that public officials face when going down that road.

# 4 Finding the Money

America's neglect of the transportation infrastructure it built at great expense in the twentieth century has not only left its roads and bridges in an inadequate condition for meeting the demands of the twenty-first. The neglect has also raised the cost of repairing and improving the country's existing infrastructure to astronomical heights. The National Surface Transportation Policy and Revenue Study Commission (NSTPRSC) estimated that between $130 billion and $166 billion per year would be needed in highway capital investments (for all federal-aid highways) from 2005 thru 2020 in order to meet a set of goals that include maintaining pavement quality at current levels, an estimate that rises to $146 to $195 billion annually for the period 2005–55. For bridges, the commission found that "simply maintaining the current overall level of bridge conditions at current levels (i.e., not allowing the backlog of existing bridge deficiencies to grow above today's levels) would require a combined investment of public and private sector resources of $650 billion over 50 years in 2006 dollars," while "the cost of eliminating all existing bridge deficiencies and addressing all such deficiencies as they arise over the next 50 years (where cost-beneficial to do so) is estimated to be $850 billion in 2006 dollars."[1] Citing figures from the Federal Highway Administration (FHWA), the American Association of State Highway and Transportation Officials (AASHTO) reported in 2008 that it would cost "$140 billion in 2006 dollars to immediately repair every bridge that is deficient in the country," including $48 billion for structurally deficient bridges.[2]

Such estimates, of course, need to be understood against the backdrop of the severe shortfalls in funding for surface transportation infrastructure generally, and for America's deficient roads and bridges in particular, discussed in chapter 2. Meanwhile, the federal Highway Trust Fund (HTF) had to be rescued from insolvency in 2008, and, according to the final report of the National Surface Transportation Infrastructure Financing Commission (NSTIFC), "this problem will only worsen until Congress addresses the fundamental fact that current HTF revenues are inadequate to support current federal program spending levels. Comparing estimates of surface transportation investment needs with baseline revenue projections developed by the Commission shows a federal highway and transit funding gap that totals nearly $400 billion in 2010–15 and grows dramatically to about $2.3 trillion through 2035."[3]

Both the NSTPRSC, which issued its final report in December 2007, and the NSTIFC, whose final report appeared in February 2009, made extensive proposals for federal responses to the need to improve the condition of the nation's roads and bridges.[4] This effort must start with solving the problem of how to finance the HTF in the future. In making its "Recommendations for Paying the Bill" of the nation's unaddressed surface transportation needs, the NSTPRSC proposed responses in three time frames: "immediate" action to keep the HTF solvent; action over the next twenty years "to finance improvements needed to enhance surface transportation system conditions and performance"; and actions "after 20 years to replace the fuel tax with a more sustainable revenue source." Noting the "growing consensus that alternatives to the fuel tax may be necessary in about 20 years," the commission concluded that, for the time being, "the fuel tax should remain an important component of surface transportation finance" and proposed raising the federal gas tax from five to eight cents per gallon per year over the next five years, with indexing to match inflation thereafter. Beyond 2025, the NSTPRSC said, the federal government and the nation as a whole must switch from a reliance on fuel taxes to mileage-based user fees.[5] The NSTIFC, for its part, also proposed increasing the federal gas tax as an immediate measure for bolstering the HTF, as well as "positioning Federal funding for the longer term" with a "more direct user charge system" to be fully deployed by 2020, gradually eliminating fuel taxes as the primary funding mechanism for surface transportation.[6]

The NSTPRSC's proposal for action between 2005 and 2025, including its recommended federal gas tax increase, stipulates that over this period, the federal government "should contribute approximately 40 percent of total surface transportation capital outlay in line with the Federal share in recent years [37 to 46 percent for highways]."[7] While it is debatable whether the federal government ought to continue to fund the nation's surface transportation programs at this level,[8] even a 40 percent federal contribution would place substantial requirements on state and local governments for raising the remainder of the necessary revenue, as the NSTPRSC recognized. Discussing the need to "remove the barriers to options for increasing state and local revenues over the next 20 years," the commission included as one of its recommended options a proposal to "increase State fuel taxes and other highway user fees"; raising state fuel taxes alone, it said, "could generate about $1.9 billion nationally for each 1-cent increase," while "indexing the fuel tax or converting to a gasoline sales tax would allow revenues to increase with rising highway construction costs."[9]

Given the commission's estimate, however, that "the State and local share of additional investment requirements could range between the equivalent of 34 and 63 cents per gallon of fuel tax," it is clear that—especially for states and municipalities that have not developed significant sources of highway revenue other than state gasoline taxes—raising taxes and fees within politically feasible limits will provide only a portion, and perhaps a small one, of the additional revenues needed. As one way of addressing the remaining gap, the NSTPRSC report—noting that tolls currently account for only 9 percent of state highway revenues, while estimating that widespread congestion pricing could contribute 30 percent of the minimum level of highway investment needed over the medium and long term—recommended that the federal government "provide new flexibility for tolling and [congestion] pricing."[10] The NSTIFC report also calls for increasing use of tolling to address both short- and medium-term needs—in particular, urging the federal government to continue and expand the pilot Interstate Highway Reconstruction and Rehabilitation Pilot Program that "allows tolling of existing Interstate capacity for reconstruction and rehabilitation."[11]

Both higher gasoline taxes and increased use of tolling by the states and local authorities would not only raise additional revenues but would also have the advantage, for overall transportation policy, of managing demand both for new and existing roads, by strengthening the link between benefits and costs for users. Increased revenues from tolling would also provide an income stream that could be leveraged by another source of funding that is likely to become increasingly important for state and local transportation departments: state infrastructure banks. Created as a pilot program in ten states by the National Highway System Designation Act of 1995, and expanded to include all the states by the Safe, Accountable, Flexible, Efficient Transportation Equity Act: A Legacy for Users (SAFETEA-LU),[12] the state infrastructure banks (SIBs) were established to function as "an umbrella under which a variety of innovative financing techniques could be implemented."[13]

Although they are a new concept for federal transportation projects, revolving funds have been used for other infrastructure investments. A SIB may consider any highway project eligible for assistance under Title 23 of the U.S. Code (which sets out the federal-aid highway system), may provide financial support to both publicly and privately sponsored projects, and may assist in financing early or later stages of a project. As the final report of the NSTIFC notes, SIBs are particularly "well positioned" to fund smaller projects than the ones of "national and regional significance" for which Congress, in the Transportation Infrastructure Finance and Innovation Act of 1998, created the federal credit program for transportation projects known as TIFIA.[14] Potential projects for SIBs specifically include construction, reconstruction, rehabilitation, resurfacing, restoration, and operational improvements for highways and bridges.

The recommendations of the NSTIFC for "Facilitating Non-Federal Investment in the Short and Medium Term" include one that the federal government "invest $500 million per year ($3 billion over a six-year authorization period) to re-capitalize State Infrastructure Banks (SIBS) and continue to allow states to use their federal program funds for this purpose as well."[15] Such programs are a partial solution for the serious funding shortfalls currently being experienced by most states. The major concern of astute analysts of similar programs to channel transportation funding is whether SIBS can prevent greedy politicians from diverting such funding for their own purposes.

Part of the rationale for SIBS has been explained by Stan Hazelroth, the executive director of the California Infrastructure and Economic Development Bank—which was established in 1994, a year before the creation of the pilot program of the U.S. Department of Transportation (DOT). Hazelroth told an interviewer in 2009 that "one of the advantages that either a state infrastructure bank has, or a federal infrastructure bank would have, is that it really takes the pork out of the process by having a standardized list of threshold criteria to distinguish different projects."[16] The need to rationalize transportation spending by tying it more closely to programmatic criteria has also been explored by the NSTPRSC, which, in addition to proposing ways of enhancing state and federal revenues for use on roads and bridges, also examined ways of rationalizing spending on this infrastructure.

The NSTPRSC report describes the juncture at which federal transportation policy now finds itself by positing three eras in the "modern history of the Federal surface transportation program": an initial era of interstate construction, a second era in which the Intermodal Surface Transportation Efficiency Act of 1991 (ISTEA) gave flexibility to the states to invest federal highway funds in "new modes and approaches," and a third era, now dawning, in which "funding flexibility will continue to have its place," although—in contrast to the era of ISTEA—federal highway dollars will have to be used "to meet specific and measurable objectives." The confused and disordered nature of the transportation funding mechanisms confronting our states is best exemplified by the report's final recommendation to mandate a simplified way to secure needed funds. In order to make federal surface transportation programs "performance-driven, outcome-based, [and] generally mode-neutral" for the first time, the commission recommended consolidating 108 existing programs under five separate DOT administrations into ten program areas.[17]

The NSTPRSC's proposal for rationalizing federal surface transportation programs—intended to provide an overarching strategy for the new federal transportation bill that Congress began working on in 2009[18]—explicitly recognized that lack of adequate funding is far from the only problem with how the nation cares for its transportation infrastructure. The lack of a "performance-driven, outcome-based" orientation in federal transportation policy that the commission identified is evident in the rules and practices for state use of federal highway funds described in chapter 2: the substitution of federal for state transportation funds by state governments; the transfer of funds among federal programs that allows states to subvert intended federal objectives; and the perverse incentives by which states can benefit financially from neglecting their roads and bridges until they require expensive, federally funded repair or reconstruction.[19] Having long recognized the need for state departments of transportation to better manage their existing transportation infrastructure, the FHWA, since the late 1990s, has been promoting the practice of asset management in those departments.

The FHWA's *Asset Management Primer*, published after the agency created an Office of Asset Management in 1999, defines asset management as "a business process and a decision-making framework that covers an extended time horizon, draws from economics and engineering theory and practice, and considers a broad range of assets."[20] This methodology incorporates an economic assessment of the different trade-offs between alternative investment options at both the project level and the network or system level, and allows agencies to make cost-effective investment decisions that best suit their project needs.

As a more recent FHWA document explains, the increasing adoption of asset management in state departments of transportation in recent years reflects an overall shift in emphasis from new construction to the preservation and operation of existing surface transportation infrastructure. It also seeks to address an increasing expectation from the public that "government should be more accountable and be managed more like a business operation." Thus the focus in transportation policy "has shifted from capital construction to one of optimizing the balance of preserving, upgrading, and replacing our highway assets through cost-effective management, programming, and informed decisionmaking."[21] Like state infrastructure banks, asset management is seen as a way to move decisions about infrastructure management out of the realm of politics and into the realm of what the FHWA has called "fact-based dialogue among system users and other stakeholders, State government officials, and managers concerned with day-to-day operations."[22]

A 2006 report from the National Cooperative Highway Research Program summarizes the core principles of asset management, which fall into several categories: policy-driven, where resource allocation decisions are based on a well-defined set of policy goals and objectives; performance-based, where policy objectives are translated into system performance measures that are used for both day-to-day and strategic management; analyzing options and trade-offs, where decisions on how to allocate funds within and across different types of investments (e.g., preventive maintenance versus rehabilitation, or pavements versus bridges) are based on an analysis of how different allocations will impact the achievement of relevant policy objectives; relying on quality information, where the merits of different options with respect to an agency's policy goals are evaluated using credible and current data; monitoring performance results for clear accountability and feedback, where results are monitored and reported for both impacts and effectiveness.[23] In spite of all the good intentions of state programs involving asset management, states still must wrestle with the ambiguities and subjectivities of installing such programs within an inspection and maintenance world that resists changes based on so much unknown as well as unfamiliar information. One significant task that must be accomplished if these programs are to succeed is the states' development of the necessary computer-based systems to successfully analyze the many variables associated with the different types of infrastructure assets.

ISTEA requires all states to produce a statewide transportation plan as well as a "financially constrained" Statewide Transportation Improvement Program (STIP) describing projects that the state intends to advance over a period of at least three years, how these projects will be funded, and how a state plans to finance the "continued operation and maintenance of the existing system."[24] In 1999, the FHWA's *Asset Management Primer* stated that "most" state departments of transportation had "some of the more common elements that provide information into the Asset Management process," the two most prevalent being "pavement and bridge management systems . . . intended to cyclically monitor the condition, measure the real-life performance, predict future trends, and recommend candidate projects and preservation treatments."[25]

Since then, according to the FHWA's more recent survey of transportation asset management around the country, "AASHTO and FHWA have made Transportation Asset Management a national priority" while "States have confirmed that asset management tools are an effective aid for negotiating political funding as well as for stabilizing the funding process over longer periods."[26] As discussed in chapter 2, Michigan's Department of Transportation has not only adopted asset management (which is required by law in that state) but has also used asset management principles to challenge the dictates of federal funding formulas. In June 2009, the final report of the New York State Commission on State Asset Maximization (a term the commission defined as essentially synonymous with asset management) made proposals for developing "sustainable asset maximization" programs in areas including transportation, where it cited "deteriorating infrastructure," "no long-term strategy for funding," "constrained fiscal capacity," and "high debt payments" as the principle challenges the state faces.[27] The FHWA, meanwhile, says that its "ultimate goal" is to "make the use of asset management the norm across the Nation for long-range transportation planning, capital program development, strategic business planning, and performance accountability."[28]

There is no question that the utilization of asset management principles by state and local departments of transportation—especially if efforts to coordinate and systematize their asset management programs for maximum effectiveness are led by respected groups such as the Transportation Research Board, AASHTO, and the FHWA—will result in better mechanisms for transportation infrastructure management. Using performance measures to rationalize decisions about resource allocation, program delivery, and so forth in areas such as road and bridge preservation will achieve savings that will be crucial to the efficient use of limited resources for transportation programs. In the short and medium term, however, no amount of increased efficiency in the deployment of available resources will be enough to remedy the effects of the currently projected gap between funding and need—even if the federal government is able to use tax and user-fee increases, federal credit programs such as TIFIA, and infrastructure banks to allocate additional funding to the remediation of deteriorated infrastructure. Indeed, a broad consensus of transportation experts now believes that no amount of increased public funding or increased public sector efficiency would be enough to address the enormous need, and that we must rely on the combined efforts of the public and private sectors in public-private partnerships.

## Public-Private Partnerships: A Definition and Some Background

"A public-private partnership," as defined by DOT, "is a contractual agreement formed between public and private sector partners, which allows more private sector participation than is traditional. The agreements usually involve a government agency contracting with a private company to renovate, construct, operate, maintain, and/or manage a facility or system. While the public sector usually retains ownership in the facility or system, the private party will be given ad-

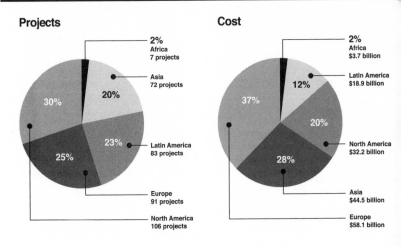

Source: FHWA

Note: The term "highway infrastructure" includes roads, bridges, and tunnels.

**Figure 4. Use of PPPs on infrastructure projects by continent.**

U.S. Department of Transportation, Federal Highway Administration,
*Case Studies of Transportation Public-Private Partnerships in the United States*, July 7, 2007
(http://www.irfnet.ch/files-upload/knowledges/FHWA_us_ppp_case_studies_
final_report_July2007.pdf, accessed May 28, 2009), 2-9.

ditional decision rights in determining how the project or task will be completed."[29] The National Council for Public-Private Partnerships, a group of private- and public-sector organizations in areas including transportation, notes that, in a private-public partnership (PPP) agreement, the public and private sectors share both "skills and assets" and "risks and rewards potential in the delivery of the service and/or facility."[30] As a recent FHWA report on transportation public-private partnerships in the United States notes: "Public-Private Partnerships (PPPs) represent a wide variety of project financing and delivery approaches which offer the potential to expedite project delivery, operations, and maintenance in a more cost-effective manner, enabling transportation agencies to effectively 'do more with less.' "[31] Another recent study succinctly describes the advantages for the public of PPPs by stating that, "at least in concept," they "allow government to capture the financial benefits of an asset without many of the operating challenges and risks."[32]

In the United States, reliance on PPPs for road construction and maintenance is a relatively new phenomenon. The American private sector was mostly responsible for building and maintaining roads up until the appearance of the automobile, at the beginning of the twentieth century. From virtually the start of the automobile age, as we saw in chapter 2, government at the federal and state levels became heavily involved in funding road construction that was performed according to standards set by the federal government. Meeting the needs of an expanding population and economy was only one reason for increasing government involvement in road provision, where the potential for graft had been demonstrated by, for example, Boss Tweed's use of street paving contracts in New York City to reward political allies and supporters. (Tweed, of course, would later be far outdone by Robert Moses in the use of public works construction in New York, although Moses' aim was to amass political power alone, not combined with personal wealth.)

The late nineteenth and early twentieth centuries, indeed, saw the first attempts by government to curb "abuses in contracting and hiring practices by sponsoring agencies" via "the strict regulation of project procurement and delivery approaches, focusing on the design-bid-build project delivery approach whereby the engineering design phase is procured separately using a qualification-based negotiated price approach, with the construction phase awarded on a low-bid basis."[33] This development received further impetus from advances in engineering that resulted in increasing separation of the design and construction phases of infrastructure projects in fields including transportation, so that "by 1933, separating the design and construction elements was a frequent, though not mandatory, occurrence in federal infrastructure development." When the interstate highway system was established in 1956, the design-bid-build approach was codified in federal procurement rules for interstate construction.[34]

The construction of the interstate, as well as the provision of funds for its maintenance by the federal government, was made possible by the existence of a dedicated revenue source in the federal Highway Trust Fund. Outside the United States, where such dedicated sources of transportation funding are rare if not nonexistent (with gasoline taxes, for example, used to fund social programs), the use of PPPs to build, operate, and maintain transportation infrastructure has a longer history. Spain began experimenting with private concessions for the construction of toll roads in the 1960s, and France did the same in the 1970s. As noted in a compilation of case studies on transportation PPPs around the world commissioned by the FHWA and published in July 2007, the "strongest impetus" for transportation PPPs came about in the United Kingdom as a result of the privatization initiatives of the Thatcher government in the 1980s.[35]

In 1992, the Conservative government of Prime Minister John Major launched its Private Finance Initiative, which involved awarding long-term contracts to private concessionaires for the operation and maintenance of public assets. Following the lead of the British, Australia, New Zealand, and Canada quickly put their own public-private initiatives into place, while countries in Central and Eastern Europe, Asia, and Latin America have also turned to PPPs for the modernization and expansion of their transportation networks (see fig. 4). As the authors of the FHWA report recognized, from the mid-1980s, "both public and private sectors in countries around the world have gained significant experience and confidence in using PPPs to get particularly large and complex infrastructure projects built. In addition, local urban governments are outsourcing maintenance of their road networks to lower costs and improve performance. Growing from a cottage industry to just under a $0.5 trillion dollar mega-industry investing in all kinds of infrastructure worldwide, including roads, railroads, airports, seaports, water/wastewater, and building, with almost $0.8 trillion dol-

# lobal and U.S. Public Private Partnership Spending

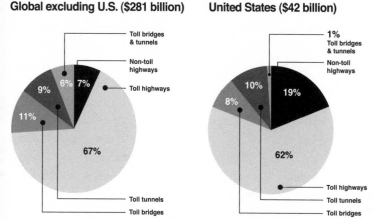

**Figure 5. Highway public-private partnerships:**
**More rigorous up-front analysis could better secure potential benefits**
**and protect the public interest of the United States.**

United States Government Accountability Office (GAO) Report to Congressional
Requestors, *Highway Public-Private Partnerships: More Rigorous Up-front Analysis Could
Better Secure Potential Benefits and Protect the Public Interest*, Washington, D.C.:
General Accounting Office, 2008, 18.

lars in PPP financing for planned project [sic] yet to be completed." The
greatest number of PPPs has been created for roadways.[36]

In the United States, experimentation with PPPs began in the early
1990s, as the highway system built soon after World War II began to
deteriorate and it became clear that the costs of redressing deferred
and neglected maintenance—not to mention the costs of perceived
needs for further expansion—were clearly outstripping the financial
capacity of the Highway Trust Fund and both the capacity and willingness of state and local governments to adequately fund their surface
transportation needs. In Virginia, plans to build a highway connecting I-95 with I-295 southeast of Richmond were running aground on
state funding constraints until, in 1995, the Virginia General Assem-

bly passed the Public-Private Transportation Act. The new highway, originally to be designated I-895 but now known as the Pocahontas Parkway, was constructed by a PPP whose tax-exempt bonds were issued on behalf of a private developer, a joint venture between the firms Fluor Daniel and Morrison Knudsen. That consortium then operated the new toll road from its completion, ahead of schedule, in 2002 until it was leased, in 2006, to the Australian toll road developer and manager Transurban LLC of Australia.

Meanwhile, the Safe, Accountable, Flexible, and Efficient Transportation Equity Act of 2003 (SAFETEA-21) included several legislative proposals designed to "facilitate public-private partnerships," including one to allow tolling on federal-aid highways and, specifically, to ease eligibility requirements for states to participate in the Interstate System Rehabilitation and Reconstruction Pilot Program—established under the Transportation Equity Act for the 21st Century (TEA-21) federal highway bill of 1998—in order to "permit selected states to collect tolls on the Interstate for the purpose of reconstructing and rehabilitating Interstate highway corridors." Another significant provision of the law amended the Internal Revenue Code to allow private activity bonds—already available for many other types of infrastructure projects—to be used for highway facilities.[37]

Soon afterward, two leasing agreements involving publicly owned roads that had long been tolled became the best known, and most controversial, transportation PPPs undertaken in the United States to date. In 2005, a joint venture between the Macquarie Infrastructure Group of Australia and Cintra, Concesiones de Infraestructuras de Transporte, S.A., of Spain paid the city of Chicago $1.83 billion for a ninety-nine-year lease to operate the Chicago Skyway, an 7.8-mile-long tollway connecting the Indiana Toll Road with the Dan Ryan Expressway. The leasing of the Chicago Skyway—the first privatization of an existing toll road in the United States—was followed a year later by the acquisition by another Macquarie-Cintra joint venture, for $3.8 billion paid to the State of Indiana, of a seventy-five-year lease to operate the Indiana Toll Road across the northern edge of the state.

PPPs come in a bewildering variety of forms, which the FHWA classifies into five major types: for the design, construction, and operation of new facilities (so-called greenfield projects) there are "alternative project delivery approaches," multimodal partnerships, and "joint development" projects; for existing facilities—where remediation of deteriorated or undermaintained infrastructure may be an issue—there are private contract fee services and long-term lease or concession agreements. Private contract services—"the most common form of private sector involvement in surface transportation project and service delivery," according to the FHWA—include, for highways, "facility and right-of-way maintenance" as well as operations.[38]

In long-term lease or concession agreements such as those for the Chicago Skyway and the Indiana Toll Road, which are supposed to be awarded in a competitive bidding process, "facility operation, maintenance, and preservation" may be among the services provided by the lessee in return for an upfront payment and the right to collect "revenues generated by the facility." Private contract services represent the minimum of private-sector involvement, and long-term concessions the maximum, along the PPP spectrum.[39] Compared with more traditional approaches to the construction and operation of infrastructure, all types of PPPs—but especially, when it comes to partnerships for operation and maintenance, long-term concessions—are distinguished by "the greater responsibility and risk taken by the private sector partners in return for an adequate return on their investment in the project or coverage of their costs."[40]

As shown in Figure 5, by late 2006, nearly two-thirds of the states seeking PPPs were interested in pursuing toll roads via this approach. This was comparable to global PPP projects, 67 percent of which entailed highway construction.

Because PPPs are relatively new to the United States, state and local government officials as well as the American public have been the audience for a debate that, so far, has often presented infrastructure PPPs as something approaching either a panacea or a plague. One of the few private, independent studies of infrastructure PPPs to date that offers analysis without advocacy notes: "The experts disagree on the true costs and benefits of these deals. . . . [M]uch of the information promoting long-term concessions comes from those who will benefit directly—the construction companies, toll operators, bankers, attorneys, and their consultants. Similarly, opposition comes from those with a vested interest such as public employee unions and consumer advocacy groups."[41]

The two public commissions created by SAFETEA-LU to explore options for financing the nation's surface transportation needs—the NSTPRSC and the NSTIFC—have both endorsed PPPs, albeit with appropriate cautions about the need to protect the public interest, while the U.S. Government Accountability Office has issued a report urging that "rigorous upfront analysis" be conducted by public entities of the potential drawbacks as well as the potential benefits of PPPs.[42] These and other relatively balanced discussions of infrastructure PPPs permit a relatively brief summary of their pros and cons for the specific purpose of dealing with the remediation of U.S. roads and bridges.

### PPPs for Existing Roads and Bridges: Pros and Cons

The rationale for PPPs to manage existing roads and bridges depends on the type of partnership. For private contract fee services—"contracts between public agencies and the private sector for services that are typically performed in-house,"[43] including operations and maintenance—the potential benefits consist mainly of enhanced efficiency and higher productivity than a public-sector agency alone could achieve. Because, as noted above, contract fee services entail the least amount of private-sector involvement among all the various types of PPPs, they are comparatively simple to negotiate and implement. Other PPPs have required the private-sector partner to hire its own contractors—which in turn assume the costs of bringing a road up to design standards and continuing to maintain it—in return for an annual payment that is above the private partner's costs but lower than what it would cost the public-sector partner to perform the work itself. Long-term lease or concession agreements, by contrast, can be highly complex, and in comparison to simple service agreements, they both offer much greater potential benefits and pose considerably greater risks for the public sector.

Because of their greater potential for enabling the nation to address the problem of its seriously deteriorated infrastructure, including both its repair and its future maintenance, we will focus our attention here on the long-term leasing of concession agreements, which the FHWA defines as agreements that involve the lease of publicly financed facilities to a private sector concessionaire for a specified time period. Under these leases, "the private sector concessionaire agrees to pay an upfront fee to the public agency in order to obtain the rights to collect the revenue generated by the facility for a defined period of time (usually from 25 to 99 years). In addition to the concession fee, the concessionaire agrees to operate and maintain the facility, which may include capital improvements in some instances."[44]

The payment of an upfront fee by the private-sector entity to the public-sector constitutes one of the two major potential benefits to state and local governments of long-term concession agreements for facilities such as roads and bridges. The second potential benefit—related to the first, inasmuch as it bears on the all-important question of what a concession agreement for a particular price is worth to both the public and private parties involved—is that, as with private contract fee services, the public partner gains from the private partner's ability to manage and improve the facility more efficiently than a state or local transportation agency can. It has become increasingly clear to the public sector that the condition of the public asset at the end of the lease is an important factor in how the public benefits from the concession. Let us examine each of these benefits in turn.

One of the principal arguments—if not the principal one—in favor of long-term leases or concessions for facilities such as the Chicago Skyway and the Indiana Toll Road is the amount of upfront money they are able to generate for the public sector at a time when government budgets in general, and transportation budgets in particular, are under severe stress. The traditional way for state and local authorities to raise large sums of capital for projects such as road and bridge construction or major renovation is through issuing tax-exempt bonds. However, as the report of the NSTIFC explains, in the economic climate created by the crash of the financial markets in 2008, the yield differential between tax-exempt bonds and private issues of debt and equity has narrowed considerably—a development that has also been advanced by the introduction of tax-exempt private activity bonds, which SAFETEA-LU made available for federal-aid highway and bridge projects, and by federal credit programs like TIFIA. In short, the cost of capital has risen significantly for state and local governments, compared with what private firms must pay. In addition, equity investments from private sources, as the NSTIFC pointed out, "may allow a greater sum to be capitalized up front than through investment grade municipal debt."[45]

When it leased the Chicago Skyway in 2005, Chicago's city government received a payment of $1.83 billion. It used this money to pay off $400 million of existing debt for a previous rehabilitation of the Skyway, reduce other municipal debt, fund a number of programs unrelated to transportation, and create an $800 million reserve fund, also for nontransportation uses. In the transaction for the Indiana Toll Road, the State of Indiana used the $3.8 billion upfront payment from the concessionaire to pay for existing road projects, pay off existing toll road bonds, and establish two transportation funds, including one to fully fund a ten-year, statewide transportation plan.

As these facts suggest, the benefits to state and local governments from the upfront payments that long-term leases or concessions can bring include income with considerable potential benefits for politicians in office at the time of the award. The upfront payment is understandably attractive to politicians whose constituents are averse to increased taxes and tolls, and who can now make vast sums of money available for programs and purposes that are popular with voters.

That the politicians can also use the PPP as a mechanism for passing the blame for future toll increases onto the private concessionaire is another benefit for elected officials. But this and other political conveniences of these partnerships have potential long-term disadvantages for the public, as we shall see.

The other benefits that private-sector involvement can theoretically bring in the case of managing existing highways and bridges include the private sector's superior expertise and capacity for innovation; its greater cost efficiency and productivity; and its greater experience with, and expertise in, risk management. As the FHWA has argued, private-sector involvement in highway projects "encourages the development of new and creative approaches to financing, economies of scale, development, implementation and operation/maintenance." It "has an incentive to ensure its operations are as cost efficient as possible" and "would also be motivated to increase the productivity and return from assets, with greater interest in implementing practices such as yield management and demand management when limited capacity exists and is expensive to create." Moreover, the private sector "may be more effective in managing the variance in construction, operating, and maintenance costs" in a highway or bridge facility and "is often better at managing third-party usage of facilities, thus reducing the net cost of a facility to transportation agencies."[46]

The NSTIFC report spells out the specific advantage of long-term concession PPPs when it notes: "A concessionaire operating a non-tolled facility supported by availability payments is more likely to consider the project's total life cycle costs, since payments are conditioned on the concessionaire maintaining asset quality." Similarly, the advantage applies to PPPs that take over a toll road "because aggregating responsibilities and control for long-term performance under a fixed incentive structure can promote efficiencies that bifurcated responsibilities inherent in conventional public-sector delivery may not. For instance, highway agencies facing near-term fiscal constraints may be more likely to follow short-term strategies that conserve cash outlays but increase asset life cycle costs over the long term."[47]

Consider the application of this approach to an aging toll bridge that has not been faithfully maintained over the course of its intended life span. Converting such a facility to a PPP concession and allowing the operator to use the tolls it takes in to improve the condition rating of the bridge and maintain the bridge at current design standards would help remove many of the bridges from the list of those rated as either functionally obsolete or structurally deficient. Compare the fate of such a bridge with that of the I-35W Bridge. Minnesota Department of Transportation (MN/DOT) personnel were told that there would be no money in the budget to fix the bridge's problems for many years to come. MN/DOT officials delayed performing needed repair work because they knew that it was not their problem to find the money for the needed work; as civil servants, they didn't see themselves facing any risk in case the bridge failed; and they had no responsibility for trying to find creative, money-saving ways to perform the repairs.

Because there have been even fewer PPPs to manage existing roads and bridges in the United States than to develop new facilities, and because the partnerships that have been set up have managed only a handful of facilities in recent years, there is little evidence available for assessing their success by any but a few, fairly limited criteria. The American public, so far, is skeptical of them. In Indiana, the state legislature authorized the leasing of the Indiana Toll Road by only a narrow margin, and in late 2008 the Pennsylvania legislature turned down a proposed $12.8 billion deal for the leasing of the Pennsylvania Turnpike. As the NSTIFC report put it, there is a "recognized concern about how best to know whether public or private delivery [of a transportation project or service] is the most cost-effective approach and about assessing whether the public sector is getting the best deal possible."[48]

If the two primary benefits of PPPs for existing roads and bridges are an upfront payment to the public sector and better, more efficient operation of the facility, each of these potential benefits brings with it a number of concerns for government, taxpayers, and the traveling public.

One obviously key issue of long-term lease or concession PPPs is the valuation of the facility in order to determine the upfront price to be paid for the concession. Although the existence of known traffic patterns and (in the case of already tolled facilities) revenue streams, along with a history of operations and maintenance, makes valuation of existing roads and bridges less uncertain than it is for greenfield projects, the brief history of long-term concessions in the United States already shows the wide range of prices possible for a given concession. For example, Macquarie-Cintra's winning bid of $3.85 billion for the Indiana Toll Road was almost twice as high as a valuation of the concession before the bid, although some critics argue that the winning bid was too low.[49] In Pennsylvania, where the winning bid for the concession that was ultimately killed by the legislature was $12.8 billion, "a number of legislators said they believed the bids would be as high as $30 billion."[50] In all, as the Keston Institute report concludes, "there is still a great deal of uncertainty regarding the value of these facilities."[51]

A second, related issue in long-term concession PPPs is the increased costs, in the form of higher tolls or other user fees, for drivers and whether the concession represents a gain for the public overall, in light of these higher costs. The Keston Institute report notes: "Traditional toll facilities financed by municipal bonds and governed by public or quasi-public agencies typically aimed to keep tolls at the minimum necessary to retire the bonds and fund needed reserves. One of the main advantages cited of switching to the concession model is the ability to raise tolls to track or exceed inflation and to keep tolls on for a long time, since the public sector has been unwilling or unable to do this."[52]

In a recent report that is highly critical of many transportation PPPs undertaken to date, the U.S. Government Accountability Office acknowledged the potential benefits of a PPP to the public sector but warned: "There are also potential costs and trade-offs to highway public-private partnerships. There is no 'free' money—while highway public-private partnerships can be used to obtain financing for highway infrastructure without the use of public sector funding, this funding is a form of privately issued debt that must be repaid to private investors seeking a return on their investment by collecting toll revenues." Yes, a carefully drawn agreement can prevent a private operator from blithely raising tolls over the concession's lifetime, but "to the extent that a private concessionaire gains market power by control of a road where there are not other viable travel alternatives that would not require substantially more travel time, the potential also exists that the public could pay tolls that are higher than tolls based on cost of the facilities, including a reasonable rate of return." The public sector could also be losing money "if the net present value of the future stream of revenues (less operating and capital costs) given up exceeds the concession payment received."[53]

That private operators are likely to increase tolls at a higher rate than public authorities would—even beyond the point of covering costs and ensuring a reasonable rate of return on investment—is simply a consequence of another fundamental shift that concession agreements for highway facilities effect. As the Keston Institute report notes, when private investment in transportation facilities was limited to the purchase of state or municipal bonds, "full and timely payment of bonds" was investors' only concern. Under the concession model, however, the private investor "hopes that revenue will exceed forecasts and yield returns greater than expected," which "transforms the operator into one that wants to maximize profit."[54] Besides maximizing revenues, a private operator will naturally want to minimize costs.

While concessions such as those for the Chicago Skyway and the Indiana Toll Road include stipulations about levels of service and maintenance for the duration of the lease, there are risks of conflict between the financial interests of the private operator and the interest of the public in a transportation system that adequately addresses public needs. Tolling policy and the possibility of windfall revenues for the private partner are not the only risks of long-term concessions. With leases as long as seventy-five or even ninety-nine years, a government's ability to respond to new or changed public needs over that length of time, especially if the private operator has won a "noncompete" clause (limiting the public sector's ability to develop new facilities that might conceivably compete with leased ones), and a number of similar concerns raise serious questions about the surrender of public control of important public facilities to private, for-profit operators. Such concerns have been heightened by the fact that the major players today in the industry of transportation infrastructure management are foreign firms such as Macquarie and Cintra.

Beyond these issues of control, there is also the fundamental question of whether the private sector can deliver the greater efficiency and productivity that proponents of PPPs promise. The FHWA correctly notes: "The premise of lower overall costs, which is a key benefit of PPPs, is highly dependent on the innovation, scale, and expertise of the private sector, with cost savings outweighing the risk premium required by the private sector."[55] However, as the Keston Institute observes, arguments can be made both for and against the proposition that "the private sector can deliver services at less cost than the public sector," especially now that "the public sector has responded to criticisms of its inefficiency by creating in-house enterprises that are better able to manage costs . . . and by outsourcing some or all of its operations without equity participation."[56]

Indeed, the widespread adoption of asset management by state and local transportation departments, discussed above, tends to reinforce the suggestion that "the concession model can bring with it many cost saving features, but that does not mean that public agencies do not have other means of achieving some or all of the benefits."[57] The fact that private operators' attempts to introduce savings and raise productivity may involve hiring nonunionized employees has aroused opposition to PPPs from the powerful public-sector unions. Such opposition may pose a major challenge for states and municipalities hoping to implement PPPs.

The concessions for the Chicago Skyway and the Indiana Toll Road illustrate both the benefits and the risks for the public of long-term

concession PPPs, as well as how only some of the risks can be miti-
gated. Both deals were undertaken primarily to monetize existing
assets in order to address budget shortfalls—for the city generally,
in the case of Chicago, and especially for transportation needs, in
the case of Indiana. The Chicago Skyway, opened in 1958, had been
operated and maintained since that time by the city's Department of
Streets and Sanitation. During the nearly fifty years in which the road
was publicly managed, "tolls changed infrequently and actually decreased by approximately 25 percent in real terms" from 1989 to 2004.
Indeed, "the Chicago Skyway had not historically increased its tolls
unless required by law, even though the Skyway had been operating
at a loss and had outstanding debt."[58]

The Indiana Toll Road, opened in 1956 and operated until its leasing by the Indiana Toll Road Commission and later (after 1981) by the
Indiana Department of Transportation, had also increased tolls infrequently over the years and was "an underperforming asset that consistently lost money."[59] Both Chicago and Indiana hired consultants
to value the assets in question prior to putting the leases out to bid,
and both obtained results indicating that the bids that were eventually
accepted amounted to approximately twice the net present value of the
roads under continued public operation. Although the winning bids
in both cases would have been significantly less had the concession
agreements not contained provisions allowing for rapid depreciation
of the assets by the concessionaires—a factor that will cost the state
and federal governments tax revenue—the size of the bids in relation
to what the public sector calculated it could obtain from the assets on
its own went far toward selling their benefits to the public.[60]

While obtaining these large upfront payments (even if, in the Indiana Toll Road concession, some argued that the payments were not
large enough), both Chicago and Indiana also imposed limits on future toll increases and required specific levels of maintenance. Under
both agreements there is an initial, preset toll schedule (expiring in
mid-2010 on the Indiana Toll Road, and in 2017 on the Chicago Skyway), after the expiration of which annual toll increases are capped

at either two percent, the increase in the Consumer Price Index, or the increase in per capita gross domestic product (GDP), whichever is highest. In the case of the Skyway, "the concessionaire must follow detailed technical specifications based on industry 'best practices,' addressing such maintenance and operational issues as roadway and drainage maintenance, safety features, toll collection procedures, emergency planning and snow removal"—no formal standards for which existed while the road was under public management. In the case of the Indiana Toll Road, "the concessionaire is contractually obligated to maintain the road," while "if Macquarie/Cintra does not meet the specified level of service standard, it can default, awarding the asset back to the public sector at zero cost."[61]

While such terms address some of the major risks to the public in turning control of roads over to private-sector interests, other features of the agreements, or of how they were vetted before being presented to the public for approval, illustrate some of the pitfalls. The Indiana Toll Road agreement, for example, includes a noncompete clause prohibiting Indiana from constructing a new highway twenty miles or longer within ten miles of the Toll Road without compensating the concessionaire. (Macquarie/Cintra did not ask for a noncompete clause in the Skyway deal only because of the unlikelihood of a new road being constructed in the vicinity, as the Skyway runs through a densely populated urban area.)

More significantly, however, beyond performing valuation studies and setting conditions for toll increases and operations and maintenance standards, neither Chicago nor Indiana performed any overall public-interest studies to determine whether their concession agreements provided what in countries such as the United Kingdom and Australia—which have used transportation PPPs extensively for many years—is called "value for money." The U.S. GAO has recently highlighted the need for states and municipalities to employ "formal public interest tests and tools" such as VFM (value for money) tests and public-sector comparators (PSCs) to determine if a given PPP ultimately serves the public interest. The GAO explains: "VFM evaluations examine total project costs and benefits and are used by some governments to determine if a public-private partnership approach is in the public interest for a given project. VFM tests are often done through a PSC, which compares the costs of doing a proposed public-private partnership project against the costs of doing that project through a public delivery model."[62] VFM tests go beyond merely examining the financial value of a project to present a detailed picture of factors that are otherwise difficult to quantify—e.g., design quality, functionality, quality of construction, and the value of any unquantifiable risks faced by the government that are to be transferred to the private sector. While such tests have been used only sparingly in the United States, they are commonly used in Australia, the United Kingdom, and Canada.[63]

It will be years before the ultimate verdict will be rendered on transactions such as the Chicago Skyway and Indiana Toll Road concessions. In Indiana, where opposition to the leasing of the Toll Road was fervid, but where major toll increases for passenger vehicles will be deferred (except for those who continue to pay by cash rather than electronically) until 2016, it remains to be seen how motorists will react to toll hikes when they come. Nor can we know now whether, as some predict, the seventy-five-year lease for the road will keep the state's hands tied with respect to an important transportation artery long after it has spent its $3.8 billion upfront payment.[64]

In Chicago, it is fortunate for proponents of the Skyway leasing that the deal was approved in the spring of 2009, long before major public dissatisfaction with the performance of the private-sector partner in a $1.15 billion parking meter concession threw the city's ability to enter into future PPPs into serious doubt.[65] The city's use of a significant portion of its $1.83 billion upfront Skyway payment for purposes other than transportation has also earned Chicago criticism from transportation policy experts who advocate PPPs as a way to fill the gap between transportation needs and resources, and to advance the policy goal of shifting more automobile transportation costs onto users, rather than as a way to divert transportation assets to other governmental purposes.

Meanwhile, late in 2008, the momentum for long-term concession PPPs for existing highways abruptly ceased when the Pennsylvania legislature killed a proposed leasing of the Pennsylvania Turnpike for seventy-five years to a consortium consisting of Citi Infrastructure Investors and the Spanish firm Abertis Infraestructuras, a deal that would have resulted in a $12.8 billion upfront payment to the state. A report on the failed transaction issued by the Pew Center on the States soon afterward found several causes for the deal's collapse, including a lack of coordination between the executive and legislative branches of the state government, overly optimistic financial assumptions, and the lack of a "clearly articulated plan for how the proceeds would have been invested and spent."[66]

Spanning all of these particular failures was also a more general one: "The debate lacked adequate consideration of the state's long-term interests," a failure with far-reaching lessons. Noting that the concept behind the leasing of the turnpike was to generate a multibillion-dollar initial payment to pay for infrastructure projects around the state that would otherwise not be affordable, the Pew report pointed out that the "short-term implications of that payment dominated the debate about whether to proceed with the lease. . . . Although it is impossible to know what ground transportation may look like decades from now, policy makers need to consider more seriously the long-term effects of a lease on their taxpayers, their economies and their environment."[67]

### The Prognosis for PPPs

Recent events have afforded legislators and policymakers a fresh opportunity for such consideration of the pros and cons of long-term concessions. In the wake of the demise of the Pennsylvania Turnpike transaction and the financial meltdown of 2008, infrastructure investors—a group that includes private equity firms and investment banks that have been amassing tens of billions of dollars in infrastructure investment funds over the past two decades—have become at least temporarily wary of entering into such partnerships. In September 2008, Missouri was forced to cancel a planned PPP—with an estimated upfront payment of $600–800 million—to repair 800 of the state's worst bridges, when private partners said that they could no longer get the credit they needed. Missouri thereupon decided to fund the repairs by issuing $700 million in bonds instead. When Florida, early in 2009, solicited bids for a long-term concession for Alligator Alley, a seventy-eight-mile, east-west highway linking Naples on the Gulf of Mexico with Broward County on the Atlantic, it did not receive a single offer.[68]

The newfound caution among infrastructure investors comes after a decade in which infrastructure fundraising and investment rose sharply. In 2007, with Europe poised to spend $350 billion a year on its failing infrastructure, India projecting $500 billion in infrastructure spending by the year 2012, China needing as much as $800 billion, and the U.S. five-year infrastructure investment need estimated at $1.3 trillion at the beginning of the twenty-first century,[69] most large investors wanted a piece of the action and infrastructure funds swelled. By 2008, however, infrastructure fundraising had fallen by slightly less than a third, from a 2007 high of $34.3 billion to $24.7 billion.[70]

In mid-2009, with a collapsing worldwide economy throwing all financial planning into turmoil, one financial commentator stated: "The bloom clearly is off the world's public-private infrastructure building boom rose."[71] Macquarie, a major infrastructure player, experienced serious losses to its funding capabilities and quickly withdrew plans to move aggressively forward on PPP projects. Both the Blackstone Group, which had planned to invest up to $4 billion in projects in India, and J. P. Morgan Chase, which had projected infrastructure investments of $2 billion, abruptly backed away from those intentions. In short, notwithstanding an overall recognition of the future importance of the PPP market, the global financial crisis was making it virtually impossible for institutional investors to offer fresh capital to governments that were desperate for these funds.

As infrastructure fundraising and investment slowed, lobbying groups such as the American Trucking Association—which has steadfastly opposed PPPs, seeing steep cost increases from the privatization of the Indiana Toll Road and other facilities—cheered the pullback. Yet despite the recent downturn, hopes for the long-term viability of private-sector infrastructure investment remain high. With the bursting of the global financial bubble and the resulting catastrophic effects on investment vehicles that had yielded outsized returns during the financial boom, the steady, low-risk, long-term profits provided by PPP transportation concessions make those concessions seem like a natural investment for pension funds, endowments, banks, and insurers.[72] (Whereas major investors in recent years have sought returns on investment of 20 percent or more, an infrastructure investment typically yields returns of 10 to 15 percent, which in the current economic environment looks most attractive.)

A report published by Kearsarge Global Advisors in January 2009 estimated that as much as $180 billion from private sources was still available for investment in infrastructure projects in the United States. If leveraged at a 60:40 debt-to-credit ratio to create a larger pool of funding for state and local government projects, private capital could generate as much as $450 billion for investment in American infrastructure.[73] As the need for this investment exists, the capital should be forthcoming once the financial markets return to a more settled state.

With states and municipalities facing enormous budget shortfalls—both in their transportation departments and overall—that can be only partially addressed, if at all, by raising taxes and tapping traditional credit markets, state and local politicians will continue to be enticed by the prospect of securing huge upfront payments in exchange for the rights to operate income-producing assets such as roads and bridges. Just as happened in the nineteenth century, when the railroads were being built in the United States and the government had to decide which railroad operators would be granted rights of way and access to valuable contiguous real estate, today investors and infrastructure firms are lobbying hard in public forums—and in some cases acting as advisors to both public-sector entities and infrastructure investors, a blatant conflict of interest—to promote infrastructure PPPs.[74]

The federal government itself has openly supported PPPs. The GAO has charged that "despite the need for careful analysis, the approach at the federal level has not been fully balanced, as DOT has done much to promote the benefits, but comparatively little to either assist states and localities weigh potential costs and trade-offs, nor to assess how potentially important national interests might be protected in highway public-private partnerships."[75] And states and municipalities do need that assistance: for public officials in the United States, who have relatively little experience with infrastructure PPPs, negotiating with investment bankers and sophisticated global players such as Macquarie and Cintra poses a classic case of information asymmetry, with great potential for harm to the public interest.

Absent the sophisticated analysis that a PPP warrants and other means for considering the legitimate interests of stakeholders (for example, motorists, commercial users, public employees, and taxpayers), a government trying to advance the overall goals of transportation and other governmental policies (in the realms of energy and environment, for instance) while protecting the public interest runs the risk of being dominated by the many powerful private-sector interests lined up behind transportation PPPs. Besides adopting measures such as limitations on toll increases, agreements specifying levels of service and maintenance, and analytical tools such VFM tests and PSCs, governments will need to maintain transparent processes, including fully competitive bidding, and engage independent advisors with private-sector experience and expertise. Even so, there remains a nagging question that the business journalist Daniel Gross may have stated best: "How is it that in the richest nation on the earth, localities simply don't have the cash to do necessary maintenance on basic infrastructure, the political will to raise such funds, or the competence to run such easily profitable operations? Why are they being forced to sell off long-term cash cows for short-term cash?"[76]

The answer to that last question can be stated easily enough, although solving the problem it describes will not be easy. First, the continuing growth of our population will see new development eclipsing anything seen since the 1950s throughout large sections of our nation, with the predominant growth coming in the south and southwest. By 2030, almost half of our residential building stock will have been constructed after 2000.[77] Second, given the need to both rehabilitate deteriorated infrastructure and provide for the transportation needs of a country that is expected to add 100 million residents by the year 2040, a combination of every financial means available—new taxes, smart toll roads and other means of collecting user fees, national and state infrastructure banks to seed additional funding from new and traditional sources, as well as PPPs—will have to be used. Meanwhile, one of the major problems that new sources of funding will need to address is the nation's backwardness in taking advantage of new forms of technology that can both provide safer, more efficient infrastructure and dramatically lower the cost of maintaining our new and old endangered infrastructure.

# 5 The Technological Imperative

For a country generally smitten with technology, it is ironic that when it comes to maintaining our nation's costly infrastructure, technology is noticeably absent. As advanced technology in the form of computer-aided design software and increasingly sophisticated project management software is widely utilized in the construction of roads and bridges, the lack of technology for maintaining our infrastructure comes as something of a surprise. How has this happened? What price is our nation paying as a consequence?

Inspection departments are the stepsisters in our state transportation agencies. The exciting work of most transportation agencies is planning, designing, and building the latest and greatest projects. Unlike projects conceived and developed by transportation departments, the ongoing inspection processes of state and local bridges required by federal law garner little, if any, publicity. Because funds are routinely siphoned off to pay for new projects and make up for other funding inefficiencies, engineers and inspectors charged with overseeing this unglamorous inspection work find themselves dealing with a huge backlog of deferred maintenance. To close this gap will require a smarter and more efficient approach to the management of the nation's infrastructure. This means that transportation agencies will need to acquire efficient and effective real-time data and knowledge resources to monitor and maintain their costly assets.

In the construction of buildings, high-tech building management systems that control heat, air conditioning, lighting, and other building systems continue to get smarter. Architects and engineers are incorporating more and more automated smart controls that an owner can utilize to manage a building and meet the changing needs of occupants. Emerging standards now enable data sharing between building systems that improve efficiency as well as provide real-time control over operating costs. There is no reason why we should not be able to convert our infrastructure to serve as smart systems that are capable of reporting incipient cracks in critical bridge members, for example, or of identifying the beginnings of potholes in roads, when such problems can be fixed at minimal cost.

Bridges are complex machines that must respond to changes in age, loading, and environmental conditions, and there is a significant contrast between the amount of technology used to design and build them and that used to maintain them. When we marvel at the flowing, poetic grace of a bridge designed by Santiago Calatrava, we begin to understand how the latest technological advances have allowed engineers and architects to shape wondrous new structures for our use and enjoyment. However, no bridge remains beautiful or stands forever if it is deprived of the funding needed to keep it aloft. To study the evolution of bridge technology is to learn how advances in the materials used to construct bridges have enabled engineers to design structures that can withstand the geometric increases in traffic volume that have accompanied the growth of the United States over the past fifty years. Yet it is stunning to learn how little technology has been used to maintain the country's bridge inventory as these structures have aged.

The transition of bridge construction from iron to steel rested upon the achievement of Andrew Carnegie, who first brought the Bessemer steel process from England to the United States and changed the face of the railroad industry.[1] During the second half of the nineteenth century, the strength of steel rails allowed for the expansion of railroads all across the country. Bridge design took advantage of this new technology to replace wood truss, cast iron, and wrought iron bridges with new steel designs. The great bridges of this era included the Eads Bridge across the Mississippi River at St. Louis (1874), the Brooklyn Bridge (1883), the first all-steel suspension bridges across the Ohio River at Rochester and Monaca, Pennsylvania (1897), and the Williamsburg Bridge in New York City (1903), whose 1,600-foot span made it, at the time, the longest suspension bridge in the world. Steel arch spans soon followed, as famous bridge engineers such as Othmar H. Ammann, the designer of the George Washington Bridge across the Hudson River; and Conde B. McCullough, the designer of the Yaquina Bay Bridge in Newport, Oregon, became names of note in the engineering world.[2]   .

By the 1960s, concrete, in combination with steel, was producing exciting composite designs. Steel box girders became a common element in the design of bridges such as the 11,179-foot Coronado Bay Bridge in San Diego, opened in 1969, during the bicentennial of the founding of San Diego. Cable-stayed bridges appeared with the Pasco-Kennewick Cable Bridge over the Columbia River in Washington State in 1978, followed by twenty-six others, including ten constructed of concrete. The design and construction of larger, structurally complex bridges brought with it a concomitant development in the sophistication of national and state codes with which designers had to familiarize themselves. Yet as bridge design became increasingly sophisticated, standards and technology for bridge inspection failed to keep pace.

## A Brief History of Bridge Inspection

As bridge design and construction developed in the nineteenth and early twentieth centuries, there were no formal inspection guidelines for engineers to follow. The results were not surprising: bridges experienced failures and significant collapses that rigorous inspection would have prevented. Famous bridge failures prompted advances in bridge design and construction, but it was not until the 1960s that bridge inspection began to be systemized at the national level.

Poor inspection was a cause of three fatal bridge failures in the United States between 1873 and 1878. The worst of these was the collapse of the Ashtabula Bridge over the Ashtabula River in northeast Ohio on the night of December 29, 1876, when a train carrying 159 passengers fell eighty feet, killing 92 people and injuring 64. A jury found that design and construction flaws had caused the bridge to weaken and sag over the eleven years between its construction and its collapse, and that regular inspection could have been prevented the tragedy. In the wake of the Ashtabula Bridge disaster, the Ohio legislature tried but failed to pass a bill that would have created statewide standards for bridge design, construction, and inspection and would have required a state-qualified bridge engineer to be in charge of all the state's bridges. Although the Ashtabula Bridge collapse not only alarmed the general public but also shook the confidence of the railroad companies that had built many of the railroad-carrying bridges,[3] the same powerful railroad companies that succeeded in blocking the introduction of national bridge inspection standards for nearly a century.[4]

Such inspections as there were occurred at irregular intervals and concentrated on easily identifiable conditions such as drainage, surface corrosion, or damage from collision. Inspections at the time focused on bridge design and avoiding future failures, rather than on maintaining bridges' health.[5] Inspectors relied solely on visual inspection techniques. Repeated calls for legislation to require annual or biannual inspections were constantly thwarted, largely due to the lobbying efforts of special interests such as the national railroads.[6] It took another catastrophic bridge collapse ninety-one years after the Ashtabula Bridge fell to spur the nation into creating national standards for bridge inspection. As a result of the December 1967 collapse of the Silver Bridge over the Ohio River—an accident that, as noted above, killed forty-six people—Congress finally recognized the need for a comprehensive and standardized bridge inspection system. The Federal-Aid Highway Act of 1968 called upon the secretary of transportation to establish national bridge inspection standards and to create a program to train bridge inspectors. An important part of the legislation was a requirement that the Federal Highway Administration (FHWA) develop inspection standards, a training program, and a manual detailing which bridge components needed regular inspections, what conditions should be reported, and, for the first time, what qualifications a bridge inspector should have. The primary purpose of the system enunciated by the new law was to identify and evaluate existing bridge deficiencies to ensure the safety of the traveling public. The law also directed the states to develop and maintain an inventory of bridges that were part of the federal-aid highway system. By 1970, the FHWA had created the National Bridge Inspection Standards (NBIS), but limited their application to bridges on the federal-aid highway system. In 1978, the Surface Transportation Assistance Act extended the NBIS requirements to all bridges longer than twenty feet and located on public roads.

In the early 1970s, the FHWA issued its *Bridge Inspector's Training Manual* (known as Manual 70), and the *Recording and Coding Guide for the Structure Inventory and Appraisal of the Nation's Bridges* (known as the Coding Guide). The new system mandated, and established procedures for, biannual inspection of bridges. Meanwhile, the American Association of State Highway and Transportation Officials (AASHTO) issued its *Manual for Maintenance Inspection of Bridges*, to serve as a companion volume to Manual 70.[7] The new manuals sought to introduce a requirement that bridge inspectors use visual inspection to provide an accurate accounting of a bridge's condition, including a record of any deterioration. Inspections of a bridge's superstructure were to include the identification of the extent of any corrosion, cracking, splitting, deformation due to overload, or damage due to collisions. Detailed procedures for assigning load ratings, which entailed both visual inspection and calculations of load analysis, were included in the AASHTO manual.

It would take many years and subsequent revisions to the manuals for the development of ratings that could be used to categorize a bridge's condition. That inspectors were not required to assign a numerical rating to a bridge would hamper many states' ability to assess accurately how much money they should allocate for bridge remediation. Two subsequent bridge collapses became the impetus for requiring state transportation departments to make improvements in the art of bridge inspection and maintenance. The late 1970s saw the end of bridge designs known as fracture-critical, bridges built with cost efficiency in mind but with the design limitation that, as noted above, a failure of one critical part would lead to the collapse of the entire bridge. The 1983 collapse of the fracture-critical Mianus River Bridge on I-95 in Greenwich, Connecticut—which was found to have been caused by corrosion, metal fatigue, and inadequate maintenance—pointed to the need for more specialized inspection procedures to address the unique needs of the thousands of similar fracture-critical bridges still in service.[8] As a consequence, bridge inspectors now had to provide reports on more bridge components and conditions as well as rate critical components.[9]

In 1987 came the failure of the Schoharie Creek Bridge in upstate New York, which, as described above, was attributed to scour and resulted in criticism by the National Transportation Safety Board (NTSB) of the New York State Thruway Authority (NYSTA) and the FHWA.[10] This investigation led to new federal requirements that states identify bridges susceptible to scour and the development of special underwater inspection procedures.

The 1990s saw the introduction of still more measures for the improvement of bridge inspection, when the FHWA replaced Manual 70 with a new *Bridge Inspector's Training Manual*, known as Manual 90. An expanded version of Manual 70 (roughly three times its length), Manual 90 included a chapter setting out advanced inspection techniques in greater detail.

However, one clear shortcoming of the inspection process was carried over to the new Manual 90. It continued the existing practice of prescribing visual inspection as the principal means of examining bridges. At the same time, it directed attention to the limitations of the visual inspection process. The new manual remained sketchy on critical issues that were hard to observe visually, such as detecting and measuring deformations.[11] A potentially more revolutionary advance came with the passage of the Intermodal Surface Transportation Efficiency Act of 1991 (ISTEA), which attempted to shift the focus of federal highway programs from construction to maintenance. The new law attempted to make bridge inspection and maintenance practices more useful for national transportation policymaking, specifically for the funding of maintenance and repair. The significance of ISTEA was its mandate that state transportation departments adopt Bridge Management Systems (BMS).

Recognizing that funding by Congress had failed to keep pace with the growing number of bridges requiring replacement or rehabilitation, the federal government required each state to use a BMS as a way to develop a more highly refined data system to track the disparate elements involved in testing a bridge's condition. A BMS was seen as a method for predicting the future conditions of each of a bridge's components. Accordingly, different repair, replacement, and maintenance constructs could be viewed with different budget analyses, providing states with a series of alternatives for their maintenance programs. In a sense, a BMS provided a state with a series of "what ifs" that enabled them to evaluate the effect of deterioration on their application of future funding, using a life-cycle cost analysis.[12]

As can be readily seen, a BMS is a useful tool for asset management programs in state and local departments of transportation (see chapter 4), which is why many departments have continued to use the systems even though the National Highway System Designation Act of 1995 repealed ISTEA's mandate for their implementation. While representing a significant improvement over the NBIS, BMS is still of limited value for bridge management—especially in today's environment of very limited financial resources—because of its overriding reliance on visual inspection.[13]

## The Limitations of Visual Inspection

According to the *Bridge Inspector's Reference Manual*, "the inspection of steel bridge members for defects is primarily a visual activity."[14] This remains true for most routine bridge inspections today, an alarming fact given that it is now well established that visual inspection is a poor method of examining steel bridges for defects. This is so because it fails to detect hidden deterioration or damage: "It is not possible to look at a bridge and determine if it has been overloaded or if it has settled unless the damage is so severe as to cause the lines of the bridge to change. Frozen bearings, corrosion, and fatigue damage can exist with no visible indications."[15]

With the advent of the interstate highway system in 1956 came dynamic testing of new bridges to determine the maximum stresses on the critical structural elements of bridges in maximum traffic conditions. In 1998, the FHWA created the Nondestructive Evaluation Center (NEC) to "improve the state of the practice for highway bridge inspection" by acting as a resource for departments of transportation, industry, and researchers. Shortly afterward, the NEC undertook a comprehensive study of the reliability of visual inspection—"the predominant nondestructive evaluation technique used for bridge inspections"[16]—which had not been studied since the NBIS was introduced in 1971. The resulting report, published in 2001 as *Reliability of Visual Inspection for Highway Bridges*, provided as disturbing a set of findings as the federal government has ever released on the nation's critical infrastructure.[17]

The NEC investigated the reliability of both routine and in-depth bridge inspections conducted by visual inspection. Alarmingly, its investigators found that "Professional Engineers are typically not present on site for bridge inspections." Moreover, even though "Visual Inspection is the most used NDE [nondestructive evaluation] technique used for concrete, steel, and timber bridges," eye examinations for inspectors were almost nonexistent.[18] In both routine and in-depth inspections conducted as part of the performance trials, most inspectors could not indicate or identify important structural aspects of the bridges under their purview. The report also found significant variability in the length of time inspectors thought they would need to perform an inspection and in how long an inspection on a bridge actually took. Finally, the report noted that many inspectors were consistently unable to detect specific types of defects.

Not surprisingly, in light of these findings, the NEC also found that "Routine Inspections are completed with significant variability . . . most prominent in the assignment of Condition Ratings, but . . . also present in inspection documentation."[19] According to the report, the definition of condition ratings was not refined enough to produce reliable inspection results. Other reasons offered for the shortcoming of the visual inspection process included: inspectors' reported fear of traffic and high winds, lack of formal bridge inspection training, poor access, and the need to rush through inspections. It became clear to federal and state transportation officials that many of the in-depth inspections required on deteriorating bridges were failing to disclose any more deficiencies than routine inspections.[20]

Working bridge engineers confirmed this view. Less than two months after the collapse of the I-35W Bridge in Minneapolis, the Committee on Science and Technology of the U.S. House of Representatives held a hearing on bridge safety. Mark Bernhardt, an engineer who has conducted more than 3,000 bridge inspections and 160 load ratings, testified that "it is the general consensus within the engineering community that visual inspection practices must be supported by rigorous training, certification and quality assurance programs, and supplemented with testing techniques to ensure reliable results."[21] Notwithstanding this consensus among bridge engineers and the alarms sounded by the NEC and others, visual inspection of bridges by minimally trained personnel who are not engineers remains the norm in state departments of transportation. Today, the FHWA only requires state bridge inspectors to participate in a three-week training program stipulated in the NBIS. This acquaints them with the nature of bridge materials, how to inspect steel superstructures generally, and how to look for fatigue and fracture in bridge components. Although it was once the norm for bridge inspections to take place during daylight hours and for inspectors to take as much time as they needed, inspections today are relegated to overnight and low-traffic periods, and inspectors report they are given limited time to perform their work.[22]

The continued reliance on visual inspection for assessing the condition of bridges, despite the now widely recognized inadequacy of this method, poses a major obstacle to the national management of transportation assets that, as we have seen, has been a principal goal of the federal government and, increasingly, of state and local departments of transportation since the early 1990s. A Transportation Research Board study found that inspections performed in accordance with NBIS standards, while useful, were "insufficient to make reliable programmatic decisions in the face of dwindling funding dollars."[23]

The improvement of the NBIS since its introduction in the early 1970s and the adoption of a BMS by many state and local departments of transportation since the early 1990s would have represented much greater advances were it not for the fact that, as the Transportation Research Board study also notes, both remain tied to the use of visual inspection: "The key to improving our bridge management and funding allocation tools is to recognize that visual inspection is the limiting variable in both NBIS and BMS."[24] To overcome the limitations of visual inspection, transportation agencies need to avail themselves of new technologies.

To be clearly valuable for the enhanced maintenance of infrastructure projects, technology must provide substantial improvement over visual inspections in the following areas: deterioration, damage, and operations. Deterioration assessment must effectively identify and measure corrosion, fatigue, water penetration, and other structural irregularities. Damage assessment needs to identify and measure impacts on a structure, overload conditions, underwater scour, seismic movement, corrosion, and inoperative bearings and other moving parts. Operational assessment needs to identify and measure ongoing traffic conditions, stresses, deflections, and displacement.[25]

New assessment technologies are central to overcoming the limiting effects of visual inspection for both bridge management and funding allocation, and offer a variety of benefits to departments of transportation and the public. Most obviously, improved technologies for assessing deterioration, damage, and vulnerability to damage or failure due to extreme or random events outside the course of normal operations have important implications for bridge safety, as was recently emphasized by a case in Maryland.

In August 2008, a truck swerving to avoid collision with an automobile on the Chesapeake Bay Bridge crashed into the railing on both sides of the bridge, displacing the railing on one side and knocking a section of it into the bay on the other side; the truck then toppled over the railing and fell into the water, killing the driver. Following the accident, the Maryland secretary of transportation appointed a panel to investigate both this particular incident and the Maryland Transportation Authority's bridge and tunnel inspection practices. In a report issued in June 2009, the panel found that "some of the railings on the Bay Bridge at the time of the crash were secured to the deck with bolts that had been weakened by corrosion," that "the majority of the bolts had been reused when the railing was replaced in 1986," and that "neither the concrete voids nor bolt corrosion had been identified as problems during prior inspection."[26]

The limitations inherent in visual inspection of bridges not only threaten the safety of the traveling public but may also, paradoxically, be costing taxpayers money for unnecessary bridge remediation and replacement. In its investigation of how state bridge inspectors assign condition ratings to bridges, the NEC report observed: "Inspectors are hesitant to assign 'low' or 'high' Condition Ratings and, as a result, tend to be grouped toward the middle of the Condition Rating scale."[27] More recently, other experts have contended that visual inspection of bridges exhibits an inherent "downward bias," as bridge inspectors err on the side of caution by giving bridges condition ratings that tend to be lower than their actual condition warrants. Peter Vanderzee and Frank Wingate of LifeSpan Technologies—a firm that provides condition assessment technology and services for infrastructure—have argued:

> Visual bridge inspection is inherently conservative by design. Consider a typical bridge inspector's mission: they are not paid to take chances with public safety, so they are rightly trained to be conservative. In addition, Federal funding for bridge replacement is biased toward ever worse condition ratings, i.e. the worst bridges get top priority for funding. And, given abundant Federal funding in the

past, there are few incentives to up-rate a bridge when lower ratings garner more Federal funds. The agency's staff structural engineer compounds the visual inspection dichotomy by using the subjective, conservative inspection data as input for a highly conservative, prescriptive analytic protocol to determine bridge sufficiency.[28]

Vanderzee estimates that, as a result of this downward bias, the number of structurally deficient bridges in the United States may be overstated by as much as one-third. An unintended consequence of visual inspection, he further argues, is that states seek and obtain federal funds to replace bridges that may not need replacement.[29] Given the chasm between needs and resources for necessary bridge remediation and replacement, the development of alternatives to the current visual inspection regimen in state departments of transportation is clearly in order.

### Technology for Bridge Monitoring and Assessment

One answer to the limitations of visual bridge monitoring and assessment is the adoption of advanced technology by those departments. The federal Long-Term Bridge Performance Program (LTBPP) is intended to develop and validate technology that can provide more quantitative and objective assessments beyond those currently available through a subjective BMS based on visual inspections. Stakeholders such as the National Academies of Sciences and Engineering, the National Institute of Standards and Technology (NIST), state departments of transportation, and industry groups have begun to fund studies to explore a wide range of technologies to be used in maintaining our roads and bridges. Each stakeholder has recognized that until reliable and real-time data can be captured and interpreted, it will be impossible to advance new methodologies that provide more efficient management of the nation's highways. The Transportation Research Board study cited above notes: "Technology development must be accompanied by improvements in decision support tools to integrate probabilistic life-cycle analysis into infrastructure management. This will require improvements in the way infrastructure assets are valued and benefits of the system are quantified. A long-term bridge monitoring program can address these needs."[30]

Technology for bridge monitoring fulfills two purposes. First, it links electronic sensors with data management systems to provide information about the condition of bridges in real time. Second, it permits inspectors to overcome visual limitations and provides information about latent conditions that will, as a bridge ages, become progressively more severe. Without technology to achieve these two goals, it is impossible for bridge inspectors to know whether exceptional stresses are affecting the structural integrity of a particular bridge. Had monitoring devices been in place on the I-35W Bridge in Minneapolis as the redecking project was proceeding in the summer of 2007, warning signals would have triggered a halt to the loading of construction materials onto the deck well before the bridge collapsed.

As Bernhardt noted in his testimony to Congress, existing inspection methods provide "a mere a snapshot of bridge conditions." Although a snapshot in time at various intervals is "generally adequate for relatively low risk structures," Bernhardt went on to say, "structurally deficient or complex structures that pose a greater risk to the traveling public" require what bridge engineers call structural health monitoring.[31]

Structural health monitoring entails the installation of various sensors and monitors onto bridge components, in order to collect and observe data remotely and around the clock. These can include strain gauges, weight-in-motion systems, fiber optics, cameras, corrosion sensors, and acoustic sensors, all linked to data servers continually monitoring bridge conditions.[32] As Steven Chase and Jeffrey Laman have explained, "the integration of the sensor with the structure creates a self-monitoring condition system that can be coupled with bridge management systems," which permits bridge officials to make immediate, informed decisions. Technology of this nature consists of piezoelectric sensors; optical sensors, including Bragg grating;

and interferometric imaging, all of which are currently being used to monitor loads in bridges, buildings, dams, and even aircraft.[33]

However, NIST reports: "Technology that could provide more quantitative data on integrity and condition of infrastructural elements is currently very expensive and is able to provide only a partial picture that is specific to the type of technology used." NIST cites examples such as ground-penetrating radar—which the Minnesota Department of Transportation (MN/DOT) declined to use for an inspection of the deck of the I-35W Bridge just months before that structure collapsed—sound-wave propagation methods, electrical impedance measurements, and other methods that can detect the presence of some subsurface defects.[34] NIST has also questioned how far the development of the sensing technology at the core of systems like structural health monitoring has come.[35] A NIST white paper, written to give the rationale for a grant competition focused on advanced sensing technologies for infrastructure, portrayed available technologies as failing to produce "real-time, in-situ data that are comprehensible for infrastructure decision-makers." In NIST's opinion, "there are currently no cost-effective, field-deployable sensing systems that are capable of providing continuous data with which to prioritize repair and renovation schedules and that provide sufficient warning of impending catastrophic failure."[36]

Not everyone agrees. Bridge technology experts like Vanderzee feel that the NBIS protocols are excessively conservative and were more appropriate when funding was adequate for repair and replacement: "In this era of severely limited federal and state funding, we are convinced that every bridge classified as structurally deficient, or that has a sufficiency rating less than fifty (the threshold for replacement), should have a technically appropriate advanced condition assessment solution deployed prior to repair or replacement funding authorization."[37] Contrary to the NIST opinion of the latest technology, numerous benefits of advanced condition assessment technology are currently available on a cost-effective basis to provide improved information, leading to better decision making. This technology can provide information to permit state agencies to remove load postings or to safely delay repairs or replacement that can reap substantial savings on maintenance. Vanderzee also points to the relatively minor cost of manual monitoring systems, which can capture peak strain data without power, monitor critical defects and suspect structural members, and measure displacements, or movements in excess of anticipated design limits.

But Vanderzee goes one step further than other technology experts. He vigorously asserts that calling for the use of proven condition assessment technologies can easily result in billions of dollars in savings over the next decade. By adapting such technology, Vanderzee believes, many of the 72,000 bridges that have been rated as structurally deficient will be shown to have less serious damage and need far fewer repairs, simply because inspectors would rather give an older bridge a lower rating—making the bridge eligible for federal funding—than provide a higher rating that would preclude such funding. In times of tight state budgets, there is a perverse incentive for states to downgrade the quality of their bridges in order to secure federal funding, which can amount to 80 percent of the cost for transportation projects. In addition, recent federal legislation has made it even easier for states to use the funding for other transportation projects that state political and transportation leaders may prefer.

State transportation agencies are of two minds when it comes to the subject of technology for bridge assessment. On the one hand, few states have adopted available assessment technology for operations or maintenance. Many transportation officials argue that limited state budgets preclude purchasing such technology for statewide use. On the other hand, states are more than ready to employ new technology and publicize its use when funding is available for its purchase from the federal government. When the replacement for the I-35W Bridge was designed, advanced technologies were built into the new structure to increase safety and cut future maintenance costs. MN/DOT added a network of 323 sensors to monitor the span for corrosion, excess strain in structural members, or other potential weaknesses;

an anti-icing system to monitor the span's temperature and, when it was cold enough to form ice, trigger sprays of potassium acetate; and a traffic monitoring system to detect not only the speed of cars but the volume of traffic, and in the event of an accident, to immediately relay information to MN/DOT's central command to reroute oncoming drivers. Considering the advanced nature of this technology, it is ironic that officials installed a wired connection rather than a state-of-the-art wireless system to transmit the data back to MN/DOT's central server.

As the story of the I-35W Bridge suggests, more than a lack of funds would seem to be involved in the slowness of transportation agencies to embrace new technology. Vanderzee and Wingate argue that, owing to the vagaries of visual bridge inspection, "bridge inspectors and DOT staff engineers are the de facto decision makers for maintenance, repair or replacement of bridges—not the Chief Bridge Engineer, CFO, or DOT Commissioner; despite their executive decision authority."[38] Silo budgeting in departments of transportation and the risk-averse culture of public agencies generally may also be a factor in the failure of many transportation agencies to make even modest investments in new technology. A recent article from HNTB Corporation—the engineering firm that advised MN/DOT about the need to add redundancy to the I-35W Bridge prior to MN/DOT's hiring of URS Corporation—summarized the situation as follows: "Funding dilemmas, community pressures, legacy contracts and relationships all conspire to place the new and improved approach on a track for next time around.[39]

Despite the existence of assessment technologies that could lead to hundreds of millions of dollars of savings from unnecessary bridge and road repairs today, federal programs have recently awarded grants to fund additional research. For example, the National Science Foundation's Sensor Innovation and Systems Program has recently funded research on advanced sensing technology. The danger is that these grants may lead state agencies to postpone adopting available technologies while they await the outcome of research. Most state transportation agencies, while professing faith in such research efforts, move slowly when they must decide whether to implement the findings, despite recommendations of consultants and technology vendors who argue that a particular technology's time has come.

In January 2009, the Michigan Department of Transportation announced a partnership with the University of Michigan to utilize a $19 million grant from NIST to test different types of surface and penetrating sensors to detect cracks, corrosion, or other infrastructure weaknesses. While the agency described the research as creating a two-way information conduit between a bridge official and the bridge, it appears that this costly effort will offer little beyond what is already available.[40]

In the case of a similar grant from NIST, the University of Texas received $3.4 million toward a $6.8 million research project to develop two wireless network systems to monitor cracks and corrosion on bridges. One system is intended to detect damages that will lead to collapse, while the other is intended to monitor early signs of corrosion. Both systems are to be powered by solar or wind energy, or kinetic energy from the bridge.[41] Spending such substantial funds in this way misses the target and may postpone the adoption of technology. If state transportation departments instead applied these funds to the growing roster of structurally deficient bridges, then more accurate assessments of bridge condition would lead to immediate savings in remediation costs.

It is ironic that NIST's call for research into advanced technologies to measure infrastructure performance characteristics, including fatigue and corrosion, was issued only after the collapse of the I-35W Bridge (of course, as we have seen, such catastrophes have supplied the impetus for most of the major advances in bridge inspection over the last forty years). Decades of progress in bridge design and construction had been accompanied by little research on technology for the all-important process of identifying the onset of fatigue or corrosion. Even as the cost of repairing the country's aging bridge stock began to rise dramatically while available funding declined, it was only with the passage of the Transportation Equity Act for the 21st Century (TEA-21) in 1998 and the Safe, Accountable, Flexible, Efficient Transportation Equity Act: A Legacy for Users (SAFETEA-LU) in 2005 that the federal government has begun to sponsor new research into this important area.[42]

The overall reluctance of federal and state departments of transportation to adopt advanced sensing technology for bridge monitoring stands in contrast to the greater willingness that states have shown to adopt new technologies for use in road monitoring, repair, and reconstruction. Obviously, road maintenance involves a far simpler process of inspection and repair than bridge maintenance. Whereas a bridge is exposed to the elements in all dimensions and includes thousands of parts that move, expand, and contract, roads are relatively simple in design, construction, and maintenance. AASHTO's 2009 *Rough Roads Ahead* describes some of the technologies for pavement monitoring and preservation now in use by various state departments of transportation: ground-penetrating radar, global positioning systems (GPS), cameras, scanning lasers, mapping technology, automated road analyzers (linked to computerized pavement management systems) for monitoring pavement condition, sealers and rejuvenators, bonded concrete overlays, dowel-bar retrofits, and pavement recycling using reclaimed asphalt, among other tools, for pavement preservation.[43]

Michigan's Department of Transportation has used ground-penetrating radar to assess conditions that could affect pavement life —such as sinkholes—and mapping technology to help assess pavements' remaining service life. Maryland has utilized an automatic road analyzer to collect information on roughness, rutting, and cracking, as well as a skid truck to collect friction data. Oregon assesses pavement conditions with a vehicle equipped with a profiler to measure roughness and scanning lasers to measure rutting. Rhode Island uses an automated distress survey to assess pavement conditions and calculate crack density, to define appropriate preventive maintenance. And Minnesota evaluates 14,000 miles of highway with a van equipped with lasers to measure the pavement's smoothness and cameras to help engineers evaluate its quality. Transportation experts foresee advances in roadway materials that will identify an incipient problem and then fix it. Nanotechnology has made possible the development of an auto-healing epoxy that recognizes concrete degradation. When a crack forms, tiny microcapsules of epoxy already embedded in the concrete are released into the crack, activating an agent embedded in the concrete that permanently seals the crack.[44]

At least one state, however, has recognized the need to utilize high-tech monitoring systems for the purpose of load testing on aging bridges. Since 2003, the Oregon Department of Transportation has found that many of the state's bridges that have passed their fifty-year life span were experiencing shear cracking, leading to load restrictions that required rerouting of heavy truck traffic from major routes through local communities. As a result, the state began to tie its bond funding for bridge repairs to a plan for structural health monitoring of selected bridges; the department currently has agreements with two nationally recognized consulting firms to design and install monitoring systems.[45]

Why haven't more state departments of transportation adopted bridge monitoring technology? According to NIST's 2008 white paper, "in general, local and state governments have significant knowledge gaps regarding quantitative assessment of infrastructure integrity, yet they do not have the funds and ability to develop more cost-effective advanced sensing tools that would eliminate the knowledge gaps."[46] Perhaps if states had a greater sense of urgency about the condition of their aging bridges, they would manage to find the funds and acquire the necessary ability.

As bridges become larger and more structurally complex, the question will no longer be whether they incorporate available technology. Rather, we will begin to ask whether the technology being used is smart. We have become accustomed to speeding through toll plazas with smart sensors, and to cities' use of advanced technology to monitor real-time information from street sensors to help reduce congestion, or to change traffic patterns in an effort to improve safety or to reduce carbon emissions. The challenge will now be to get owners of bridges to better monitor and manage their infrastructure as a means of improving the allocation of limited resources.[47]

What are the obstacles to the more aggressive adoption of commercially available technology? Outside consultants to state transportation agencies are highly attuned to the needs and demands of the officials who decide whether to award lucrative contracts to study and design bridges, and to whom. State officials dispense the patronage to those best attuned to how the agency works and to what it does or does not want from a consultant. These same consulting firms offer experienced engineers and inspectors who leave governmental service secure employment that is far more remunerative than a civil service career. It is a close, symbiotic relationship at best, and an incestuous one at worst. How else could one characterize the timing of the retirement of Don Flemming, head of the MN/DOT's central bridge division, and his immediate hiring by URS, which thereupon secured a four-year contract to study the I-35W Bridge? Sensing that a state's budget will not permit costly repairs to structurally deficient bridges, or knowing that a state transportation department has been instructed to devote most of its efforts to building new roads and bridges as opposed to repairing its aging infrastructure, a consultant who desires to do business with the state would be wise not to suggest approaches at odds with such policies. As a result, despite the overwhelming likelihood that engineering consultant firms are well aware of the ongoing deterioration of a state's bridges, or that there is little or no money in the transportation budget to accommodate the introduction of technology to provide better bridge assessments, few consultants are willing to risk censure by recommending that a bridge be closed or to fight for funds for technology that are unlikely to be made available from politicians and managers with other agendas.

The ambivalence of transportation consultants who work on these challenges daily is obvious from the statements of experts such as those at the transportation giant HNTB, which acts as engineering advisor on transportation issues to federal and state agencies. The president of this employee-owned company recently acknowledged: "The lack of funding and oversight is forcing us to maintain the world's greatest transportation system with patches and prayers. Today, as we most recently witnessed in Minneapolis, our roads and bridges are accidents waiting to happen."[48] At the same time, the company, in a recent collection of thoughtful commentaries on infrastructure— after describing many of the advantages that technology brings to the infrastructure world of today—cautions, in words that technology experts around the nation have repeatedly heard from transportation agencies: "Even the most eager adopters of technology often are stopped in their tracks due to simple economic and political pressure to save tomorrow's problems for tomorrow."[49]

What will be needed in the future is a move away from what one expert who works with public agencies calls a "silo mentality" that leads the staff of a transportation agency to be disinclined to exhibit even the slightest evidence of entrepreneurial bent. Such a mentality is most evident when it appears as the silo budgeting of departments of transportation, whose bridge managers constantly complain that they "don't have the money, and there's no way to go upstairs to try to get the money."[50]

In short, most transportation employees recognize that they cannot obtain funds that will permit the adoption of advanced condition assessment technology without a long, drawn-out fight. Thus, the message being communicated to employees is that, even though the adoption of sound, commercially available technology may well serve the long-term interests of the agency, promoting such change is risky.

This silo mentality could become a thing of the past if transportation agencies began to view the implementation of technology as an opportunity to enhance state revenues. In one of the most sophisticated analyses of our nation's transportation system, the National Surface Transportation Infrastructure Financing Commission (NSTIFC) recognized that the use of technology provides new revenues as well as avenues for creative financing: "New technologies, such as electronic transponders, video recognition tolling, and satellite based payment systems, are creating new options for funding the transportation system that simply have not been available before."[51] Efficiencies provided by this technology free up other resources and enhance a state's ability to collect revenues on an expedited basis.

Thus, as we have seen before, the challenge of restoring the nation's deteriorating roads and bridges comes down to two things: money, certainly, and a more intangible factor including elements such as management, politics, and culture. In the end, the need to invest in technology for the maintenance and remediation of our transportation infrastructure reflects the need not just to spend more but to spend smarter. The chasm between needs and resources also fuels the rise of innovative financing techniques, such as public-private partnerships.

Perhaps the NSTIFC report says it best: "In the twentieth century, surface transportation was largely about steel and concrete: extending and expanding the physical network of roads, bridges, and rail systems and the cars, buses, and trucks that operated on it. The goal was to raise the money needed, from whatever sources, to build a robust enough system to meet the nation's mobility needs."[52] Today, with our federal highway system completed and aging, as are the 600,000 bridges on our public roads, finding the resources to manage and maintain these assets has become more critical than ever. In fact, the costs associated with this challenge will exceed the cost of building these assets in the first place.

The vulnerabilities of our infrastructure are not being adequately addressed by the current reliance on visual inspection methodologies. Reluctance to introduce available technologies cannot simply be attributed to a Luddite mind-set on the part of transportation agencies. Other issues are affecting the slow adoption of these modern tools for detecting structural deficiencies. In one sense, it resembles the unwillingness of the construction industry to adopt technology, which has left that trillion-dollar industry the most inefficient in the nation.[53] Can it be that transportation agencies—faced with continual budget cuts from political leaders who see neither photo ops nor political gain from spending money on remediating aging bridges—no longer have the clout to secure the funding needed to repair the assets that are their responsibility? Perhaps the lack of a sense of urgency about introducing technology is a result of the federal government's failure to fund the implementation of available technology. Or is it because many of today's bridge engineers fall short of honoring their professional oath to serve the larger public interest? Is it all of the above?

In order for the nation to do better and become truly smarter about the way that it maintains and protects its critical road and bridge infrastructure, it will need to change its ways. This will entail exploring and applying innovative management systems, methods of finance, and technologies, many of which will probably require a changed perspective as well as leadership on the part of the federal government. Public assets require public solutions. We turn to these in chapter 6.

# 6 The Way Forward

A country that does not have a public planning system simply turns that function over to a network of private enterprise—domestic or foreign—which then becomes the true seat of economic power. . . . If the future is to be provided for, you must have a community of planners and some way must be found to support them, to permit them to develop their plans and resolve their differences, and to give them access to the levers of public power. To walk away from this problem with a shrug about "markets" is to disenfranchise the future. . . .

In New Orleans . . . the price of failing to plan properly was, in the first place, unnecessary death, and in the second, a vast and costly improvisation after the fact. And as with the levees, the main issue was not a failure to think: it was the absence of public authority, will, and money to run thought into execution. —James K. Galbraith, *The Predator State*

Implicit in any understanding of the problems our nation faces with its ailing infrastructure is that we must make significant changes in how we fund, build, and manage these critical assets. It would be inconceivable for the nation to allocate the massive amounts of money needed to bring our roads, bridges, airports, power grid, and levees up to acceptable standards, only to have those assets begin a downward slide toward a new deterioration for future generations to correct. To address current needs and make the required structural changes in our system, we need to educate our politicians and our citizens about the critical state of our nation's infrastructure and infect them with a renewed sense of urgency about acting before it is too late. We need to apply the latest available technology to ensure that how we design, construct, and maintain our nation's transportation infrastructure will produce enough cost efficiencies to offset the staggering costs of the past few decades' deferred maintenance. And we need to use creative management in overseeing the trillions of dollars of assets in our nation's transportation inventory. To do all this will require a renewed commitment to restoring our infrastructure's lost prominence.

In short, we need across-the-board revisions of the approaches that have led us to this crossroad in the history of our transportation system. Set out below is a series of recommendations to address the current problems, along with new ideas for our nation to consider, discuss, and debate.

### Finding New Financial Resources and Doing Better with Them

The amount of money needed to fix and sustain our nation's infrastructure exceeds $2 trillion, according to the American Society of Civil Engineers (ASCE).[1] It is a daunting amount, which cannot be collected for use to fix these problems on a piecemeal basis. Finding the money will require the federal government to play an active role. It will entail the development of new, creative relationships between the public and private sectors. It will require a renewed sense of urgency on the part of politicians.

And it will involve an extensive reeducation of our leaders and the public on what will be needed for the future. The annual level of federal highway and transportation spending required to meet the "need to maintain" level under the base-case scenario of the National Surface Transportation Infrastructure Financing Commission (NSTIFC) is $59 billion, while another $19 billion is needed if we are to bring infrastructure up to design standards, or a total of $78 billion. Estimated average annual revenues available under current law generate approximately $32 billion, resulting in an annual revenue gap of $46 billion (in 2008 dollars). The annual level of federal highway and transit spending required to meet the "need to improve" level climbs to $74 billion and $22 billion, respectively, for a total of $96 billion. This translates into an annual revenue gap of $64 billion (in 2008 dollars).[2]

Despite recent pronouncements by the U.S. Department of Transportation (DOT) that have urged the expansion of investment from the private sector, most experts believe that this approach does not represent a "free lunch" alternative. In fact, according to the excellent study prepared by the NSTIFC, when it comes to our nation's ability to pay for our infrastructure's various new and remediation needs, there is no "silver bullet."[3] But whatever solutions are developed will need to address the following imperatives: (1) the establishment of new priorities that accomplish national and regional, as opposed to state-specific, goals; (2) establishing more carefully defined objectives that those seeking funding from national resources must conform to; (3) revising the mechanisms for distributing transportation monies to the states by eliminating the discretionary use of such funds by state and local politicians for nontransportation purposes; and (4) the application of much-needed technology in how we design and construct new infrastructure facilities, to ensure that we build more efficiently and—even more important—achieve defined goals of minimizing the repair and replacement costs that are currently draining our transportation budgets.

There is widespread agreement among those who have studied the present system that the current federal procurement procedures in our transportation network produce comparatively inferior results and are in a state of crisis.[4] Recent support by the DOT of the role of public-private partnerships (PPPs) in infrastructure funding has failed to address the growing concern that PPP projects that cross state boundaries have significantly greater risks than those that are limited to projects within a single state. And, although few commentators have raised the issue, the construction industry—the most inefficient industry in our nation—negatively contributes to those risks via cost overruns that are estimated to total at least $120 billion a year.[5] The industry currently shifts the risk for project delays and cost overruns onto federal, state, and local governments. Until our nation faces up to the need for true fixed-price contracts, those overruns and delays will continue to plague taxpayers and soak up even more resources.

## The Need for a Federal Infrastructure Bank

A federal infrastructure bank for spurring major new private investment is needed to jump-start funding for urgent transportation projects. Historically, America's infrastructure programs were created to establish and build national networks for expanding commerce and transportation. These fundamental goals have been realized. The challenge now is to maintain, upgrade, and replace infrastructure facilities in a manner that optimizes the return on the public dollars invested in our highways, power grid, and other infrastructure assets. In the face of rising demand and aging facilities across a range of transportation modalities—from highways to dams and wastewater systems—the federal government must act to define priorities and generate competition among investors from the private sector.

But our revamped infrastructure policy needs be more than a vehicle for funding new construction: "It should promote non-structural solutions for relieving congestion (such as congestion pricing on highways and in the skies). It must also articulate new missions to meet current realities."[6] An overhaul of our national transportation policy should encompass a full range of programs, from our deteriorating public schools to investment in broadband. One of the latest ideas for funding infrastructure is the proposal now before Congress for a National Infrastructure Bank (NIB). President Barack Obama, California Governor Arnold Schwarzenegger, Pennsylvania Governor Ed Rendell, New York City Mayor Michael Bloomberg, and many other big-city mayors have endorsed the idea, as have a number of trade associations favoring increased infrastructure investment and Felix Rohatyn, the investment banker who headed the citizens' group that saved New York City from bankruptcy in the late 1970s. A new bill was introduced into the House of Representatives in May 2009 by Representative Rosa DeLauro of Connecticut.

While supporters of the NIB laud the idea of such a funding vehicle, critics like Robert Poole of the Reason Foundation have challenged the idea as naive and falling short of the goal the federal government should have in mind. They see such a bank as lacking in several critical ways. First, they point to the fact that the $60 billion currently being proposed is inadequate and represents the proverbial drop in the bucket. Second, they contend that the bank would not really be a bank, in that it would not lend money on a sustainable basis, requiring borrowers to pay it back. Poole notes that the proposed NIB fails to show that it would be a source of revenue bonds, through which users would pay for services provided by the new infrastructure.[7]

During his campaign, President Obama promised that what was then called a National Infrastructure Reinvestment Bank would invest $60 billion over ten years, which would be leveraged into almost half a trillion dollars of additional infrastructure spending while generating nearly two million new jobs. The key for any such bank is that the concept must be premised upon the need for payback.[8] The structure for investing in the rebuilding of our ailing infrastructure must also contain a program for repayment, in much the same way that the gasoline taxes imposed by President Eisenhower to fund construction of the interstate highway system meant that the system paid for itself. At present, no assertions made by the NIB's proponents call for specific repayment mechanisms. If the goal of the federal government in creating an NIB is to generate economic growth, the expenditure of billions of dollars on infrastructure in our financially constrained times may not be fiscally prudent.

Nor have any current proposals for an NIB included a clear understanding that once large projects are completed, they will need a defined and funded plan for operation and maintenance to keep them from falling into disrepair. Current NIB proposals fail to propose the use of the latest technology to minimize the maintenance needed to protect the long-term value of these assets. Central to the discussion of whether an NIB will meet all needed objectives is the question raised by Felix Rohatyn and Everett Ehrlich in an article in *The New York Review of Books* in favor of the NIB. They wrote: "The issue here is not the efficiency of capital markets but rather the efficiency with which federal programs work and spend funds. The purpose of the

National Infrastructure Bank would be to use federal resources more effectively and to raise additional funding."[9]

We should be careful not to assume that PPPs represent some kind of silver bullet for our nation's funding shortfall. Despite the promise that PPPs hold out as an important new source of funding for transportation projects, public officials considering investment by the private sector for state and local transportation projects must be certain to ask, as part of their due diligence, questions such as:

- Should private funds be limited to public projects that could otherwise not go forward, because states do not have sufficient funding for critically needed transportation projects?
- Should PPP funding be limited to transportation projects, or should we consider such funding for other types of socially needed projects?
- Should federal support go only to those transportation projects that are needed to solve critical congestion, or should states—especially those in the South and Southwest, which will be experiencing the most population growth over the next fifty years—also be permitted to receive funding before problems arise?
- Should PPP funding be limited to new projects, which by their nature represent more risk to the private sector and, hence, will demand greater concessions from the public sector? Or should such funding include remediation, where current federal funding has had no appreciable effect in recent decades?
- How can state and federal governments ensure that the billions of dollars available from the private sector fund multistate transportation issues, as well as single-state projects?
- Will the PPP agree to accept financial responsibility if the project it invests in fails to improve traffic flow or provide the promised number of jobs for local workers? Will the PPP provide funds to ensure the maintenance of the asset it bids on over the projected life of the concession, which may be as long as ninety-nine years?

These and other questions must be debated in public forums at the federal, state, and local levels to address the challenging issues posed by the use of an NIB and PPPs to address the growing shortfall of transportation funding.

### Transportation Funding:
### Achieving Better Outcomes and Greater Impact

The current system for overseeing the distribution of federal aid for state highway projects through the Federal Highway Administration (FHWA) is clearly broken. Once funds are distributed to the states, it is hard to determine where the money went. More significantly, it is nearly impossible to identify whether the money was well spent.[10] For example, recent criticisms of the current system charge that DOT, which has set national goals for improving safety and reducing traffic congestion, lacks any mechanisms to link funding levels with specific performance-related goals and outcomes. Both the U.S. Government Accountability Office (GAO) and the Office of Management and Budget (OMB) have urged the FHWA to introduce programs to establish measurable project oversight goals and communicate them through all levels of the agency, to ensure improved oversight of the projects that it funds. In addition, the FHWA must establish improved accountability systems to control cost overruns, where it exercises direct oversight of transportation funding.[11] We can no longer afford the massive cost overruns that routinely plague our infrastructure projects. For every Big Dig and Ground Zero project whose costs soar billions of dollars beyond initial estimates, thousands of smaller projects add additional millions and billions that drain the public exchequer.

It is difficult to accept excuses from FHWA officials who state that "costs cannot be accurately estimated early because issues such as public opposition to a project or unforeseen environmental mitigation procedures that are determined necessary are likely to drive up the cost of a project."[12] Cost estimates are developed as the design for a project proceeds. Once the design is substantially defined, which can be during what is known as the design development phase or during the later construction documents phase, almost all elements and details of the design and all reasonably anticipatable risks should have been incorporated into the plans. As one authoritative commentator has written, promoters of large-scale transportation projects do not use "honest numbers." These projects, which routinely exceed initial estimates by 20–40 percent or more, represent "a field where little can be trusted, not even—some would say especially not—numbers produced by analysts."[13]

With the assistance of experienced cost estimators, competent project overseers can accurately anticipate the range of bids from prospective contractors. In fact, the best way of estimating a project's cost is to await the completion of the construction documents phase by the architect or the engineers, so as to ensure that all design details and risks have been incorporated into the documents and will form the basis for a true fixed-price contract that protects against cost overruns.[14]

The important work of developing a series of cost estimates by the completion of the construction documents phase results in exceedingly accurate budgets and eliminates unanticipated cost overruns, unless there are later revisions that reflect an owner's change in scope or materials. In any case, the budgeting process would then be faithfully completed, federal agencies would no longer face state requests for additional funding, and the true risk for completing each project on time and on budget will have been assumed by capable and efficient contractors who are willing to perform their work for a fair profit, without unwarranted change orders or delays that affect the project's completion date.[15]

As one example of the types of problem that currently exist, the FHWA's efforts to contain costs have not succeeded. As highlighted by a GAO report, cost growth on FHWA projects could not be determined because the FHWA's information system for highway projects could not track total costs over the life of a project.[16] In 2002, the GAO reported that this information was still not available and noted that recent congressional attempts to gather accurate information about project overruns had not been provided by the agency.[17] Amazingly, the FHWA acknowledged that it tracks project costs via use of an accounting system, when what is needed for multimillion dollar transportation projects is a sophisticated project management system.[18] In view of the fact that, as the FHWA certainly knows, most large infrastructure projects are performed under a series of linked contracts, the use of an accounting system is certainly an imperfect mechanism for achieving the business goal of preparing accurate estimates and monitoring ongoing construction costs.

If we are to succeed in reining in costs on infrastructure projects in the years ahead, while ensuring that we get the best value for the funding dispersed by the federal government, a national symposium of transportation and asset management experts should be convened to recommend the best tools and practices to enable our federal and state agencies to better monitor their infrastructure assets.

## A New Rating System for Our Nation's Bridges

Current methodologies that define the condition and ratings of the 600,000 bridges in the National Bridge Inventory (NBI) provide inadequate information for transportation authorities to prioritize the allocation of remediation funds. In addition to being subjected to regular condition inspections, all bridges are analyzed for their capacity to carry vehicular loads. Critical measurements needed to support these analyses are recorded during the bridge inspection process. Bridges that cannot safely carry heavy vehicles, such as some tractor-trailers, are posted with weight limits. Based upon inspection and load capacity analysis, any bridge deemed unsafe is to be closed.

Federal ratings, which utilize a scale of 1 to 9 (9 meaning in excellent condition and 5 meaning in fair condition), result from overall average condition assessments of a bridge's three or four major components. Bridges are considered "structurally deficient," according to the FHWA, if the condition rating of one of its major components is less than 5, the bridge has inadequate load capacity, or repeated bridge flooding causes traffic delays. The fact that a bridge is structurally deficient does not imply that it is unsafe or likely to collapse. However, as we have seen with the I-35W Bridge, that rating is a warning sign that closer examination is needed to determine if a bridge is safe for the traveling public.

As noted previously, a comprehensive study performed in 2001 by the FHWA highlighted the fact that visual-only inspections were largely unreliable. With regard to localized defects in superstructure members, the study found that "the overall accuracy rate for this group at correctly identifying crack indications was only less than 8.0 percent"[19] As noted above, Mark Bernhardt—an engineer who has participated in more than 3,000 bridge inspections and 160 load ratings—believes it is generally acknowledged within the engineering community that "visual inspection practices must be supported by rigorous training, certification and quality assurance programs, and supplemented with testing techniques to ensure reliable results."[20] The inability of inspectors to utilize advanced technology as a result of inadequate transportation funding almost guarantees that we can no longer be certain that bridge inspections identify the true condition of a bridge. Inadequate inspections also make it likely that our more seriously impaired bridges will fall into further disrepair. This, in turn, triggers massive additional repair costs instead of the much smaller ones that would have been needed if technology had been used to detect problems years earlier. Most significantly, the FHWA study enables us to conclude that current bridge ratings systems are largely inaccurate, that inspectors are not being given sufficient time to conduct inspections, and because ratings are improperly calculated, transportation agencies cannot take appropriate remedial action in a timely fashion.[21]

The FWHA, in conjunction with the American Association of State Highway and Transportation Officials (AASHTO), needs to prepare a new set of examples for bridge inspections, as well as new requirements for inspectors' hands-on experience. The agency should prepare formal programs—to be presented to all transportation agency personnel around the nation—that include visual presentations of precisely what inspectors should observe under situations ranging from the earliest detection of signs of wear and tear to the appearance of conditions that require a structurally deficient bridge to be reclassified as unsafe. Senior officials in state transportation agencies—even those who are not licensed engineers—should be required to attend these sessions and join their staffs on inspections to become personally acquainted with various bridge conditions, in an effort to improve their agencies' ratings of bridge conditions.

The most experienced engineers and inspectors must be identified and asked to share their understanding of how bridges work and how to apply engineering principles to aging infrastructure. This experience will translate into more comprehensive bridge manuals and working guidelines for ensuring that inspections accurately assess and track ongoing bridge conditions. In addition, mechanisms must be put in place to guide state transportation agencies in identifying critical deficiencies, in order to minimize costs and ensure the protection of the traveling public. Standardizing bridge ratings alone will not be sufficient.

Today's subjective rating system does not include triggers and thresholds that require federal and state transportation agencies to take immediate action when warranted. By simplifying and refining the current system used to document condition ratings, we would be able to coordinate the disbursement of federal funds with the rating system for bridges' conditions. Such coordination would ensure that defective bridges are repaired immediately, when the necessity arises.

Most important, the latest technology for condition assessment must be introduced and applied without delay. The federal government should set aside funding for making this technology available and training state transportation personnel in its use; the use of grant money merely to research available technologies should no longer be approved. The National Institute of Standards and Technology (NIST) should be authorized to develop programs for expanding the use of new generations of technology applicable to the early recognition of road and bridge deterioration. With the prompt adoption of such technology, experts estimate that we could save hundreds of millions of dollars in unneeded repairs and minimize the extent of repairs.

As noted earlier, in his testimony before Congress, Mark Bernhardt sets out a strong case why visual inspections are inadequate records of the true condition of structurally deficient or complex bridges. Like other experts, Bernhardt recommended the use of sensors and monitors connected to central servers, giving bridge owners the equivalent of a cardiograph for all critical structural members on a 24/7 basis.[22] The relevant commercial technology is readily available and only needs to be approved by state agencies to be put into use on a widespread basis.

If visual examination is as arbitrary and subjective as the FHWA study has shown, how can transportation agencies—and the people who travel across our nation's bridges—have confidence in the ratings given by these inspectors? Why do federal, state, and local bridge owners consistently refuse to introduce available technology to check out the details of a bridge's true condition, which inspectors acknowledge cannot be seen even at close range? How can our national transportation leaders not recognize the importance of gathering information into a central database that state and local transportation agencies can access, to determine how to protect and preserve their individual assets? And why do some federal agencies, such as NIST, provide millions of dollars in grant money to study the feasibility of such technology, thereby promoting the idea that it is still a work in progress, and not commercially available for immediate use? Indeed, the replacement for the collapsed I-35W bridge in Minneapolis used sophisticated modern technology, as discussed above.

Technology has become commonplace in virtually every aspect of our lives. The future health of our critical infrastructure can best be managed by the immediate implementation of structural health monitoring systems that provide transportation officials with immediate feedback on the structural integrity of our roads and bridges. This is a twenty-first-century need that is waiting to meet up with available twenty-first-century technology.

## A National Clearinghouse for Bridge Information

As Peter Vanderzee has said: "First and most importantly, subjective information simply cannot support objective decision-making. Visual inspection of bridge condition is simply not sufficient to support major financial investments. Multi-million dollar decisions should be supported by more objective information not 'eyeballs and estimates.'"[23]

In the aviation industry, one of the safest in the world, the Federal Aviation Administration (FAA) has long been a leader in collecting and communicating data on the quality and inspection results of all types of aircraft. When a problem arises in one type of aircraft, all the planes in that type are immediately grounded until they are recertified as safe in accordance with strict inspection standards. The existence of a central database for this information permits uniform standards for safety and ensures that airplanes meet maintenance requirements to keep the traveling public safe.

The fact that our nation does not have a similar centralized database for tracking the defects in and deterioration of our aging bridges, so that necessary corrective action can be taken immediately, is unacceptable. The 600,000 bridges in the NBI can be divided into types such as suspension or cable bridges, and then further subdivided into other categories. The FHWA has no current mechanism for identifying common characteristics within such categories of deterioration leading to failure, which could serve as an early warning system for every state and local transportation agency in the country. Such a system would allow the agencies to use such information to prioritize the repair and replacement of their bridge assets.

Here's what two experts have said about this issue: "While the inspections associated with this [NBIS] effort provided useful information about the nation's bridge inventory and their condition, it was insufficient to make reliable programmatic decisions in the face of dwindling funding dollars."[24] The federal government now requires asset management agencies to participate in a nationwide effort to coordinate the information to be gleaned from utilizing new technology, which will alert the agencies to problems at an early stage and save billions of dollars a year in federal and state funding. A national infrastructure database could be part of this initiative, suggesting a host of better ways to safely defer unnecessary repairs and replacements, drive life-cycle maintenance costs down, and safely extend the life of our aging roads and bridges.

In 1998, the FHWA created the Nondestructive Evaluation Center (NEC). The incentive for its development was the realization that visual inspections made by bridge inspectors and engineers across the nation as part of the annual inspections required by the National Bridge Inspection Standards (NBIS) left much to be desired. The new center was charged with determining what improvements were needed. It was designed to act as a resource for state transportation agencies, industry, and researchers concerned with the development and testing of innovative, nondestructive evaluation (NDE) technologies. The long-term goals of the center were to provide state transportation agencies with independent evaluation and validation of NDE technologies, develop new NDE technologies, and give states technical assistance in exploring the use of these technologies.[25] The NEC's report highlighted the fact that 60 percent of state respondents noted that a professional engineer conducted less than 40 percent of bridge inspections. For routine inspection tasks, the report noted a wide variability of condition rating assessments and observed that the ratings were generally not assigned in a systematic fashion. As a result of these findings, the report concluded that the current system for providing condition ratings "may not be refined enough to allow for reliable Routine Inspection results."[26]

With a national database, there would no longer be any uncertainty about what inspections should be performed across the country after a bridge failure anywhere in the nation. A national alert would go out immediately, urging transportation agencies to inspect all similarly designed or constructed bridges within their purview. Exchanges of information on engineering expertise needed to ensure a full range of consulting services for unusual types of inquiries would be centralized and furnished to transportation agencies of any size. Immediate warnings to close bridges in a type found to be in jeopardy would be forwarded from the centralized database, and information from follow-up investigations to ensure compliance and corrective work would be gathered and recorded there. Engineers would be able to easily learn from past design or construction errors as they designed tomorrow's new, improved roads and bridges.

Creating a national clearinghouse for the collection and widespread dissemination of information to transportation agencies about the different types, conditions, remedial alternatives, and inspections relevant to the vast number of bridges in our nation's infrastructure is long overdue.

### Improving the Role of the NTSB

Following the collapse of the I-35W Bridge in Minneapolis, the nation turned its attention to the investigation undertaken by the National Transportation Safety Board (NTSB) into the cause of the tragedy. The NTSB is an independent federal agency charged by Congress to investigate every civil aviation accident in the United States and significant accidents in the other modes of transportation—railroad, highway, marine, and pipeline. The NTSB also promulgates safety recommendations aimed at preventing future accidents.

The NTSB serves as an investigative and reporting agency, whose reports provide recommendations to other federal agencies, as opposed to an agency that has the ability to mandate needed changes when it comes to federal and state transportation agencies. Since its inception, the NTSB has issued numerous recommendations to federal agencies following its investigations of traffic accidents, airline crashes, road and bridge collapses, and other transportation incidents. However, its report on the I-35W Bridge collapse highlights in significant ways the importance of expanding the agency's charter so that it can play a larger role in protecting our fragile infrastructure and ensuring immediate corrective action to avoid future disasters.

The final NTSB Report on the I-35W Bridge noted that AASHTO had failed to advise state transportation agencies to include gusset plates as part of load rating inspections. It can be argued that gusset plates, as important connections, should have been specifically included in all bridge inspections, or at the very least as part of inspections of fracture-critical bridges. Following the I-35W Bridge collapse, the NTSB did recommend that states include gusset plates in future inspections. But why did neither the NTSB nor AASHTO recommend this after earlier bridge failures in which gusset plates were identified as a cause of failure?

What the NTSB report appears to have dismissed entirely was any responsibility on the part of the Minnesota Department of Transportation (MN/DOT). This exoneration is inexcusable, based on the maintenance history of the I-35W Bridge's extensive wear and tear, corrosion, and signs of incipient failure for many years prior to its collapse. Inspections dating back to 2001 (at least eight years after the bridge was first rated structurally deficient) by outside consultants had identified widespread corrosion and fatigue caused by weather and the volume of traffic that pounded at the bridge's fracture-critical members. Recognizing the fragility of the bridge's original fracture-critical design, consultants such as HNTB and URS—both of which had extensive analytical bridge experience—had stressed the need for added redundancy to strengthen the bridge and had pointed out that the safety factor would be very low in the event of a future unanticipated additional load.

The inspection completed by MN/DOT inspectors in June 2006—the last one before the bridge's collapse—found cracking and fatigue problems and gave the bridge a sufficiency rating of 50 percent. A rating of 50 percent or lower pursuant to federal standards is interpreted to mean that the bridge should be considered for replacement.

In December 2006, pursuant to the recommendation of URS, which had spent the better part of two years studying the bridge's critical members, the structure was scheduled to undergo a $1.5 million steel reinforcement project. However, MN/DOT chose to ignore all three of URS's proposed strengthening recommendations and cancelled the project, amid concerns that drilling for the retrofit could weaken the bridge. Instead, MN/DOT chose to implement a program of periodic inspections to monitor the bridge, a bizarre decision given that the structure was already subject to constant review as a fracture-critical bridge. Yet the NTSB reported none of these facts.

While bridge failures may result from a multitude of causes, they can generally be attributed to one or more of a defined group of causes. A bridge may have been badly designed, or weakened by being subjected to heavier loads and greater amounts of stress than it was designed to bear. In either of these cases, and even if a bridge has been well designed and properly used, it can also be weakened if inadequate maintenance allows the effects of ordinary wear and tear to develop into structural defects. As the era of the construction of the interstate system of highways and bridges gives way to the era of preventive maintenance, and as increasing traffic loads and over-sized vehicles continue to be the norm, bridge collapses and other failures have become common. In fact, more than 500 failures have been documented since 1989.

With the increasing number of bridge failures, NTSB's investigative teams have taken on an increasingly prominent role in determining the historical background and causes for each failure. The agency's reports have presented findings of fact in each case and have recommended future action by appropriate federal and state transportation agencies. And while the reports have been highly successful in alerting the aviation industry to critical changes affecting it, the impact of the NTSB on our roads and bridges has been less successful, even as they deteriorate further with each passing year.

Just as important as a central clearinghouse for information on the status of our nation's 600,000 bridges is a federally chartered agency to analyze each bridge failure, put it into historical perspective to help prevent similar failures in the future, and disseminate the information to federal, state, and local bridge owners. In the final analysis, engineers are only as good as the sum of the experience they and those who came before them have acquired, along with the personal and professional judgment they bring to each project. They need to know about bridge failures that took place centuries ago, and they must address the challenge of designing new and better ways to make today's structures strong—all the while realizing that each advance represents embarking on a journey into the uncharted waters of innovation. As Henry Petroski so sagely noted: "Emulating success risks failure; studying failure increases our chances of success."[27]

Despite the Silver Bridge collapse in 1967 and several other major failures, the dissemination of information to state and local bridge agencies in order to avoid similar disasters has been less than successful. Highlighting this shortcoming was the notable failure of the NTSB and the FHWA to translate the lessons learned from these events into FAA-type directives that required state and local bridge owners to certify that they were following up on the investigative findings of the NTSB. That agency's investigations of the collapses of the Mianus River Bridge in Connecticut in 1983 and the Grand River Bridge in Ohio in 1996 are most instructive. The failure of the Grand River Bridge was caused by deterioration of the structure's gusset plates. If the NTSB had required owners of similar bridges to inspect their gusset plates, MN/DOT officials would have realized that the bowing of the plates shown in photographs taken in 1999 and 2003 was a sign of incipient failure and could have prevented the tragic collapse of the I-35W Bridge.

A careful reading of the history of analogous bridge failures during the years following construction of the I-35W Bridge reveals that (1) there was a nationwide recognition that fracture-critical bridges required more care and inspection than more modern bridges, designed to include redundancies in case a critical structural member should fail; (2) MN/DOT failed to revise the bridge's load ratings because of the addition of new lanes or the substantial increase in the size and number of vehicles that crossed the bridge over the years; (3) when the bridge was rated structurally deficient due to an identifiable lack of maintenance, MN/DOT failed to use federal funding for a higher level of maintenance to improve the bridge's rating; and

(4) during the years when the funding needed to redress the causes that placed the bridge at risk of failure was not available from either the federal or state government, MN/DOT failed to acknowledge the serious nature of the bridge's problems and demand that state leaders find the money to correct the problems before tragedy struck. The NTSB report addressed none of these facts.

All of the above raises some key questions. Why has no federal agency been charged with carrying out the lessons learned from the major bridge failures of the past half-century? Why are the recommendations of the NTSB sent to state and local transportation agencies without concomitant mandates that immediate action be taken to identify similar circumstances around the nation? Why hasn't the public been advised that there are currently 7,980 U.S. bridges that are both structurally deficient and fracture-critical, and in as much danger of failing as the I-35W Bridge did? How can federal officials read about the NTSB findings in the collapses of the Mianus River and Grand River Bridges and not fault MN/DOT officials for not having learned the lessons of those tragedies—or for not even being aware of these prior failures?

Congress should require either the NTSB or the FHWA to immediately mandate the relevant inspections and corrective measures on similar bridges after a bridge has failed, and to ensure that bridge owners comply immediately where necessary, or at the very least in a timely fashion. Bridge owners must be required to acknowledge receipt of such instructions and supply a clear statement of the specific information they gleaned from the new inspections and what steps they will take if corrective action is warranted. The traveling public deserves no less.

Although that last suggestion goes beyond the current purview of the NTSB, and even the FHWA, it nevertheless is only practical in light of the perilous state of our bridge inventory. As mentioned earlier, our nation has experienced nearly 600 bridge failures in the twenty years since 1989. Over 150,000 bridges on the National Bridge Inventory are rated structurally deficient or functionally obsolete. There are 7,980 structurally deficient and fracture-critical bridges, many of them weakened and moved closer to failure by years of inadequate maintenance. No engineer would take issue with the fact that many of these bridges are as close to collapse as the I-35W Bridge was in the years leading up to its failure.

As a result of these ineluctable facts, and until major efforts are taken to remediate the condition of our fragile bridges, the Federal Emergency Management Agency, in conjunction with the Department of Homeland Security and all fifty state transportation agencies, should be required to conduct mock disaster emergency drills, rehearsing the actions that the government of one state and the nation will undoubtedly be required to take when the next bridge failure occurs. By going through the precise steps that simulate a bridge collapse involving the death of dozens of people in cars that fall a hundred feet or more, along with injuries to hundreds of other people, as well as being forced to confront the massive cost of restoring traumatized communities, transportation officials as well as federal and state politicians will be forced to recognize the impending nature of the tragedies that could be avoided by immediately funding the addition of structural support to all of the nation's fracture-critical bridges and attending in due course to the remediation of our other neglected bridges.

## A New Federal Commission on Infrastructure Remediation

Throughout our nation's history, we have always been able to marshal the intellectual resources of our best and brightest to identify needed solutions to our problems. Today it is time for us to gather the transportation world's best and brightest to find ways to upgrade our deteriorating infrastructure.

Our nation lacks a defined national transportation policy that outlines goals similar to those that President Eisenhower laid out for the interstate highway system in the 1950s. In that case, the federal government became the strategic planner of a nationwide (as opposed to a state-focused) system of roads, funded predominantly by a gasoline tax imposed by the federal government. Now, however, our national infrastructure is strangled by politicians' annual distribution of hundreds of billions of dollars for transportation funding within their state borders without regard to ongoing remediation.

Why do we need a coordinated national, as opposed to local, transportation strategy?

Just as we once stopped relying chiefly on railroads to move passengers and freight, now we need to reconfigure our freight networks, ports, and airports so that they all work together as parts of an international transportation and commerce system, joined by a state-of-the-art, high-speed rail network. In comparison to many other developed nations, in some ways we are a true "third world country, that is saddled with outdated infrastructure that screams out for updating."[28] At present, by generally accepted parameters, the federal government has moved away from acting as the coordinator of a national strategy for developing and remediating our nation's infrastructure. In fact, only in a series of speeches by the former secretary of transportation, Mary Peters—who championed the need for public-private partnerships to fund transportation projects throughout the nation—can we see a federal official expressing a broad view of national infrastructure policy.

As Robert Puentes of the Brookings Institution stated in 2008: "The federal transportation system lacks any overarching vision, goals, or guidance."[29] Without that leadership, transportation policy will be fractured and governed only as a series of fiefdoms controlled at the state level, without any consideration for regional and national imperatives that impact our freight, railroad, airport, national security, or environmental programs—all of which should, in the best interests of the nation, be viewed from a federal perspective.

What would a national transportation strategy look like? Much as the canals and railroads built during the nineteenth century led to the advances in communication and commerce that grew our nation exponentially, continued U.S. economic growth is becoming increasingly dependent on how we choose to plan for it over the next thirty to fifty years. During this first half of the twenty-first century, our country will grow by over 100 million people. We will build over "427 billion square feet" of new and rehabilitated homes, offices, hospitals, hotels, and schools, as well as roads, bridges, and airports in places not on the map today.[30] We have gone from a mostly rural to a largely urban society. Our near-total reliance on the automobile has placed an inordinate stress on roads into, out of, and around metropolitan areas, which has led to unprecedented congestion. The major metropolitan areas contain almost 60 percent of the total U.S. population, yet they have over 85 percent of three critical transportation signifiers: traffic congestion, transit ridership, and population exposure to auto-related air pollution.[31]

Without "overarching vision, goals, or guidance," we will inevitably make mistakes in the planning and execution of future transportation development that will cost our nation dearly. It is essential that we recognize the full importance of our largest metropolitan areas, which account for a major portion of our transportation needs. Although our nation is not totally comprised of cities, neither is it chiefly rural. Yet our transportation funding is managed as if the roads and bridges in the most sparsely populated places in our nation are just as critical to our commercial interests as urban roads and bridges. Accordingly, we need to develop a framework for a national policy on transportation that links our metropolitan areas, redesign needed flows of goods and traffic to minimize congestion, and allocates funding where it can best be used to meet national as well as regional objectives.

Such an approach would not hurt rural Americans. On the contrary, it turns out that half of those who live in rural areas actually live within the boundaries of identifiable metropolitan areas. We need to redefine the relationship between Washington and these areas in order to improve the interstate transfer of goods from ports to highways into metropolitan areas, where such commerce is coming to a standstill. We need the federal government to create agencies equivalent to regional Federal Reserve Banks, which would monitor transportation needs in each region of the country and make needed adjustments when imbalances in the national marketplace occur. These regional transportation agencies would be able to lobby for new, high-speed rail lines to connect growing population centers or to ensure that needed remediation funding is provided in a timely fashion for roads and bridges that transport the most traffic on multistate commuting, rail, and freight routes. Current statistics show that these transportation networks are becoming truly inefficient, which argues that we must begin to develop these regional transportation centers within the next few years.

How would a national transportation strategy spur innovation? Urging Washington to work with private enterprise and regional partners would spur substantial additional investment and maximize the impetus for greater innovation. As is readily apparent, current transportation policies do not provide substantial incentives for technological innovation. We build the same way today as we did hundreds of years ago, and the notorious inefficiencies of the construction industry and its nearly total failure to use available technology cost our nation's economy over $120 billion a year, as noted above. We fail to use available technology to identify the first signs of deficiencies in roads, bridges, and tunnels, which has led to the geometric explosion of additional costs for remediating our infrastructure.

By empowering state and regional transportation agencies to invest more smartly in building and maintaining their infrastructure assets, we would encourage greater private investment in ways that would give investors the incentive to use the most modern technologies. Demanding that bidders for PPP projects show how they would implement the latest technologies as a part of their proposals would create a competitive environment that would spur innovation in the traditionally moribund world of the transportation industry.

To oversee a national transportation strategy, we need a national infrastructure commission. This new group should include our most experienced transportation experts, finance experts, engineers, and scientists, who would be asked to define the nation's needs during the twenty-first century from a host of perspectives. It would propose ways to restore the most vulnerable 50 percent of our infrastructure stock to health. It would identify the latest in structural analyses and methodologies to determine if a bridge, tunnel, or highway is dangerously defective. It would assign qualified engineers and contractors to develop both a full remediation and an ongoing maintenance program; determine the actual cost needed to repair each structure; and ensure that qualified contractors with successful track records for on-time performance perform all work under true fixed-price contracts.

As a nonpartisan group, the commission would be charged with identifying the structures most critically in need of corrective work and publicizing that list to the general public. It would have full authority to secure previously authorized funding to oversee the work and would ensure that it was carried out on time and on a cost-effective basis.

The federal government would pay 90 percent of the costs of this corrective work, and the state or local infrastructure owner would be responsible for the remaining 10 percent. These funds could not be diverted to any project not on the commission's list of most urgent projects. Where appropriate, any tolls or other revenue-generating measures recoverable from such projects would be redistributed to the federal government and the owner in the same proportion that they paid for the costs.

In addition, the new commission would be charged with coordinating large-scale projects, such as ports, airports, high-speed rail lines, power grids, and multistate transportation programs, working with the often competing interests that are involved in these projects. Too often, as Ehrlich and Rohatyn pointed out, such projects can be held hostage by the "iron triangle" of lobbyists, Congress, and a host of bureaucrats who have learned to game the system by manipulating government agencies such as the Highway Trust Fund and the Army Corps of Engineers.[32] As increasing numbers of large infrastructure projects impact other modes of transportation, the commission will act as a coordinating overseer to ensure that no competing interests that arise will be permitted to dilute or eliminate worthy programs. For example, an expansion to the port of Long Beach, California, or a new international airport in Providence, Rhode Island, where heavily trafficked interstate highways merge, would certainly need an infrastructure coordinating agency to unravel the disparate interests that would undoubtedly arise during the planning and funding phases for such projects.

The new commission would be empowered to raise capital, issue tax credit bonds, provide grants and loans, and give loan guarantees for states and local governments seeking approval for large infrastructure projects. Rating the viability of these projects would include attention to payback provisions, as well as allocated funding through the life of the facility for the maintenance required to ensure that the asset's value will remain high for decades to come.

Finally, we need to ensure that a national transportation policy mandates the need to hold state and local recipients of federal funding to higher standards of financial accountability. Spurred by the legislation of the past two decades, federal transportation policy has largely abdicated its role as overseer of how states spend the federal funds they receive. Greater transparency in the use of such money would go a long way to restoring the public's faith that earmarks and so-called bridges to nowhere will become relics of a politicians-gone-wild past. We can no longer afford a federal government that boldly authorizes billions for transportation projects, yet glibly ignores how such monies are spent.

In the absence of a national infrastructure commission and a national transportation policy, we will continue our profligate ways, ensuring that trillions of dollars for the remediation of our roads, bridges, and other aging infrastructure will be misspent, driving up the cost for future generations, while politicians at all levels of government continue to use the public purse for their own agendas.

## Restoring the Engineering Profession to Its Traditional Role

In no small part, the inability of our nation's engineers to play a larger role in transportation infrastructure policy has been a major reason for the profession's decline over the past few decades. Today the engineer toiling in the public sector must juggle the competing interests of honoring his or her professional oath while completing projects with political and economic constraints.

This is because everyone in the transportation sector is aware of the financial constraints that limit the alternatives available to fixing our ailing infrastructure. How else to characterize the fumbling efforts of MN/DOT officials and employees who testified following the I-35W Bridge collapse about the need to put off clearly warranted remediation for the bridge to 2017 and beyond? One MN/DOT official was strikingly candid when he publicly stated that because labels such as "intolerable" and "deficient" alarm the public, experts reassuringly say that the labels don't necessarily mean a bridge is unsafe. This same official, Dan Dorgan, MN/DOT's chief engineer, probably would have made similarly reassuring statements regarding the I-35W Bridge in the weeks and months prior to its collapse.[33]

Restoring the engineers in our transportation system to positions where they can exercise their professional judgment free of political or financial constraints is a critical step toward ensuring that work on our most deteriorated roads and bridges is performed according to their needs, rather than treating all infrastructure equally. Engineers tend to be conservative in how they design the structures they work on. They are taught how to factor in margins of safety and, above all else, to protect the health and welfare of the public. Yet engineers are also mindful of the culture and political mind-set of the corporation, institution, or governmental entity for which they work. And if that organization works closely with state transportation departments that are strapped for funding, the message that engineers receive is clearly one of "don't rock the boat."

If an engineering firm's clientele is comprised largely of governmental agencies whose budgetary limitations will not permit a full range of needed corrective actions or alternatives to be performed, then the risk exists that compromise remedies taken in light of such restrictions will be more risky, though less costly. While there is nothing wrong with pursuing a wide range of less costly alternatives, when engineers in public service allow financial constraints to affect their judgment as to what is right and wrong, then public safety may be compromised.

The engineers who currently oversee remediation of the 150,000 U.S. bridges that are rated structurally deficient or functionally obsolete are aware that in every year that these bridges receive only cosmetic attention or no attention at all, they move one step closer to failure. These engineers would be hard-pressed to provide assurances that the 7,980 bridges that are both fracture-critical and structurally deficient[34] are safe for the traveling public. Why? Because they understand the limitations of bridge design and the many unknown factors regarding these bridges. Without technology that monitors such bridges and gives early warning of any threats to a structural member, without technology that can identify the extent of fractures that can spontaneously cause failure of a critical structural member, no engineer can claim to know whether a bridge built fifty or seventy-five years earlier will fail in the near future. Any engineer would admit that it's a possibility. But the public is not told of this, nor will any inspection report hint at it.

Increasingly, the engineers in our state transportation departments have been marginalized, moved further from the public eye, and replaced by budget specialists or political appointees with no engineering backgrounds. Engineering decisions should be left to engineers, whose judgment and experience must be allowed to come to the fore as our aging roads and bridges reach an even more critical state in the years ahead. The inadequate amount of funding for remediation is, and will be for the near future, an important element in how we address this serious problem. But financial concerns should not outweigh the professional judgments of the engineers who are the true stewards of our transportation system, and who are charged with protecting the welfare of the traveling public.

Our nation has found the money needed to fix the levees in New Orleans and Mississippi only after they were devastated by Hurricane

Katrina. Congress immediately provided nearly $300 million to re-place the I-35W Bridge with a state-of-the-art structure, after MN/DOT had decided to defer needed replacement of the original bridge's deck for a decade or longer. Today, we need to race to ensure that every one of the remaining 18,857 fracture-critical bridges in this nation are given needed redundancy. No engineer working on these bridges would recommend anything less, were funding available. Engineers must prove themselves capable of returning to their role of master builder and accepting the responsibilities that follow. They have been pushed aside for too long. In turn, we must learn to trust in their judgment and experience and not let it be compromised by budgetary constraints.

In an op-ed piece for the *New York Times* in October 2008, David Brooks drew attention to the many ways that conventional decision-making processes affecting our nation's financial management have gone awry, leading to the collapse of our economy. He pointed out that most decisions require that we first perceive a problem, next consider possible solutions, and calculate which is best, before proceeding to act. When it came to our financial systems, that standard approach failed, and even the oracle of the economic world, Federal Reserve Chairman Alan Greenspan, acknowledged that he was shocked that the financial markets did not work as economists had expected.

Brooks called for altering the way we address problems, switching from a reliance on rational calculation and reassessing how we per-ceive problems in the first place. But he warned that perceiving a situ-ation, while seemingly a simple operation, begins a process that in-cludes perceptual biases, which tend to distort our thinking. He cited the writings of Nassim Nicholas Taleb, who warned in *The Black Swan* about, as Brooks put it, the "tendency to see data that confirm our prejudices more vividly than data that contradict them; our tendency to overvalue recent events when anticipating future possibilities; our tendency to spin concurring facts into a single causal narrative." But Brooks strikes his most strident note about problem solving when he notes that "government officials are probably going to be even worse perceivers of reality than private business types. Their information feedback mechanism is more limited, and, being deeply politicized, they're even more likely to filter inconvenient facts."[35]

It is easy to see how officials in state transportation agencies, faced with a massive shortfall in funding and the urgent need for corrective action on thousands of roads and bridges, would misperceive the importance of relying upon their experienced teams of professional engineers, who must be free to make decisions free from political or financial constraint.

It is long past time to return the engineering profession to its rightful place as the independent ombudsman for our nation's infrastructure. Promoting such a change should be various groups, including the American Society of Professional Engineers, AASHTO, members of Congress, and state transportation commissioners—all of whom should prefer to see the responsibility for fixing our national infrastructure crisis placed squarely upon the one group that can address the crisis dispassionately, and without the need to do what is politically expedient.

We can no longer afford to ignore the fact that we are in the midst of a transportation funding crisis, which has been exacerbated by an even larger and longer-term problem: how we choose to invest in our infrastructure. It is not difficult to imagine the serious consequences that will unfold if we fail to address the deplorable condition of our bridges and roads, including the increasingly higher costs we will pay for the goods and services that rely on that transportation network, and a concomitant reduction in our standard of living. We can no longer afford to treat our all-important infrastructure system as a second- or third-tier priority. Not only is public safety at risk, but by inaction, we are greatly increasing the risk of jeopardizing our national destiny and damaging the heritage we will leave for generations to come. Failure is no longer an option.

# Notes

## Introduction

1. U.S. Department of Transportation, Research and Innovative Technology Administration, Bureau of Transportation Statistics, "Condition of U.S. Highway Bridges by State: 2008 (as of March 2009)" (http://www.bts .gov/current_topics/2009_03_18_bridge_data/html/bridges_by_state.html, accessed March 23, 2010).

2. Affiliated with Texas A&M University, the Texas Transportation Institute is an agency of the state of Texas that since 1950 has provided research and reports on highway, air, water, rail, and pipeline transportation issues.

3. Gary S. Becker, "The Infrastructure 'Crisis' Once Again," the Becker-Posner blog, August 26, 2007 (http://www.becker-posner-blog.com/archives/ 2007/08/the_infrastruct.html, accessed May 1, 2009).

4. Quoted in Clifford D. May, "Board Faults Thruway Unit on Collapse," *New York Times*, 27 April 27 1988 (http://www.nytimes.com/1988/04/27/ny region/board-faults-thruway-unit-on-collapse.html?pagewanted=all, accessed March 23, 2010).

5. Edward V. Regan, "Holding Government Officials Accountable for Infrastructure Maintenance," *Proceedings of the Academy of Political Science 37*, no. 3 (1989).

6. George E. Peterson, "Financing the Nation's Infrastructure Requirements," in *Perspectives on Urban Infrastructure*, edited by Royce Hanson (Washington: National Academy Press, 1984), 130.

## 1. A Tale of Two Bridges

1. Quoted in William D. Eggers and John O'Leary, *If We Can Put a Man on the Moon: Getting Big Things Done in Government* (Boston: Harvard Business School Press, 2009), 138.

2. Kumalasari Wardhana and Fabian C. Hadipriono, "Analysis of Recent Bridge Failures in the United States," *Journal of Performance of Constructed Facilities 17*, no. 3 (August 2003): 144–50.

3. Gray Plant Mooty, "Investigative Report to Joint Committee to Investigate the I-35W Bridge Collapse," May 2008 (http://www.commissions.leg

.state.mn.us/jbc/GPM_Report/InvestigativeReport.pdf, accessed September 9, 2008), 3. Hereinafter cited as Gray Plant Mooty, *Investigative Report*.

4. See Charles Seim, "Why Bridges Have Failed throughout History," *Civil Engineering* 78, no. 5 (May 2008): 66–67.

5. John Brandon, "A Bridge That Monitors Itself," *Popular Science*, October 16, 2008 (http://www.popsci.com/john-brandon/article/2008-10/bridge-monitors-itself, accessed March 16, 2010). According to the data contained in the 2009 National Bridge Inventory and analyzed by Steven Chase, formerly of the FHWA, there are 18,857 bridges that require a fracture-critical inspection (U.S. Department of Transportation, Federal Highway Administration, "Deficient Bridges by State and Highway System" [http://www.fhwa.dot.gov/bridge/deficient.cfm accessed March 4, 2010]).

6. *Bridge 9340, I-35W Over Mississippi River, Fatigue Evaluation and Redundancy Analysis, Draft Report*, URS Corporation, July 2006, p. 2–15.

7. The "design load" of a bridge represents the amount of "dead load" (the physical weight of the bridge) plus its expected "live load" (the anticipated load of the traffic to be borne by the bridge) plus a factor of safety built into the design to handle unexpected contingencies.

8. Don North, "What Could Make the Skyway Bridge Fall Down?" *St. Petersburg Times*, June 4, 1978 (reprinted at http://news.google.com/newspapers?nid=1346&dat=19800513&id=fdEvAAAAIBAJ&sjid=5P0DAAAAIBAJ&pg=6786,5047958, accessed February 22, 2010).

9. Richard A. Walther and Steven B. Chase, "Condition Assessment of Highway Structures: Past, Present, and Future," in Transportation Research Board of the National Academies, Structures Section, *50 Years of Interstate Structures: Past, Present, and Future* (Transportation Research Circular E-C104, September 2006, http://onlinepubs.trb.org/onlinepubs/circulars/ec104.pdf, accessed June 23, 2009), 69. Hereinafter cited as Walther and Chase, "Condition Assessment."

10. Joseph E. Krajewski, "Bridge Inspection and Interferometry" (master's thesis, Worcester Polytechnic Institute, 2006), 11–12. Hereinafter cited as Krajewski, "Bridge Inspection," 22.

11. Ibid., 24.

12. Ibid., 23–24.

13. National Transportation Safety Board, *Highway Accident Report: Collapse of the U.S. 43 Chickasawbogue Bridge Spans near Mobile, Alabama, April 24,*

1985, Washington: U.S. National Transportation Safety Board, 1986, (http://openlibrary.org/b/OL17833256M/Highway_accident_report, accessed March 22, 2010).

14. Ibid., 4.

15. Ibid.

16. National Transportation Safety Board, *Highway Accident Report: Collapse of the I-35W Highway Bridge, Minneapolis, Minnesota, August 1, 2007*, 2008 (http://www.ntsb.gov/publictn/2008/HAR0803.pdf, accessed January 22, 2009), 134. Hereinafter cited as NTSB, *I-35W Bridge.*

17. The weight of an empty 747–400 is approximately 395,000 pounds. The weight of a fully loaded 747–400, which carries between 416 and 524 passengers, is 875,000 pounds. See (http://www.boeing.com/commercial/747family/pf/pf_400_prod.html, accessed on August 7, 2009). The Gray Plant Mooty report observed that NTSB's calculation of the weight distribution on the bridge when it collapsed showed that the total weight of the aggregate and construction equipment in the closed southbound lanes (578,735 pounds) represented approximately 82 percent of the total weight (700,485 pounds) on the center (main) span of the bridge (Gray Plant Mooty, *Investigative Report,* 71). See also the NTSB chart at http://www.ntsb.gov/dockets/Highway/HWY 07MH024/default.htm, accessed March 22, 2010).

18. NTSB, *I-35W Bridge,* 150.

19. "Contributing to the design error was the failure of [design firm] Sverdrup & Parcel's quality control procedures to ensure that the appropriate main truss gusset plate calculations were performed for the I-35W Bridge and the inadequate design review by Federal and State transportation officials. Contributing to the accident was the generally accepted practice among Federal and State transportation officials of giving inadequate attention to gusset plates during inspections for conditions of distortion, such as bowing, and of excluding gusset plates in load rating analyses" (NTSB, *I-35W Bridge,* 152).

20. Jim Carlson, "An Engineer's View on the NTSB Findings," news release, January 25, 2008 (http://www.senate.leg.state.mn.us/members/member_pr _display.php?ls=86&id=1357, accessed March 23, 2010).

21. This listing included all bridges longer than twenty feet on all public roads.

22. Abba G. Lichtenstein, "The Silver Bridge Collapse Recounted," *Journal of Performance of Constructed Facilities* 7, no. 4 (November 1993): 249–50.

23. MN/DOT *Bridge Inspection Manual*, 6. Hereinafter cited as MNDOT, *Manual*.

24. Ibid.

25. MNDOT, *Manual*, Section 3.7.11.

26. Theodore V. Galambos, *The Safety of Bridges*, in National Academy of Engineering, *The Bridge*, Vol. 38, No. 2 (Summer 2008), 23.

27. Raymond Hartle, *Bridge Inspector's Training Manual/90*, rev. ed. (Washington: U.S. Department of Transportation, 1995), 21.

28. AASHTO, Manual for Condition Evaluation of Bridges, 2nd ed. 2003 (interim, single user digital publication).

29. Raymond Hartle, *Bridge Inspector's Training Manual/90*, rev. ed. (Washington: U.S. Department of Transportation, 1995), 21; MNDOT *Manual*, 70.

30. Quoted in Gray Plant Mooty, *Investigative Report*, 35.

31. Ibid., 45–46.

32. Ibid., 26.

33. Heather M. O'Connell, Robert J. Dexter, and Paul Bergson, *Fatigue Evaluation of the Deck Truss of Bridge 9340: Final Report* (St. Paul, Minn.: Minnesota Department of Transportation, March 2001; http://www.lrrb.org/pdf/200110.pdf, accessed March 22, 2010), 4.

34. Quoted in Gray Plant Mooty, *Investigative Report*, 27.

35. Ibid., 57–58.

36. Ibid., 27.

37. URS Corporation, "Fatigue Evaluation and Redundancy Analysis Draft Report for Bridge #9340," prepared for MN/DOT January 2007, 6.

38. HNTB Corporation, "Proposal to MN/DOT," October 2001, attachment C, "Estimate of Hours and Costs."

39. Gray Plant Mooty, *Investigative Report*, 28.

40. Gray Plant Mooty, *Investigative Report*, 60 (emphasis in original).

41. Ibid., 60, citing Dorgan's comments on URS's preliminary report.

42. Ibid., 65.

43. Ibid., 63.

44. Quoted in ibid., 64–65.

45. Ibid., 46–47.

46. Quoted in ibid., 65–66.

47. Ibid.

48. Internal MNDOT e-mail, quoted in ibid., 67.

49. Ibid., 68.

50. Referring to the conditions at the time of the collapse, Wiss, Janney, Elstner Associates, Inc. (WJE), the consultant hired by MnDOT to do a detailed investigation in conjunction with that being performed by the NTSB, stated: "The dead load carried by the critical elements, both at the time of the collapse and in the previous years, represented a large fraction of available capacity. Therefore, small changes in strength, such as those associated with static versus dynamic loading, would cause a relatively large change in load capacity. Conversely, the static nature of the construction loads made them significantly more severe than moving loads of a comparable magnitude" (Wiss, Janney, Elstner Associates, *I-35W Bridge over the Mississippi River: Collapse Investigation; Bridge 9340, Minneapolis, Minnesota* (Northbrook, Ill.: Wiss, Janney, Elstner Associates, November 2008; http://www.ntsb.gov/dockets/Highway/HWY07MH024/404995.pdf, accessed March 22, 2010), 154.

51. Pam Louwagie, James Walsh, and Paul McEnroe, "Should This Bridge Be Open?" Minneapolis-St. Paul *Star Tribune*, August 11, 2007 (http://www.startribune.com/local/11593656.html, accessed December 29, 2008).

52. Ibid.

53. New York City Department of Transportation, "Frequently Asked Questions" (http://www.nyc.gov/html/dot/html/faqs/faqs_bridge.shtml, accessed June 8, 2009).

54. Ross Sandler and Samuel I. Schwartz, *Spanning the 21st Century: Reconstructing a World Class Bridge Program* (New York: New York City Department of Transportation, 1988), 23.

55. Richard Levine and Kirk Johnson, "Chronicle of City's Neglect of Williamsburg Bridge," *New York Times*, June 10, 1988.

56. For more on the scandal, see Jack Newfield and Wayne Barrett, *City for Sale: Ed Koch and the Betrayal of New York* (New York: Harper and Row, 1988).

57. Mo Sharif, "Protecting New York City's Bridge Assets," *Public Roads*, May–June 2005 (http://www.tfhrc.gov/pubrds/05may/06.htm, accessed December 3, 2008).

58. Interviews with Sam Schwartz, September 25, 2008, and November 19, 2008.

59. Williamsburg Bridge Technical Advisory Committee, "Summary Report to the Commissioners of Transportation of the City and State of New

York," June 30, 1988, 3. I have drawn on the report for several of the details in this account.

60. Steinman, Boynton, Gronquist & Birdsall, which Blair Birdsall joined in 1964, was the successor firm to Robinson & Steinman, founded in 1921 by Holton D. Robinson (1863–1945), who served as assistant engineer in charge of cable construction on the Williamsburg Bridge, and the legendary D. B. Steinman (1886–1960). Steinman, whose crowning achievement was the Mackinac Bridge connecting the upper and lower peninsulas of Michigan, worked as a young man alongside Othmar H. Ammann (1879–1965), the designer of the George Washington, Verrazano-Narrows, and Bayonne Bridges. Both Steinman and Ammann were then in the employ of Gustav Lindenthal (1850–1935), who succeeded L. L. Buck as chief engineer of the Williamsburg Bridge in 1902, served as New York City's commissioner of bridges in 1902–3, and designed the Hell Gate Bridge that connects the Astoria neighborhood of Queens with Randall's Island in the East River. Blair Birdsall died in 1997 at the age of ninety.

61. Interview with Sam Schwartz, March 10, 2008.

62. This condition would be deemed by some engineering consultants to be a contributory cause to the failure of the I-35W Bridge.

63. Richard Levine and Kirk Johnson, "Chronicle of City's Neglect of Williamsburg Bridge," *New York Times*, June 10, 1988.

64. Sarah Lyall, "The Williamsburg Bridge Is Shut for 2 Weeks as Cracks Are Found," *New York Times*, April 13, 1988 (http://www.nytimes.com/1988/04/13/nyregion/the-williamsburg-bridge-is-shut-for-2-weeks-as-cracks-are-found.html?pagewanted=1, accessed March 22, 2010).

## 2. Following the Money

1. Quoted in Laurie Blake, Paul McEnroe, Pat Doyle, and Tony Kennedy, "MNDOT Feared Cracking in Bridge but Opted against Making Repairs," *Minneapolis-St. Paul Star Tribune*, August 3, 2007 (http://www.startribune.com/local/11593616.html, accessed August 2, 2009). The Gray Plant Mooty report states: "Both current and former MNDOT employees universally expressed the view that the Department would not allow the condition of a bridge to jeopardize the safety of the public; when a high risk situation becomes known, MNDOT will remove that risk without regard to cost or other implications. We found no reason to challenge the veracity of this assertion with re-

gard to a clear and immediate danger. We did find instances, however, where cost was a factor in determining courses of action with respect to the Bridge at points in time when immediate risk was not obvious" (Gray Plant Mooty, *Investigative Report*, 30–31).

2. Quoted in Mike Kaszuba and Laurie Blake, "As State Money Diminished, So Did Goals for Bridge Safety," *Minneapolis-St. Paul Star Tribune*, August 16, 2007 (http://www.startribune.com/local/11552281.html?elr=KArks:DCiUHc3E7_V _nDaycUiacyKUUr, accessed August 3, 2009).

3. American Society of Civil Engineers, *Report Card for America's Infrastructure*, 2009, (http://www.infrastructurereportcard.org/sites/default/files/RC2009_ full_report.pdf, accessed August 3, 2009), Table B, 7.

4. David Levinson, "Case Study: Road Pricing in Practice," California PATH Research Report, November 1997 (http://escholarship.org/uc/item/ 0w06s4n2?query=Case Study, accessed March 23, 2010).

5. Ellis L. Armstrong, Michael C. Robinson, and Suellen M. Hoy, [eds.], *History of Public Works in the United States, 1776–1976* (Chicago: American Public Works Association, 1976), 55–67.

6. Owen D. Gutfreund, *Twentieth-Century Sprawl: Highways and the Reshaping of the American Landscape* (New York: Oxford University Press, 2004), 20.

7. Kenneth T. Jackson, *Crabgrass Frontier: The Suburbanization of the United States* (New York: Oxford University Press, 1985), 167.

8. Owen D. Gutfreund, *Twentieth-Century Sprawl*, 143, 155, and 157.

9. Quoted in Richard F. Weingroff, "June 29, 1956: A Day in History" (http://www.fhwa.dot.gov/interstate/thisday.htm, accessed March 13, 2010).

10. Owen D. Gutfreund, *Twentieth-Century Sprawl*, 57.

11. Philip Dearborne, quoted in Heywood T. Sanders, "Politics and Urban Public Facilities," in Royce Hanson, ed., *Perspectives on Urban Infrastructure* (Washington: National Academy Press, 1984), 170.

12. Kenneth T. Jackson, *Crabgrass Frontier*, 163.

13. Ibid., 164.

14. Owen D. Gutfreund, *Twentieth-Century Sprawl*, 16–17 (emphasis in original).

15. As noted above, from the time it was instituted in 1932 until the creation of the Highway Trust Fund for financing the construction of the interstate highway system, revenues from the federal gasoline tax went into the federal government's general fund rather than being set aside for highway-related expenditures.

16. By this time, Moses had enacted state legislation authorizing him to collect tolls on the many new roads and bridges he had built through his powerful Triborough Bridge Authority (Robert A. Caro, *The Power Broker: Robert Moses and the Fall of New York* [New York: Vintage Books, 1975], 634).

17. Owen D. Gutfreund, *Twentieth-Century Sprawl*, 39.

18. Mark H. Rose, *Interstate: Express Highway Politics 1939–1989*," rev. ed. (Knoxville: University of Tennessee Press, 1990), 42.

19. On the battle over toll versus toll-free highways, see ibid., 37–56.

20. Ibid., 58.

21. Richard F. Weingroff, "Origins of the Interstate Maintenance Program" (http://www.fhwa.dot.gov/infrastructure/intmaint.cfm, accessed March 4, 2009). Hereinafter cited as Weingroff, "Origins."

22. Committee on Transportation and Infrastructure, U.S. House of Representatives, "Report to Accompany H.R. 3999," July 10, 2008, 5. Hereinafter cited as Committee on Transportation and Infrastructure, "Report."

23. Congress of the United States, *New Directions for the Nation's Public Works* (Washington: Congressional Budget Office, September 1988), 2.

24. Fred W. Frailey, "America's Highways Going to Pot," *U.S. News & World Report*, July 24, 1978, 36. The article also reported: "The Department of Transportation figures that to maintain the levels of highway quality that existed in 1975 will cost an average of 21.8 billion dollars a year in capital outlays until 1990—or twice as much as is being spent in 1978. That estimate does not take into account inflation since 1975, and the cost of resurfacing has risen 9.7 percent in the past year alone." As we shall see, a later DOT study would revise this estimate to $16 billion between the years 1980 and 1990—still an extraordinary projection.

25. Quoted in Weingroff, "Origins."

26. Edward Weiner, *Urban Transportation Planning in the United States* (New York: Springer, 2008), 129.

27. Fred W. Frailey, "America's Highways Going to Pot," *U.S. News & World Report*, July 24, 1978, 36.

28. Melinda Beck et al., "The Decaying of America," *Newsweek*, August 2, 1982, 12–18.

29. Congress of the United States, Congressional Budget Office, *The Interstate Highway System: Issues and Options*, June 1982 (http://www.cbo.gov/ftpdocs/53xx/doc5332/doc19b-Entire.pdf, accessed March 5, 2009), xv, re-

ported that only 1,575 miles remain to be completed on the 42,944-mile interstate system.

30. Ibid., xv, 16–17, 4.

31. U.S. Government Accountability Office, "Limited Funds and Numerous Deficient Off-System Bridges Create Federal Bridge Program Dilemma," GAO/RCED-84–66, December 8, 1983, 1.

32. Congress of the United States, Congressional Budget Office, *New Directions for the Nation's Public Works*, September 1988, (http://www.cbo.gov/ftpdocs/55xx/doc5544/doc09b-Entire.pdf, accessed March 5, 2009), xv.

33. "Dwight D. Eisenhower National System of Interstate and Defense Highways," October 5, 2009 (http://www.fhwa.dot.gov/programadmin/interstate.cfm, accessed February 28, 2010). See also Weingroff, "Origins."

34. Memo from King W. Gee, Program Manager, Infrastructure, Federal Highway Administration, U.S. Department of Transportation, January 11, 2002 (http://www.fhwa.dot.gov/preservation/011102.cfm, accessed April 8, 2009). The memorandum reads in part: "Under the legislation establishing the HBRRP, Congress intended the funds to be used to replace or rehabilitate deficient highway bridges so they would no longer be deficient. We implemented the program in accordance with this concept. However, in 1995, Congress added subsection (d) to 23 U.S.C. 116: (d) PREVENTIVE MAINTENANCE—A preventive maintenance activity shall be eligible for Federal assistance under this title if the State demonstrates to the satisfaction of the Secretary that the activity is a cost-effective means of extending the useful life of a Federal-aid highway." It goes on to state that although, in 1996, the FHWA had issued "guidance" for division administrators and others in the field to the effect that "Federal-aid highway funds could be used for projects to extend the service life of existing . . . bridges," to date, HBRRP funds had "not been used for this purpose." The author of the memorandum went on to emphasize that "*routine maintenance remains the responsibility of the State and is not eligible for HBRRP or other Federal-aid highway funding. The division office is responsible for making the determination on what can be considered as a cost-effective means of extending the service life of a bridge*" (emphasis in original).

35. Ellen Schweppe, "Legacy of a Landmark: ISTEA After 10 Years," *Public Roads*, November–December 2001 (http://www.tfhrc.gov/pubrds/novdec01/legacy.htm, accessed February 24, 2009).

36. Quoted in ibid.

37. Alan Altshuler and David Luberoff, *Mega-Projects: The Changing Politics of Urban Public Investment* (Washington: Brookings Institution Press, 2003), 115.

38. Weingroff, "Origins."

39. The law was so named in fulfillment of a promise by Congressman Don Young, an Alaskan Republican who was then chairman of the House Transportation and Infrastructure Committee, to his wife Lu, to name a piece of legislation for her.

40. Robert Puentes, "Getting Infrastructure Bang for the Buck" (reprinted from "Road Blocked," *The New Republic*, November 13, 2008, at http://www .brookings.edu/opinions/2008/1113_infrastructure_puentes.aspx, accessed March 19, 2010).

41. For more information on these statistics, see U.S. Department of Transportation, Federal Highway Administration, Federal Transit Administration, *2006 Status of the Nation's Highways, Bridges, and Transit: Conditions & Performance* (http://www.fhwa.dot.gov/policy/2006cpr/pdfs/cp2006.pdf, accessed March 19, 2006). Hereinafter cited as FHWA, *Conditions*.

42. Matt Helms, "Proposal Overhauls Funding for Michigan's Roads," *Detroit Free Press*, November 20, 2008 (http://www.drivemi.org/PDFs/Detroit FreePresseqk.pdf, accessed March 17, 2010).

43. Congress of the United States, Congressional Budget Office, *The Interstate Highway System: Issues and Options*, June 1982 http://www.cbo.gov/ftp docs/53xx/doc5332/doc19b-Entire.pdf, accessed March 5, 2009), 11.

44. Kenneth T. Jackson, *Crabgrass Frontier*, 248–49, 174–75.

45. The twentieth century's consummate practitioner of the politics of road and bridge construction—which he conducted in a manner that both trampled on democratic governance and led to the shameless neglect of infrastructure maintenance and repair familiar from the story of the Williamsburg Bridge in chapter 1—was Robert Moses in New York City. Robert Caro writes in his biography of Moses that one of the ways he helped bankrupt the city was "draining away for new construction so much of the city's resources that it could not pay to keep up maintenance on its existing $12,000,000,000 physical plant." Caro continues: "Not only subways but highways fell into this category; even Moses' own roads could not be kept up. And the cost of neglected maintenance is astonishingly high: the West Side Highway, for

example, could have been kept in perfect repair during the 1950s for about $75,000 per year; because virtually no repairing was done, by the 1960s, the cost of annual maintenance would be more than $1,000,000 per year; and in 1974 the highway had begun literally to fall apart—a condition that would take tens of millions of dollars to repair. By the time Moses left power in 1968, the city would be utterly unable to make even a pretense of keeping its physical plant in repair" (Robert A. Caro, *The Power Broker: Robert Moses and the Fall of New York* [New York: Vintage Books, 1975], 796). For more on the "astonishingly high" cost of neglected maintenance, see chapter 3 of this book.

46. Congress of the United States, Congressional Budget Office, *New Directions for the Nation's Public Works*, September 1988, (http://www.cbo.gov/ftpdocs/55xx/doc5544/doc09b-Entire.pdf, accessed March 5, 2009), xvi. Although it specified highways as one of only two federal infrastructure programs in which "fees" (i.e., the federal gasoline tax) were "high enough to defray most of the federal spending," the CBO report also stated that "even in [the federal highway and aviation] programs, some users—notably, operators of heavy trucks and private planes—pay less than their share of costs, while other users—light truck operators and airline passengers—make up the difference by paying fees that recover more than the costs they create. In each of these programs, below-cost pricing leads users to request more infrastructure services than they are willing to pay for, while planners get an exaggerated perception of investment needs from these misleading signals about infrastructure demand" (xvi–xvii).

47. National Surface Transportation Infrastructure Financing Commission, *Paying Our Way: A New Framework for Transportation Finance*, February 2009 (http://financecommission.dot.gov/Documents/NSTIF_Commission_Final_Report_Mar09FNL.pdf, accessed February 28, 2010), 4. Hereinafter cited as NSTIFC, *Paying Our Way*.

48. The notion of below-cost pricing as a factor in creating pressure for new construction and capacity expansion is given a different, more acerbic treatment by the European planning and transportation scholars Bent Flyvbjerg, Nils Bruzelius, and Werner Rothengatter, who argue in their book *Megaprojects and Risk: An Anatomy of Ambition* (Cambridge: Cambridge University Press, 2003) that "cost underestimation and overrun" are not only endemic in large-scale public projects such as roads, bridges, and tunnels, but

"cannot be explained by error and seem to be best explained by strategic misrepresentation, namely lying, with a view to getting projects started" (16).

49. Cambridge Systematics, Inc. with Michael D. Meyer, "Crashes vs. Congestion: What's the Cost to Society?," March 5, 2008, (http://www.aaanews room.net/Assets/Files/200835920140.CrashesVsCongestionExecutiveSum mary2.28.08.pdf), accessed March 19, 2010) ES-1.

50. U.S. Government Accountability Office, *Federal-Aid Highways: Trends, Effect on State Spending, and Options for Future Program Design*, August 2004 (http://www.gao.gov/new.items/d04802.pdf, accessed on March 19, 2010), 5.

51. Ibid., 3–4, 87, 32. In an interesting aside, this report notes that "increases in federal grant funding for non-highway purposes, such as health, education, and welfare, are also associated with reduced effort on the part of the states to fund highways"—i.e., "states with a higher percentage of their non-highway spending funded by federal grants reduced their effort to fund highways, presumably, to provide matching funds for programs like Medicaid, which is an open-ended matching program." The GAO study also found that "high per capita income states make less effort [on highways] than states with lower incomes," owing to the fact that "the same effective tax rate (level of effort) generates more revenues in high-income states than in states with lower incomes. Thus, the same level of highway spending can be funded with less effort in high-income states and low-income states compensate by undertaking a greater effort to fund highways from state resources" (87–88).

52. Surface Transportation Policy Project, "The $300 Billion Question: Are We Buying a Better Transportation System?" January 2003 (http://www .transact.org/library/300B/Executive_Summary.pdf, accessed March 19, 2010), 1. Hereinafter cited as Surface Transportation Policy Project, "The $300 Billion Question."

53. Ibid., 3.

54. Ibid., 2.

55. Ibid.

56. Surface Transportation Policy Project, "The $300 Billion Question." The sections on roads and bridges, respectively, are available at http://www.trans act.org/library/decoder/roadconditiondecoder.pdf and http://www.transact .org/library/decoder/Bridge-Decoder.pdf (accessed March 10, 2009).

That the flexibility given to the states in spending federal highway money is a factor in the states' neglect of needed road and bridge repair is also indicated by data in FHWA, *Conditions*. For federal-aid roads (i.e., all public roads, excluding "rural minor collectors" and local roads), FHWA figures show that, as of 2004, ride quality on pavements (measured in terms of vehicle miles traveled, or VMT, rather than mileage per se) on the NHS, which includes the interstates and for which there are dedicated FHWA programs such as the NHS program and the IM program, was better than on federal-aid roads off the NHS. For example, 67 percent of VMT on rural NHS roads was on pavement rated good in 2004, as compared with 46 percent on non-NHS roads. For roads in small urban areas (those with populations between 5,000 and 50,000), the percentages were 54 percent and 31 percent, respectively, while only in large urban areas were the figures roughly equal for NHS and non-NHS roads (37 and 34 percent, respectively). Moreover, the data for federal-aid highways over this period show that the condition of pavement on most roads in the NHS improved between 1995 and 2004, while that on most non-NHS roads declined. For bridges the picture is similar. Data in the National Bridge Inventory for 2008 show that only 5.2 percent of bridges in the NHS were structurally deficient, compared with 13.5 percent of non-NHS bridges. In 2004, the last year for which data were available for the 2006 FHWA report, only 5 percent of the structurally deficient bridges in rural areas (where 14 percent of all bridges fell into this category) were in the NHS, although 40 percent of the structurally deficient bridges in urban areas (where only 9 percent of all bridges were so classified) were. It would appear that, for both roads and bridges, being in the NHS is a stronger guarantee of sound condition in rural than in urban areas—which is not surprising, considering that NHS roads and bridges in urban areas take the most punishment in terms of traffic volumes, speeds, and weights, while federal highway funding formulas, reflecting the composition of the U.S. Senate, contain a degree of bias in favor of less-populated states. See FHWA, *Conditions*, Exhibits 3-5 and 3-17 (in both of which interstates, other freeways and expressways, and principal arterials represent roads in the NHS), and http://www.fhwa.dot.gov/Bridge/nbi/defbr08.xls (hereinafter cited as FHWA, *Conditions*, spreadsheet).

57. Surface Transportation Policy Project, "The State of Our Nation's Roads: Half of All Major Roads Are in Less Than Good Condition; Decoding Transportation Policy & Practice #9," January 30, 2003 (http://www.transact.org/library/decoder/roadconditiondecoder.pdf, accessed March 23, 2010), 3.

58. FHWA, *Conditions*, spreadsheet.

59. Surface Transportation Policy Project, "The $300 Billion Question," 9.

60. Surface Transportation Policy Project, "The State of Our Nation's Roads: Half of All Major Roads Are in Less Than Good Condition; Decoding Transportation Policy & Practice #9," January 30, 2003 (http://www.transact .org/library/decoder/roadconditiondecoder.pdf, accessed March 23, 2010), 3.

61. For structural deficiency rates in 2008, see FHWA, *Conditions*, spreadsheet. For HBP obligation-to-apportionment ratios for 2003–7, see Committee on Transportation and Infrastructure, "Report," 8. The report also discusses the problem of states' making disproportionate amounts of the highway program rescissions that Congress routinely requires between the authorization and appropriation processes from their HBP funds: "In implementing congressionally-mandated rescissions of unobligated contract authority balances in highway program funds, States have chosen to disproportionately rescind contract authority from a few programs, including the Highway Bridge Program. Although the Highway Bridge Program represents approximately 11 percent of the overall program funding level in SAFETEA-LU [the 2005 federal transportation act], rescissions of contract authority available for this program have totaled approximately one-third of total rescissions" (7).

62. Interview with Sam Schwartz, May 10, 2009.

63. Ibid.

64. Samuel I. Schwartz, "Catch Me, I'm Falling," *New York Times*, August 13, 2007 (http://query.nytimes.com/gst/fullpage.html?res=9905E5DC1538F 930A2575BC0A9619C8B63&sec=&spon=&pagewanted=all, accessed March 19, 2010). As noted above, it took eleven years after the enactment of ISTEA before the FHWA determined that federal HBRRP funds could be used for preventive maintenance under restrictive conditions.

In the late 1980s, New York State Comptroller Edward V. Regan made the following statement to the National Council on Public Works Improvements: "When highways and bridges are regularly maintained there is no press coverage. When they are rebuilt it is an 'event.' There is a ribbon-cutting and plenty of press coverage. The incentives, therefore, are for public officials to purposefully starve the maintenance budget. . . . Until this motivation . . . is acted upon [sic], we will be treated to recurrent infrastructure crises. In fact, proposals for infrastructure bonds, banks, etc. only abet this whole process" (quoted in Robert W. Poole, Jr., "Incentives for Mobility: Using Market Mechanisms to Rebuild America's Transportation Infrastructure" [Reason Foundation Policy Insight no. 116, August 1989, revised May 1991; http://reason.org/files/c2b063df9ecc318b20969c4deofdfa12.pdf, accessed March 1, 2010], 7).

65. Testimony of Michigan Department of Transportation Director Kirk Steudle, in *Structurally Deficient Bridges: Hearing before the Committee on Transportation and Infrastructure, House of Representatives; One Hundred Tenth Congress, First Session, September 5, 2007* (Washington: Government Printing Office, 2007; (http://frwebgate.access.gpo.gov/cgi-bin/getdoc.cgi?dbname=110_house_hearings&docid=f:37652.wais, accessed on March 19, 2010).

66. American Society of Civil Engineers, *Report Card for America's Infrastructure*, bridges (http://www.infrastructurereportcard.org/fact-sheet/bridges, accessed March 17, 2010). Hereinafter cited as ASCE, *Report Card*.

67. American Association of State Highway and Transportation Officials, *Bridging the Gap: Restoring and Rebuilding the Nation's Bridges*, July 2008 (http://www.transportation1.org/BridgeReport/scarce.html, accessed August 6, 2009).

68. ASCE, *Report Card*, 3, 4, and 7.

69. Economists and political scientists who have studied infrastructure issues have found barriers to the adequate maintenance of infrastructure in the nature of the American political process itself, and Gary S. Becker, an economist at the University of Chicago, has noted: "Those parts of the infrastructure that are not supported by pressure groups will suffer more from the cutbacks in spending" ("Economic Viewpoint: Why Potholes and Police Get Such Short Shrift," *Business Week*, July 25, 1988,12). This argument is also made in a recent report from the Transportation Research Board, which states: "The long lives and slow aging of highways and other infrastructure mean that the effects of neglect may not be revealed for many years. Policy makers and the public at large, confronted with multiple demands for public funds, are easily persuaded to devote resources to issues for which there are vocal constituencies. Maintenance offers few opportunities for responsible officials to garner public recognition and support of the sort that comes when programs are initiated or new facilities are opened for service" (Transportation Research Board of the National Academies, "Public Benefits of Highway System Preservation and Maintenance: A Synthesis of Highway Practice,"

2004 [http://onlinepubs.trb.org/Onlinepubs/nchrp/nchrp_syn_330.pdf, accessed May 1, 2009], 3).

In a paper published in 1984, the economist George E. Peterson of the Urban Institute dismissed the then-prevalent arguments that inadequate federal aid and a downturn in the market for long-term government bond issues were responsible for inadequately maintained infrastructure, and pointed to political factors rather than financial or economic ones. Peterson found merit in the argument that "infrastructure spending has been unable to compete effectively with other budget claims for political reasons," observing that "Budget reductions that trigger employment layoffs, wage freezes, and or cancellation of public services meet immediate and vigorous opposition. At least in the past, maintenance deferrals and cancellation of underground capital projects have been much less visible to the electorate." Yet a more plausible argument, in Peterson's view, was that inadequate infrastructure investment, including for maintenance, reflected "a deliberate budget choice exercised by public officials and by voters," even though "[i]t is possible—indeed, likely—that with better and more plentiful information as to the condition of facilities and the consequences of deferring repair investment, local governments would have chosen to spend more for these purposes" (George E. Peterson, *Financing the Nation's Infrastructure Requirements*, in *Perspectives on Urban Infrastructure*, 130 and 122).

70. See Jeffrey Ang-Olson, Martin Wachs, and Brian D. Taylor, "Variable-Rate State Gasoline Taxes," Institute of Transportation Studies, University of California at Berkeley, working paper UCB-ITS-WP-99–3, 1999 (http://repositories.cdlib.org/cgi/viewcontent.cgi?article=1072&context=its, accessed August 6, 2009). See also Robert Puentes, "A Bridge to Somewhere: Rethinking American Transportation for the 21st Century," The Brookings Institution, June 12, 2008, (www.brookings.edu/reports/2008/06_transportation _puentes.aspx, accessed June 25, 2009), 39.

71. According to a 2008 report by the National Surface Transportation Infrastructure Financing Commission, "today, drivers pay less than half as much per mile traveled as they did at the end of the 1950s. . . . The share of state government highway funding paid by user fees has declined by nearly 20 percent since 1965, putting more pressure on states' general revenues to close that gap" (quoted in The Pew Center on the States, *Driven by Dollars: What States Should Know When Considering Public-Private Partnerships to Fund Transpor-*

*tation*, March 2009 [http://www.pewcenteronthestates.org/uploadedFiles/ PA_Turnpike_FINAL_WEB.pdf, accessed August 6, 2009], 5).

72. David T. Hartgen and Ravi K. Karanam, "17th Annual Report on the Performance of State Highway Systems (1984–2006)," July 2008 (http://www .reason.org/files/9bbbda199a9e7c16b2d877e42fdc5b53.pdf, accessed April 4, 2009), 16, 18, and 20.

73. Michigan Department of Transportation, *State Long-Range Transportation Plan, 2005–2030: Conditions and Performance Technical Report*, December 11, 2006, Table 11, 23.

74. FHWA, *Conditions*, spreadsheet.

75. FHWA Highway Statistics Series 2007. In November 2008, the Michigan Infrastructure and Transportation Association, a construction industry group, proposed that the state replace its flat-rate tax on gasoline and diesel fuel with a percentage-based levy that would fluctuate with the price of fuel. See Matt Helms, "Proposal Overhauls Funding for Michigan's Roads," *Detroit Free Press*, November 20, 2008.

76. Susan Mortel, "Financial Challenges Ahead! MDOT Five Year Program Adjustment Alternatives," September 26, 2008 (http://www.semcog.org/ uploadedfiles/Programs_and_Projects/Transportation/SMortelExecPPT.pdf, accessed March 18, 2010).

77. The *Detroit Free Press* recently reported on a survey by the County Road Association of Michigan, which showed that twenty-three counties had allowed paved roads to revert to gravel because they lacked the resources to keep the pavement in safe condition (Matt Helms, "More Michigan Roads Allowed to Crumble into Gravel, Study Says," *Detroit Free Press*, February 9, 2009).

78. David T. Hartgen and Ravi K. Karanam, "17th Annual Report on the Performance of State Highway Systems (1984–2006)," July 2008 (http://www .reason.org/files/9bbbda199a9e7c16b2d877e42fdc5b53.pdf, accessed April 4, 2009), 16, 18, and 20.

79. *Transportation 2030: New Jersey's Long-Range Transportation Plan* (draft for public discussion), October 2008 (http://www.nj.gov/transportation/works/ njchoices/pdf/2030plan.pdf, accessed April 16, 2009), 28.

### 3. No Sense of Urgency

1. John B. Miller, "Life Cycle Delivery of Public Infrastructure: Precedents and Opportunities for the Commonwealth," *Pioneer Institute* 44 (December 2008): 23.

2. David Westerling and Steve Poftak, "Our Legacy of Neglect: The Longfellow Bridge and the Cost of Deferred Maintenance," Pioneer Institute White Paper, July 2007 (www.pioneerinstitute.org/pdf/070731_poftak_longfellow .pdf, accessed March 23, 2010), 13. Deferring paving maintenance also costs more in the long term, as deterioration accelerates rapidly. Because of this, deferred repairs can cost up to five times as much as early repairs (Metropolitan Transportation Commission, Bridge and Highway Operations Section, "The Pothole Report: An Update on Bay Area Pavement Conditions," March 2000 [http://www.mtc.ca.gov/library/pothole/pothole.pdf, accessed March 23, 2010]).

3. Gray Plant Mooty, *Investigative Report*, 78.

4. Interview with Peter Vanderzee, February 26, 2009.

5. Gray Plant Mooty, *Investigative Report*, 30–32.

6. Ibid., 31.

7. Ibid., 77.

8. Willa Cather, *Alexander's Bridge* (Cambridge, Mass.: Riverside, 1912), 11.

9. Hart Crane, *The Bridge* (London: Liveright, 1992), 1. And who can forget the role of the bridge engineer in the movie *The Bridge over the River Kwai*, where the officer played by Alec Guinness was so highly valued by his Japanese captors for his ability to construct a needed bridge for their war effort?

10. Andrew Abbott, *The System of Professions: An Essay on the Division of Expert Labor* (Chicago: University of Chicago Press, 1988), 232.

11. At the outset of World War I, Hoover volunteered to head international relief efforts for Belgium, later serving as food administrator in the Woodrow Wilson wartime government: "As much as any man could, he got the credit for reorganizing the war-shattered European economy" (David M. Kennedy, *Freedom From Fear: The American People in Depression and War, 1929–1945* [New York: Oxford University Press, 1999], 45–46).

12. Robert A. Caro, *The Power Broker: Robert Moses and the Fall of New York* (New York: Vintage Books, 1975), 273.

13. Mark H. Rose, *Interstate: Express Highway Politics, 1939–1989*, rev. ed. (Knoxville: University of Tennessee Press, 1990), 115–17.

14. Ibid., 115.

15. Ibid., 117.

16. Interview with Sam Schwartz, May 10, 2009.

17. Interview with Sam Schwartz, September 25, 2008; the Order of the Engineer (http://www.order-of-the-engineer.org/?page_id=6, accessed March 30, 2010).

18. Edwin T. Layton, Jr., *The Revolt of the Engineers: Social Responsibility and the American Engineering Profession* (Cleveland, Ohio: Press of Case Western Reserve University, 1971), 1–2. In describing how American engineers managed the transition, beginning very early in the twentieth century, from independent professional practice—the norm for American professionals such as doctors and lawyers—to employment in corporate or government organizations, another historian, Terry S. Reynolds, states that "they did this by increasingly aligning themselves with the aims and aspirations of their companies. By midcentury, professional standing for many engineers had become identical with corporate standing. The approval of one's superiors in corporate or government hierarchies became more important than the approval of one's technical peers, contrary to the values of the traditional professions of law, medicine, and the clergy" ("The Engineer in 20th Century America," in *The Engineer in America: A Historical Anthology from Technology and Culture*, edited by Terry S. Reynolds [Chicago: University of Chicago Press, 1991], 174).

19. Quoted in Henry Petroski, *Engineers of Dreams: Great Bridge Builders and the Spanning of America* (New York: Vintage Books, 1996), 208–9. Hereinafter Petroski, *Engineers of Dreams.*

20. The sociologist Andrew Abbott points out that as the rise of scientific management—coupled with the invention of the first serious mechanical calculating devices—placed great importance on the discipline of cost accounting in manufacturing enterprises in the early twentieth century, engineers and accountants competed for jurisdiction over this task (*The Systems of Profession: An Essay on the Division of Expert Labor* [Chicago: Chicago University Press, 1989] 226–33).

21. It is not clear that isolating transportation management from politics is necessarily good for infrastructure maintenance, at least in certain settings. Heywood T. Sanders, for example, argues that applying formal engineering standards to determine what urban infrastructure gets repaired can serve the public less well than political standards: "One of the problems in

applying a formal standard to public facility renovation decisions is that the standard suggests nothing of the specific problems or failures that should generate public action. The need for a load limit on a bridge that serves an industrial park, the overloading of a combined sewer in a residential neighborhood, and the deterioration of a concrete pedestrian walkway are examples of specific needs that affect the decision-making process. Needs provide far more substantive support for funding because they are tangible items, with clear costs and benefits" (Sanders, "Politics and Urban Public Facilities," in Royce Hanson, ed., *Perspectives on Urban Infrastructure* [Washington: National Academy Press, 1984], 160).

22. Richard P. Feynman, "Personal Observations on the Reliability of the Shuttle," Appendix F to *Report of the Presidential Commission on the Space Shuttle Challenger Accident* (http://science.ksc.nasa.gov/shuttle/missions/51-l/docs/rogers-commission/Appendix-F.txt, accessed May 8, 2009).

23. Ibid.

24. Ibid.

25. Ibid.

26. Henry Petroski, *Success through Failure: The Paradox of Design* (Princeton, New Jersey: Princeton University Press, 2006), 114.

27. *Report of the Presidential Commission on the Space Shuttle Challenger Accident*, chap. 5 (http://history.nasa.gov/rogersrep/v1ch5.htm, accessed on March 22, 2010), 1.

28. Ibid.

29. NTSB, *I-35W Bridge*, xiii.

30. Ibid., 130.

31. Ibid., 61, 63.

32. Toader Balan, a structural engineer and a former structural engineering professor, told me in an interview that the failure sequence occurred as follows:

1. Too much weight on the bridge (in a nonsymmetric loading pattern, resulting both from construction materials and traffic) caused excessive compressive force on a nonredundant truss member. [As noted earlier, MNDOT acknowledged that ensuring a symmetric loading of construction materials was a concern that they brought to the attention of URS in a memo well before the concrete deck overlay project was begun in 2007.]

2. The truss member buckled under the excessive compressive force and began to bend, resulting in an outwardly directed force on the gusset plate in question (which is why the gusset plate was found bent after the failure). Before the failure, since there was no excessive compressive force, there was no outward force on that gusset plate, which is why it did not fail earlier.

3. The outward force on the gusset plate caused it to bend or buckle, which weakened the entire connection, causing the connection to fail.

4. That gusset plate connection failure caused a cascading failure of the entire bridge, since the connection wasn't redundant.

Other engineering consultants such as Thornton Tomasetti, retained by the families of those killed or injured in the collapse of the I-35W Bridge, have given similar analyses and pointed to the summer heat and the fact that the bearings below the deck truss had been frozen from rust and other debris for years. As of the date of this writing, these engineers have not provided a written report, but interviews and press releases indicate their belief that the bottom chord of the truss, not the gusset plates, was the location of the initial failure. In sum, other experts would agree with Balan: "It is not possible for a failure of this nature to occur unless excessive forces in the members exceed the resistance capacity of the material, in this case steel. However, once the force exceeds the resistance capacity (past the yield point of the material), the failure cannot be stopped. Blaming the design or construction of forty-five years ago ignores what MnDOT could have done to predict and reduce the risk of this failure mechanism" (interview with Toader Balan, June 24, 2009).

33. Quoted in "NTSB: Design Flaw 40 Years Ago, Factor in Collapse," Associated Press, January 15, 2008 (http://wcco.com/bridgecollapse/ntsb.bridge.collapse.2.629831.html, accessed March 3, 2010).

34. Triggered by the I-35W Bridge collapse, the Ohio Department of Transportation (ODOT) looked for defective gusset plates on the Main Avenue Bridge spanning the Cuyahoga River in Cleveland, a bridge similar in design to the failed Minnesota bridge. Instead of a gusset plate problem, during inspections in September 2007, department workers discovered that two steel plates along the bottom chords had rusted to such a thinness that one of the chords had a four-inch hole. ODOT added new steel plates to provide additional structural support (Damon Sims, "ODOT Withheld Fears about

Danger of Main Avenue Bridge Collapsing in 2007," June 28, 2009 [http://blog.cleveland.com/metro/2009/06/odot_withheld_fears_about_dang.html, accessed June 30, 2009]).

35. Gray Plant Mooty, *Investigative Report*, 3 and 4.

36. Tony Kennedy, Mike Kaszuba, Paul McEnroe, and Dan Browning, "Possible Flaw Detected in Bridge Design," *Minneapolis-St. Paul Star Tribune*, August 9, 2007(http://www.startribune.com/local/11592746.html, accessed March 22, 2010).

37. Mike Kaszuba and Kevin Diaz, "Bridge Collapse: 'Working Theory' Blames Design, Weight," *Minneapolis-St. Paul Star Tribune*, November 1, 2007 (http://www.startribune.com/local/11594406.html, accessed March 23, 2010).

38. Quoted in ibid.

39. National Transportation Safety Board, "NTSB Urges Bridge Owners to Perform Load Capacity Calculations before Modifications; I-35W Investigation Continues," press release, January 15, 2008 (http://www.ntsb.gov/pressrel/2008/080115.html, accessed on March 17, 2010).

40. Mark V. Rosenker, "Opening Remarks at the Minnesota I-35W Bridge Collapse Press Conference," Washington, January 15, 2008 (http://www.ntsb.gov/speeches/rosenker/mvr080115.html, accessed on March 17, 2010).

41. Quoted in "NTSB: Design Flaw 40 Years Ago, Factor in Collapse," Associated Press, January 15, 2008 (http://wcco.com/bridgecollapse/ntsb.bridge.collapse.2.629831.html, accessed on March 18, 2010).

42. Letter from James L. Oberstar to Mark V. Rosenker, January 23, 2008 (http://www.timescape.us/graphics/NTSB-OberstarLetter.pdf, accessed on March 18, 2010).

43. Tony Kennedy, "NTSB Won't Hold Open Hearing on I-35W Bridge Collapse," *Minneapolis-St. Paul Star Tribune*, March 26, 2008 (http://www.startribune.com/local/16796896.html, accessed March 18, 2010).

44. Ibid.; National Transportation Safety Board, "Notation 7975A, Member Deborah A.P. Hersman and Member Kathryn O'Seary Higgins, Dissenting," March 3, 2008 (http://minnesota.publicradio.org/features/2008/03/ntsb_dissenting.pdf, accessed November 14, 2008); and Kevin Diaz, "NTSB Chief Has Political Job but Says Politics Don't Define Him," *Minneapolis-St. Paul Star Tribune*, January 16, 2008 (http://www.startribune.com/local/13852836.html, accessed March 23, 2010).

45. NTSB, *I-35W Bridge*.

46. Wiss, Janney, Elstner Associates, *ı-35w Bridge over the Mississippi River: Collapse Investigation; Bridge 9340, Minneapolis, Minnesota* (Northbrook, Ill.: Wiss, Janney, Elstner Associates, November 2008; http://www.ntsb.gov/dockets/ Highway/HWY07MH024/404995.pdf, accessed March 22, 2010).

47. A former NTSB board member described the normal NTSB investigative process for Minnesota Public Radio in a report aired on October 15, 2007 (Sea Stachura, "Three Investigations Search for Cause of I-35w Bridge Collapse," http://minnesota.publicradio.org/display/web/2007/10/12/ntsbupdate, accessed May 15, 2009).

48. National Transportation Safety Board, *Highway Accident Report: Collapse of U.S. 35 Highway Bridge, Point Pleasant, West Virginia, December 15, 1967*, synopsis (http://www.ntsb.gov/Publictn/1971/HAR7101.htm, accessed May 15, 2009).

49. Charles Seim, "Why Bridges Have Failed throughout History," *Civil Engineering* 78, no. 5 (May 2008): 87.

## 4. Finding the Money

1. National Surface Transportation Policy and Revenue Study Commission, *Transportation for Tomorrow*, December 2007 (http://transportationfortomorrow.org/final_report/pdf/final_report.pdf, accessed June 1, 2009), Exhibit 4–6, 4-9–4-10. Hereinafter cited as NSTPRSC, *Transportation for Tomorrow*.

2. American Association of State Highway and Transportation Officials, *Bridging the Gap: Restoring and Rebuilding the Nation's Bridges*, July 2008 (http://www.transportation1.org/BridgeReport/scarce.html, accessed August 6, 2009).

3. NSTIFC, *Paying Our Way*, 3–4; see also Exhibit ES-3, 4

4. The work of both the NSTPRSC and the NSTIFC was commissioned by Congress in SAFETEA-LU, enacted in 2005.

5. NSTPRSC, *Transportation for Tomorrow*, 38, 40–42, and 50–54.

6. NSTIFC, *Paying Our Way*, 9. From the outset of the Obama administration, through the passage of the American Recovery and Reinvestment Act of 2009 and into the allocation of stimulus funds for highway and bridge projects, debate raged about the possibility of reconciling the need for immediate job creation via "shovel-ready" projects with effective infrastructure investment. The NSTIFC report made what is probably the definitive statement on this issue when it noted: "An economic stimulus spending package that includes investments in surface transportation, while helpful, will not

solve the immediate or the longer-term problems of funding system needs. The current investment shortfall is just too great. . . . For instance, a stimulus package that includes nearly $40 billion for highway and transit infrastructure, while important in addressing the short-term economic crisis, will pay for only about three months of the identified annual national funding gap to maintain and improve the system—a gap that repeats itself and compounds year after year" (7).

7. NSTPRSC, *Transportation for Tomorrow*, 41.

8. Three members of the NSTPRSC, in fact, challenged the majority's views on this point while also disputing other conclusions reached in the final commission report. See ibid., 59–68.

9. Ibid., 44.

10. Ibid., 44 and 5-24.

11. NSTIFC, *Paying Our Way*, 12. The report explains: "If tolling the existing Interstate System is determined to be the appropriate solution by a particular state, this pilot program enables the state to use this option to help meet its funding gap. States that participate in the pilot program must ensure that there are appropriate protections for system users and interstate commerce." Early in 2009, the Washington State legislature voted to make Washington the first state in the nation to convert an existing bridge, the state Highway 520 bridge across Lake Washington, into a tolled facility. Tolling on the bridge was slated to begin in October 2010, while construction simultaneously started on a replacement, with tolls from the existing bridge intended to reduce the amount of borrowing required for the replacement project. See Aubrey Cohen, "520 Bridge Tolls To Be a Nationwide First?" *Seattle Post-Intelligencer*, June 2, 2009 (http://www.seattlepi.com/transportation/406806_tolls03.html, accessed June 3, 2009).

12. SAFETEA-LU authorized state infrastructure banks to enter into agreements with the U.S. secretary of transportation to establish separate financial entities that would provide transportation infrastructure credit assistance for fiscal years 2005–9.

13. U.S. Government Accountability Office, "State Infrastructure Banks: A Mechanism to Expand Federal Transportation Financing," report to congressional requestors, October 1996 (http://www.gao.gov/archive/1997/rc97009.pdf, accessed March 23, 2010), 8.

14. NSTIFC, *Paying Our Way*, 13.

15. Ibid.

16. Stan Hazelroth, interview by Tom McNamara, *Blueprint America: Building the National Infrastructure Bank*, PBS (http://www.pbs.org/wnet/blueprint america/reports/building-the-national-infrastructure-bank/transcript-cali fornia-i-bank-interview/554/, accessed June 3, 2009).

17. NSTPRSC, *Transportation for Tomorrow*, 10 and 15.

18. As a result of the economic crisis and national issues such as health care, Congress has repeatedly pushed the proposed transportation bill to the background, even though it recognizes that many fragile state economies are heavily dependent on this funding.

19. In addition to the NSTPRSC report, another call for a fundamental reorientation of U.S. transportation policy has come from the bipartisan National Transportation Policy Project (NTPP), whose report, *Performance Driven: A New Vision for U.S. Transportation Policy*, was issued in June 2009. Stating that "U.S. transportation policy needs to be more performance-driven, more directly linked to a set of clearly articulated goals, and more accountable for results," the report criticizes the emphasis of previous transportation policy on "revenue sharing and process, rather than on results." It advocates consolidating the 108 existing federal transportation programs into six, four of which—accounting for 75 percent of all federal transportation funds—would be for "system preservation" (*Performance Driven*, http://www.bipartisanpolicy .org/sites/default/files/ntpp_performance%20driven_june%209%2009_2 .pdf, accessed March 22, 2010).

20. U.S. Department of Transportation, Federal Highway Administration, Office of Asset Management, *Asset Management Primer*, December 1999 (http://www.fhwa.dot.gov/infrastructure/asstmgmt/amprimer.pdf, accessed June 9, 2009), 5. Hereinafter cited as U.S. DOT, *Asset Management Primer*.

21. U.S. Department of Transportation, Federal Highway Administration, Office of Asset Management, *Asset Management: Overview*, December 2007 (http://www.fhwa.dot.gov/asset/if08008/assetmgmt_overview.pdf, accessed June 10, 2009), 6 and 1.

22. U.S. DOT, *Asset Management Primer*, 9.

23. Cambridge Systematics, Inc., et al., National Cooperative Highway Research Program, *Performance Measures and Targets for Transportation Asset*

*Management*, NCHRP Report 551 (Washington: Transportation Research Board of the National Academies, 2006), I:ii. Hereinafter cited as Cambridge Systematics, *Performance Measures*.

24. U.S. DOT, *Asset Management Primer*, 13.

25. Ibid.

26. U.S. Department of Transportation, Federal Highway Administration, Office of Asset Management, *Asset Management: Overview*, December 2007 (http://www.fhwa.dot.gov/asset/if08008/assetmgmt_overview.pdf, accessed June 10, 2009), 10 and 24.

27. New York State Commission on State Asset Maximization, *Final Report*, June 1, 2009 (http://esd.ny.gov/Subsidiaries_Projects/SAM/Data/SAM_FINAL_REPORT.pdf, accessed March 23, 2010) 1, 26–27 and 35.

28. U.S. Department of Transportation, Federal Highway Administration, Office of Asset Management, *Asset Management: Overview*, December 2007 (http://www.fhwa.dot.gov/asset/if08008/assetmgmt_overview.pdf, accessed June 10, 2009), 29. Of the ten program areas for surface transportation that the NSTPRSC proposed creating to consolidate and rationalize federal transportation policy, the first—which the commission also said "underlies all of the other recommended programs"—is named "Rebuilding America: A National Asset Management Program." The commission states: "To assure the maximum effectiveness of Federal capital investment support, States, local governments, and other entities accepting Federal capital support must develop, fund, and implement a program of asset maintenance and support over the useful life of the asset that conforms to nationally accepted standards and that is independently audited" (NSTPRSC, *Transportation for Tomorrow* 16–17). Background information about the individual and combined initiatives of the FHWA, AASHTO, the Transportation Research Board of the National Academies, and other organizations can be found in Cambridge Systematics, *Performance Measures*, and in Cambridge Systematics, Inc., et al., *Transportation Asset Management Guide: Final Report Prepared for National Cooperative Highway Research Program (NCHRP) Project 20–24(11)*, November 2002(http://knowledge.fhwa.dot.gov/cops/pm.nsf/All+Documents/E39768AC30F32E298 5256E00005B257C/$File/AssetMgmtGuide.pdf, accessed June 11, 2009). See also ASCE, *Report Card*, which advocates as one of its "Five Key Solutions" that departments of transportation "Address Life Cycle Costs and Ongoing Maintenance" (12–13).

29. U.S. Department of Transportation, *Report to Congress on Public-Private Partnerships*, quoted in U.S. Department of Transportation, Federal Highway Administration, *Case Studies of Transportation Public-Private Partnerships in the United States*, July 7, 2007 (http://www.irfnet.ch/files-upload/knowledges/FHWA_us_ppp_case_studies_final_report_July2007.pdf, accessed May 28, 2009), 2-2. Hereinafter cited as U.S. DOT, *Case Studies*.

30. National Council For Public-Private Partnerships (http://ncppp.org/howpart/index.shtml, accessed March 23, 2010).

31. U.S. DOT, *Case Studies*, abstract.

32. The Pew Center on the States, *Driven by Dollars: What States Should Know When Considering Public-Private Partnerships to Fund Transportation*, March 2009 (http://www.pewcenteronthestates.org/uploadedFiles/PA_Turnpike_FINAL_WEB.pdf, accessed June 16, 2009), 8. Hereinafter cited as Pew, *Driven by Dollars*.

33. U.S. DOT, *Case Studies*, 2-1.

34. John B. Miller, "Engineering Systems Integration for Civil Infrastructure Projects," *Journal of Management in Engineering*, September–October 1997, 64 and 62.

35. U.S. Department of Transportation, Federal Highway Administration, *Case Studies of Transportation Public-Private Partnerships around the World*, final report, prepared for the Office of Policy and Governmental Affairs, July 7, 2007 (http://www.fhwa.dot.gov/ipd/pdfs/int_ppp_case_studies_final_report_7-7-07.pdf, accessed 5/28/09), 2-1.

36. Ibid., 2-1–2-2.

37. Federal Highway Administrator Mary Peters, "Excerpts from Remarks as Prepared for Delivery," Canal Road Intermodal Connector Meeting, October 21, 2003, Gulfport, Mississippi (http://www.fhwa.dot.gov/pressroom/re031021.htm, accessed May 28, 2009). In 1998, TIFIA established a federal program for "eligible transportation projects of national or regional significance" to receive secured loans, loan guarantees, or standby lines of credit from USDOT. "The program's fundamental goal," according to the FHWA, "is to leverage Federal funds by attracting substantial private and other non-Federal co-investment in critical improvements to the nation's surface transportation system."

38. U.S. DOT, *Case Studies*, 2-3. What the FHWA calls "alternative project delivery approaches" for the construction and expansion of highways in-

cludes various types of arrangements in which the private sector entity is responsible for operating and maintaining a facility that has also been privately planned, financed, and/or constructed (2-4–2-9).

39. Ibid., 2-3.

40. U.S. Department of Transportation, Federal Highway Administration, *Synthesis of Public-Private Partnership Projects for Roads, Bridges & Tunnels from around the World—1985–2004*, August 30, 2005 (http://www.ncppp.org/councilinstitutes/fhwappp.pdf, accessed May 28, 2009), 1.

41. Jeffrey N. Buxbaum and Iris N. Ortiz, "Protecting the Public Interest: The Role of Long-Term Concession Agreements for Providing Transportation Infrastructure," Keston Institute for Public Finance and Infrastructure Policy, University of Southern California, Research Paper 07-02, June 2007, (http://www.usc.edu/schools/sppd/keston/pdf/20070618-trans-concession-agreements.pdf, accessed May 28, 2009), 4. Hereinafter cited as Buxbaum and Ortiz, "Protecting the Public Interest."

42. See NSTPRSC, *Transportation for Tomorrow*, 48–51 and 5-28–5-30; NSTIFC, *Paying Our Way*, 14 and 173–83; and U.S. Government Accountability Office, *Highway Public-Private Partnerships: More Rigorous Up-front Analysis Could Better Secure Potential Benefits and Protect the Public Interest*, report to congressional requestors, February 2008 (http://www.gao.gov/new.items/d0844.pdf, accessed March 23, 2010). Hereinafter cited as U.S. GAO, *Highway Public-Private Partnerships*.

43. U.S. DOT, *Case Studies*, 2-4.

44. Ibid., 2-8 and 2-9.

45. NSTIFC, *Paying Our Way*, 179. The NSTIFC report also notes: "The borrowing capacity of government issuers is constrained by the market requirement that tax-exempt bonds demonstrate sufficient debt service coverage to receive an investment grade rating. Private investors' ability to draw on non-rated bank debt and investor equity can potentially allow a larger amount of a project's costs to be financed" (178). With the recent failures of major monoline bond insurers—insurers operating a single line of insurance business that insures the timely payment of interest and principal on bonds—public entities with less than a AA credit rating are finding it difficult to access the tax-exempt bond market at all.

46. U.S. DOT, *Case Studies*, 2-17–2-18.

47. NSTIFC, *Paying Our Way*, 178.

48. Ibid., 179.

49. According to an article in *Mother Jones*, a retired Notre Dame economics professor analyzed the deal for the plaintiffs in a lawsuit aimed at stopping the transaction and found that "the value of the road, over a 75-year term, could be as much as $11.38 billion" (Daniel Schulman and James Ridgeway, "The Highwaymen," *Mother Jones*, January–February 2007 (http://www.motherjones.com/politics/2007/01/highwaymen, accessed June 16, 2009). The assumptions behind the $11 billion estimate are explained in U.S. GAO, *Highway Public-Private Partnerships*, 32.

50. Pew, *Driven by Dollars*, 11.

51. Buxbaum and Ortiz, "Protecting the Public Interest," 6.

52. Buxbaum and Ortiz, "Protecting the Public Interest," 2.

53. U.S. GAO, *Highway Public-Private Partnerships*, 7–8.

54. Buxbaum and Ortiz, "Protecting the Public Interest," 2.

55. U.S. DOT, *Case Studies*, 2-22.

56. Buxbaum and Ortiz, "Protecting the Public Interest," 2.

57. Ibid. Just before Pennsylvania's Governor Ed Rendell, in 2007, proposed the leasing of the Pennsylvania Turnpike as a means of dealing with that state's serious transportation funding gap, the Pennsylvania legislature had passed Act 44, which increased tolls on the road and provided for the introduction of tolling on I-80, subject to federal approval. The plan would have provided the state with an estimated $116 billion in revenues over fifty years, although the FHWA denied authorization for the tolling of I-80 because some of the resulting revenues would have been used for transit. See Pew, *Driven by Dollars*, 10–13.

58. U.S. GAO, *Highway Public-Private Partnerships*, 31.

59. Pew, *Driven by Dollars*, 7.

60. Daniel Schulman and James Ridgeway question the integrity of the consultant's report that found that the bid offered by Macquarie/Cintra would yield approximately double the revenue that the state could have hoped to realize by continuing to manage the Indiana Toll Road on its own. They cite internal e-mails from the administration of Governor Mitch Daniels, who pushed hard for the concession agreement, which suggest that the valuation study, commissioned not long before the PPP agreement was finalized, was concocted by an accounting firm friendly to the administration to shield officials from the charge that there had been no independent analysis

of the proposed transaction (Schulman and Ridgeway, "The Highwaymen," *Mother Jones*, January–February 2007 [http://www.motherjones.com/politics/2007/01/highwaymen, accessed June 16, 2009], 2).

61. Pew, *Driven by Dollars*, 6 and 7. The U.S. GAO also notes that, as an alternative or supplement to upfront payments, the public interest in PPPs can be protected by revenue-sharing agreements by which "the higher the return on investment of the private concessionaire, the higher the share" of revenue that the concessionaire must share with the state or municipality (*Highway Public-Private Partnerships*, 44). Neither the Chicago Skyway nor the Indiana Toll Road concession involves revenue sharing.

62. U.S. GAO, *Highway Public-Private Partnerships*, 53.

63. See Robert Poole, "Adding More Transparency to Public-Private Partnership Infrastructure Projects: Ways to De-politicize the Process," Reason Foundation, March 31, 2009 (http://www.reason.org/news/show/1007209.html, accessed June 17, 2009).

64. Tom Coyne, "Indiana Lawmakers at Odds Over Toll Road," *Washington Post*, June 27, 2007 (http://www.washingtonpost.com/wp-dyn/content/article/2007/06/27/AR2007062700395.html, accessed June 18, 2009).

65. See Cezary Podkul, "Public Parking Pains," *Infrastructure Investor Week in Review*, June 11, 2009, and Leslie Wayne, "Politics and the Financial Crisis Slow the Drive to Privatize," *New York Times*, June 4, 2009 (http://www.nytimes.com/2009/06/05/business/economy/05private.html, accessed March 23, 2010).

66. Pew, *Driven by Dollars*, 3.

67. Ibid. See also endnote 57 above, on projections that an earlier plan for tolling both the Pennsylvania Turnpike and I-80 could have earned the state nearly ten times more revenue over fifty years than the Citi-Abertis deal would have garnered.

68. David A. Lieb, "Credit Crisis Forces Missouri to Revamp Bridge Funding, *Missourian*, September 18, 2008 (http://www.columbiamissourian.com/stories/2008/09/18/credit-crisis-forces-missouri-revamp-bridge-funding/, accessed June 19, 2009); Lloyd Dunkelberger, "Florida moves ahead on privatizing roads," *Herald-Tribune*, May 26, 2009 (http://www.heraldtribune.com/article/20090526/ARTICLE/305269998/2055/NEWS?Title=Florida-moves-ahead-on-privatizing-roads, accessed June 18, 2009).

69. See the ASCE, *Report Card*, 2.

70. Michael Kapoor, "Out with the Old," *Infrastructure Investor*, April 9, 2009, 24.

71. John Schulz, "Public-Private Partnerships for Infrastructure: RIP," Gerson Lehrman Group, May 1, 2009 (http://www.glgroup.com/News/Public -Private-Partnerships-for-Infrastructure--RIP-38127.html, accessed March 23, 2010).

72. Michael Kapoor, "Out with the Old," *Infrastructure Investor*, April 9, 2009, 25.

73. "Benefits of Private Investment in Infrastructure," Kearsarge Global Advisors, January 2009.

74. On the conflict of interest posed by the role of the investment bank Goldman Sachs in several major transportation PPPs in the United States, see Daniel Schulman and James Ridgeway, "The Highwaymen," *Mother Jones*, January–February 2007 (http://www.motherjones.com/politics/2007/01/high waymen, accessed June 16, 2009). A recent poll that showed increasing public support for private investment in the nation's infrastructure was sponsored by the investment banking firm Lazard (see Michael Erman, "Poll: U.S. Voters Back Privatized Infrastructure, *Reuters*, June 8, 2009 (http://www.reuters.com/ article/rbssFinancialServicesAndRealEstateNews/idUSN0832108520090608, accessed June 19, 2009).

75. U.S. GAO, *Highway Public-Private Partnerships*, 72.

76. Daniel Gross, "Lost Highway: The Foolish Plan to Sell American Toll Roads to Foreign Companies," *Slate*, March 29, 2006 (http://www.slate.com/ id/2138950/, accessed June 19, 2006).

77. Arthur C. Nelson, "Toward a New Metropolis: The Opportunity to Rebuild America," December 2004 (http://www.brookings.edu/metro/pubs/ 20041213_RebuildAmerica.pdf, accessed March 23, 2010).

## 5. The Technological Imperative

1. See David Nasaw, *Andrew Carnegie* (New York: Penguin Press, 2006).

2. John Fisher, Dann Hall, Ray McCabe, Ken Price, Chuck Seim, and Stan Woods, "Steel Bridges in the United States: Past, Present, and Future," in *Fifty Years of Interstate Structures: Past, Present, and Future*, Transportation Research Circular E-C104, Transportation Research Board, Structures Section, September 2006 (http://onlinepubs.trb.org/onlinepubs/circulars/ec104.pdf, accessed June 23, 2009), 27–32.

3. Petroski, *Engineers of Dreams*, 97.

4. Beside the Ashtabula Bridge, the other bridge collapses in the United States in the 1870s were those of the Truesdell Highway Bridge over the Rock River in Dixon, Illinois, on May 4, 1873 (fifty-six dead and thirty injured), and the Tariffville Railroad Bridge over the Farmington River in Tariffville, Connecticut, on January 15, 1878 (thirteen dead and seventy injured). The 1870s also saw one of the most notable bridge collapses in history when the Tay Bridge, a wrought iron truss bridge in Scotland completed in 1878, collapsed only nineteen months after its opening, in December 1879, killing all seventy-five people aboard a train that fell a hundred feet into the Firth of Tay. An investigation indicated that certain details in the design of the bridge—details that gone undetected even after it had gone into use—had contributed to the collapse.

5. Krajewski, "Bridge Inspection," 11–12.

6. Ibid., 39.

7. Ibid., 15.

8. Walther and Chase, "Condition Assessment," 69.

9. Krajewski, "Bridge Inspection," 22.

10. Ibid., 23–24.

11. Ibid., 26–27.

12. Walther and Chase, "Condition Assessment," 74–76.

13. Ibid., 71 and 76.

14. *Inspection and Evaluation of Common Steel Superstructures*, FHWA NHI 03–001 and FHWA NHI 03–002, revised December 2006, topic area 8.18, "Inspection Procedures and Locations," section 8.

15. Walther and Chase, "Condition Assessment," 76. Chase and Jeffrey Laman of Pennsylvania State University point out, with reference to the all-important task of determining load ratings, that "an analysis of the reported design load for structurally deficient bridges reveals that the design load for most bridges is often unknown. This suggests that the load ratings in the NBI are based more on engineering judgment than on detailed calculation and testing." Among other conclusions they reach in their study on field testing of bridges is that "technologies and methods exist to perform these tests but are not widely used" (Steven B. Chase and Jeffrey A. Laman, "Dynamics and Field Testing of Bridges" [http://onlinepubs.trb.org/onlinepubs/millennium/00029.pdf, accessed on March 22, 2010], 2–3; hereinafter cited as Chase and Laman, "Dynamics").

16. U.S. Department of Transportation, Federal Highway Administration, "FHWA NDE Center Research & Development: Evaluating Visual Inspection" (http://www.tfhrc.gov/hnr20/nde/vi.htm, accessed March 22, 2010).

17. U.S. Department of Transportation, Federal Highway Administration, Nondestructive Evaluation Center, *Reliability of Visual Inspection for Highway Bridges*, June 2001 (http://www.tfhrc.gov/hnr20/nde/01020.htm, accessed July 2, 2009). Hereinafter cited as U.S. DOT, *Reliability of Visual Inspection.*

18. U.S. Department of Transportation, Federal Highway Administration, "Highway Bridge Inspection: State-of-the Practice Study," April 2001 (http://www.tfhrc.gov/hnr20/nde/pdfs/01033.pdf, accessed March 22, 2010), 39 and 41.

19. U.S. Department of Transportation, Federal Highway Administration, "FHWA NDE Center Research and Development: Visual Inspection Study Update" (http://www.tfhrc.gov/hnr20/nde/visual.htm, accessed March 22, 2010).

20. With respect to fracture-critical bridges, where the need for adequate inspection is particularly acute, the training of inspectors had been deemed "adequately available" by a Transportation Research Board study, although the same report also found that "a general knowledge gap exists with respect to fatigue and fracture design, evaluation, and behavior in the engineering community" and that, in American departments of transportation, "many of the most experienced engineers are retiring and with their departure will be lost the years of experience acquired during the period when most of the issues with fatigue and fracture were foremost (1970–1990)" (Robert J. Connor, Robert Dexter, and Hussam Mahmoud, *Inspection and Management of Bridges with Fracture-Critical Details: A Synthesis of Highway Practice* [Washington, DC: Transportation Research Board of the National Academies, 2005; http://onlinepubs.trb.org/Onlinepubs/nchrp/nchrp_syn_354.pdf, accessed June 25, 2009], 34).

21. Mark E. Bernhardt, "Bridge Safety—Next Steps to Protect the Nation's Critical Bridge Infrastructure," testimony before the Committee on Science and Technology, U.S. House of Representatives, September 19, 2007 (http://democrats.science.house.gov/Media/File/Commdocs/hearings/2007/full/19sept/bernhardt_testimony.pdf, accessed July 3, 2009), 3. Hereinafter cited as Bernhardt, "Bridge Safety."

22. Krajewski, "Bridge Inspection," 39.

23. Walther and Chase, "Condition Assessment," 67.

24. Ibid., 76.

25. Ibid., 76–77. In addition, service assessment methodologies, Walther and Chase explain, "need to be capable of detecting and measuring congestion, accidents, traffic bottleneck, rerouting due to clearance issues, etc." (77).

26. Bridge and Tunnel Inspection Peer Review Panel, "Review of the Maryland Transportation Authority's Bridge and Tunnel Inspection Practices," final report, June 1, 2009, (http://cdm26690l.cdmhost.com/cgi-bin/showfile.exe ?CISOROOT=/p266901coll7&CISOPTR=2329&filename=2330.pdf, accessed March 22, 2010) 3.

27. U.S. DOT, *Reliability of Visual Inspection*, 1:477.

28. Peter J. Vanderzee and Frank B. Wingate, "Structural Health Monitoring for Bridges," LifeSpan Technologies White Paper, 2008, 3. Hereinafter cited as Vanderzee and Wingate, "Structure Health Monitoring."

29. Interview with Peter J. Vanderzee, February 26, 2009.

30. Walther and Chase, "Condition Assessment," 77–78.

31. Bernhardt, "Bridge Safety," 4.

32. Ibid.

33. Chase and Laman, "Dynamics," 4.

34. Technology Innovation Program, National Institute of Standards and Technology, "Advanced Sensing Technologies for the Infrastructure: Roads, Highways, Bridges and Water," June 2008 (http://www.nist.gov/tip/cnn_white_paperfinal.pdf, accessed March 22, 2010), 4. Hereinafter cited as Technology Innovation Program, "Advanced Sensing Technologies."

35. It is worth noting that the technology discussed here, including structural health monitoring, is distinct from the technology of computer modeling for analyzing the performance of bridges. Wherever a bridge is located, it experiences flexing of its parts whenever a car or truck crosses it. When traffic increases over time, or when the size of automobiles and trucks increases over a bridge's lifetime, cracks will emerge and begin the process of corrosion that will, if not addressed in a timely fashion, lead to a loss of structural integrity—i.e., fatigue. In spite of the increasing use of computers to design and evaluate bridges in recent decades, all bridge engineers know that the factors that make up a bridge's unique structural profile are too complex to be fully analyzed through calculations. As a result, all computer analyses, no matter how fully developed, are simulations that rarely match the actual conditions of a bridge that is in use.

36. Technology Innovation Program, "Advanced Sensing Technologies," 1 and 5.

37. Quoted in "Infrastructure Assessment Technologies Show 30+% Savings Potential: White Paper Explains a Less Expensive Way to Fix the National Bridge Problem," press release, October 28, 2009, LifeSpan Technologies (http://www.lifespantechnologies.com/eclublinks.asp?PublicPage=true, accessed March 25, 2010).

38. Vanderzee and Wingate, "Structure Health Monitoring," 3.

39. HNTB Companies, "Think: Innovative Solutions; Intelligent Infrastructure," 2007 (http://think.hntb.com/assets/thinkmagazine/documents/Think01_Web.pdf, accessed July 3, 2009), 8.

40. "MDOT Partners with U-M on Bridge Technology Research," January 22, 2009 (http://www.michigan.gov/mdot/0,1607,7-151-9620_11057-207299--,00.html, accessed March 22, 2010).

41. The Daily Texan, "Engineering Team Receives $3.4 Mil for Bridge Project," *Daily Texan*, January 20, 2009.

42. "SAFETEA-LU will bring needed funding to research so that shortcomings of NBIS and BMS can be studied and overcome. Key initiatives in SAFETEA-LU include the Long-Term Bridge Research Program wherein the Innovative Bridge Research and Deployment Program is continued, with a new set-aside for high performance concrete bridge technology research and development. In addition, several new initiatives to address bridge life and performance have been funded" (Walther and Chase, "Condition Assessment," 77).

43. American Association of State Highway and Transportation Officials, *Rough Roads Ahead: Fix Them Now or Pay for It Later*, 2009 (http://roughroads.transportation.org/RoughRoads_FullReport.pdf, accessed March 22, 2010), 31–32.

44. HNTB Corporation, "Responsible Infrastructure" (http://www.hntb.com/sites/default/files/issues/Mon,%2004/13/2009%20-%2015:43/Think03_Web.pdf, accessed June 25, 2009), 11.

45. According to Bruce Johnson, State Bridge Engineer in Oregon's Department of Transportation, "in addition to the structural health monitoring program, we conducted in depth investigations and re-scoped many of the 35 bridges to assure that we only strengthened or replaced those that were actually in need of work. As a result of that effort, approximately 82 of the 355 bridges were re-scoped to no work and many of the planned replacements

were re-scoped to strengthening projects." Letter from Bruce Johnson to Peter J. Vanderzee, January 16, 2009.

46. Technology Innovation Program, "Advanced Sensing Technologies," 6.

47. See NSTIFC, *Paying Our Way*, 15–16.

48. Paul Yarossi, "Taking the Road Less Traveled: The Top Transportation Issues Facing President Obama," January 2009, (http://www.hntb.com/ sites/default/files/issues/Taking%20the%20Road%20Less%20Traveled_Tech Paper.pdf, accessed June 25, 2009), 3.

49. HNTB Companies, "Think: Innovative Solutions; Intelligent Infrastructure," 2007 (http://think.hntb.com/assets/thinkmagazine/documents/ Think01_Web.pdf, accessed July 3, 2009), 8.

50. Interview with Peter Vanderzee, February 26, 2009.

51. NSTIFC, *Paying Our Way*, 26.

52. Ibid., 15.

53. See Barry B. LePatner, with Timothy Jacobson and Robert E. Wright, *Broken Buildings, Busted Budgets: How to Fix America's Trillion-dollar Construction Industry* (Chicago: University of Chicago Press, 2007), 98–105. Hereinafter LePatner, *Broken Buildings*.

### 6. The Way Forward

1. ASCE, *Report Card*.

2. NSTIFC, *Paying Our Way*, 22.

3. Ibid., 24.

4. U.S. GAO, *Highway Public-Private Partnerships*, 78.

5. LePatner, *Broken Buildings*, 34.

6. John J. Castellani et al., "Guiding Principles for Strengthening America's Infrastructure," March 27, 2006 (http://www.csis.org/media/csis/pubs/ 060327_infrastructure_principles.pdf), accessed March 24, 2010), 2.

7. Robert Poole, "A National Infrastructure Bank?" Reason Foundation, February 3, 2009 (http://reason.org/news/show/a-national-infrastructure-bank, accessed March 23, 2010).

8. "Obama's Economic Policy Speech Excerpts," *Time*, March 27, 2010 (http://thepage.time.com/obamas-economic-policy-speech-excerpts, accessed March 27, 2010).

9. Everett Ehrlich and Felix G. Rohatyn, "A New Bank to Save Our Infrastructure," *New York Review of Books*, October 9, 2008 (http://www.nybooks .com/articles/21873, accessed August 21, 2008).

10. U.S. Government Accountability Office, *Federal-Aid Highways: FHWA Needs a Comprehensive Approach to Improving Project Oversight*, report to the chairman, Committee on Transportation and Infrastructure, House of Representatives, January 2005 (http://www.gao.gov/new.items/d05173.pdf, accessed March 23, 2010). Hereinafter cited as U.S. GAO, *Federal-Aid Highways*.

11. Ibid., 21.

12. U.S. GAO, *Federal-Aid Highways*.

13. Bent Flyvbjerg, Nils Bruzelius, and Werner Rothengatter, *Megaprojects and Risk: An Anatomy of Ambition* (Cambridge: Cambridge University Press, 2003; http://assets.cambridge.org/052180/4205/sample/0521804205ws.pdf, accessed March 24, 2010), 5.

14. See LePatner, *Broken Buildings*.

15. For more detailed treatment of how true fixed-price contracts can reform the inefficiencies of the construction industry, see *The LePatner C³ Method* (www.lepatner.com).

16. U.S. Government Accountability Office, *Transportation Infrastructure: Managing the Costs of Large-Dollar Highway Projects*, report to the chairman, Subcommittee on Government Management Restructuring, and the District of Columbia Committee on Governmental Affairs, U.S. Senate (Washington: Government Accountability Office, 1997).

17. U.S. Government Accountability Office, *Transportation Infrastructure: Cost and Oversight Issues on Major Highway and Bridge Projects*, 21GAO-02–702T (Washington: Government Accountability Office, 2002).

18. U.S. GAO, *Federal-Aid Highways*, 28.

19. U.S. Department of Transportation, Federal Highway Administration, Nondestructive Evaluation Center, *Reliability of Visual Inspection for Highway Bridges*, June 2001 (http://www.tfhrc.gov/hnr20/nde/01o20.htm, accessed July 2, 2009), 371. Hereinafter cited as U.S. DOT, *Reliability of Visual Inspection*.

20. Bernhardt, "Bridge Safety," 3.

21. U.S. DOT, *Reliability of Visual Inspection*.

22. Bernhardt, "Bridge Safety," 3.

23. Peter J. Vanderzee and James D. Cooper, P.E., "A Bridge Too Near," *Pittsburgh Engineer*, June 2005 (http://www.eswp.com/PDF/PE_summe05_9-11.pdf, accessed March 23, 2010), 9.

24. Walther and Chase, "Condition Assessment," 67.

25. U.S. DOT, *Reliability of Visual Inspection*.

26. Ibid.

27. Henry Petroski, *Success through Failure: The Paradox of Design* (Princeton, New Jersey: Princeton University Press, 2006), 114.

28. Lawrence H. Summers, "Informal Transcript of Opening Session Remarks," Hamilton Project Infrastructure Forum, the Brookings Institution, July 25, 2008, 3. Summers also said: "I don't see how anyone who has spent any time looking at American public schools, 75% of which have structural deficiencies, 25% of which have problems in the ventilation systems, or who has had the opportunity to compare Kennedy Airport with almost any international airport to which one can fly from Kennedy Airport, could be satisfied with the state of America's infrastructure."

29. Robert Puentes, "A Bridge to Somewhere: Rethinking American Transportation for the 21st Century," Brookings Institution, June 12, 2008, (www.brookings.edu/reports/2008/06_transportation_puentes.aspx, accessed June 25, 2009), 6.

30. Arthur C. Nelson, "Toward a New Metropolis: The Opportunity to Rebuild America," December 2004 (http://www.brookings.edu/metro/pubs/20041213_RebuildAmerica.pdf, accessed March 23, 2010).

31. NSTPRSC, *Transportation for Tomorrow*, 2:6–20.

32. Everett Ehrlich and Felix G. Rohatyn, "A New Bank to Save Our Infrastructure," *New York Review of Books*, October 9, 2008 (http://www.nybooks.com/articles/21873, accessed August 21, 2008), 4.

33. Pam Louwagie, James Walsh, and Paul McEnroe, "Should This Bridge Be Open?," *Star Tribune*, August 11, 2007 (http://www.startribune.com/local/11593656.html, accessed December 29, 2008).

34. Of the 18,857 fracture-critical bridges mentioned above (see note 5 to chapter 1), 7,980 are structurally deficient according to our original research.

35. David Brooks, "The Behavioral Revolution," *New York Times*, October 27, 2008 (www.nytimes.com/2008/10/28/opinion/28brooks.html?_r=1, accessed August 2, 2009).

# Index